The Soviet Intelligentsia

By the same author

Contemporary Soviet Government (1968)

The Soviet Intelligentsia

An essay on the
social structure
and roles of Soviet
intellectuals
during the 1960s

L G Churchward

Reader in Political Science
University of Melbourne

Routledge & Kegan Paul

London and Boston

First published 1973
by Routledge & Kegan Paul Ltd
Broadway House, 68–74 Carter Lane,
London EC4V 5EL and
9 Park Street,
Boston, Mass. 02108, U.S.A.
Printed in Great Britain by
W & J Mackay Limited, Chatham

ISBN 0 7100 7475 1

Contents

Contents

Tables

Preface

My aim in writing this book has been to produce a brief account of the contemporary Soviet intelligentsia which will prove useful both to the specialist and to the general reader. While a great deal has been published in English on the subject of the Russian and the Soviet intelligentsia very little of it deals with the contemporary intelligentsia as a whole. It has been mainly concerned with the intelligentsia in pre-revolutionary Russia or in the early Soviet period. What has been published outside these limits deals mainly with small sections of the intelligentsia (such as writers or artists) rather than the intelligentsia as a whole. To the best of my knowledge this is the first book in English devoted to the subject of the contemporary Soviet intelligentsia.

My original interest in the subject of the contemporary Soviet intelligentsia was a by-product of my general interest in Soviet politics. From the appearance of Professor John N. Hazard's *The Soviet System of Government* early in 1957 various general studies of the Soviet political system have speculated on the political role of the Soviet intelligentsia. I have not found the generalizations of my American colleagues satisfactory, mainly because they so obviously over-simplify a very complex social and political problem.

I first thought of the idea of writing a short book on the Soviet intelligentsia early in 1967. Although my close colleague and friend at the Australian National University, Dr T. H. Rigby, advised caution and amplified the difficulties of the undertaking, I persisted with the notion. I commenced the systematic collection of material in 1967 and took a short leave late in 1968 to hasten the process. The really intensive work for the book was done during this leave (December 1968–June 1969) when I visited the Toronto Centre for Russian and East European

Studies, St Antony's College (Oxford), the Centre for Russian and East European Studies (Birmingham), and Moscow.

In the writing of this book I have been greatly encouraged and helped by friendly criticism from colleagues in all the above places. In particular I wish to express my thanks to the Council of the University of Melbourne for making it possible for me to take this short leave and to Professor A. F. Davies of the Department of Political Science, University of Melbourne, for adjusting my teaching load in the first half of 1970 to enable me to write this book. I acknowledge the assistance that I have received from A. D. Grishin, Grey Hodnett, H. Gordon Skilling, Franklyn Griffiths, Bob Davies, Geoff Barker, Mosha Lewin, Michael Kaser, Sheila Bruce and colleagues in Moscow. I owe a special debt to Harry Rigby and others who read and criticized the first draft of this book during 1970. I believe that the present text is better and more accurate than the original draft, thanks to this friendly criticism. I am also deeply indebted to my wife Mary, for her patient checking of the manuscript and for her criticism.

The book itself is my own responsibility. I have sought to make it a general account of the Soviet intelligentsia in the sixties, a study in breadth rather than in depth. It is not primarily a book for political scientists. It is a very personal mixture of current history and sociology. Nevertheless I have endeavoured to emphasize problems of great concern to Western political scientists, such as the growth of social sciences in the Soviet Union and the political role of the Soviet intelligentsia. I have tried to make the book factual and descriptive rather than theoretical. I have also sought to reduce the documentation. However, the Bibliography provides a fairly full coverage of the material used for preparing the book. Unless otherwise acknowledged, the translations in the book are my own.

The original draft of this book was written over February–April 1970. It has been extensively revised, enlarged and reorganized during February–August 1971. This delay in publication enabled the inclusion of some statistical material taken from the 1970 census. Unfortunately the more relevant material was still unpublished when the manuscript was completed.

I wish to thank Mrs Jan Rubenstein for her accurate typing of the manuscript.

Glossary

Aktiv	The leading cadres and most active members of a particular organization or society. The party *aktiv* of the CPSU—the leading party cadres and active workers at all levels right down to the party primary organization.
Apparat	Apparatus, staff. Typically the apparatus of the CPSU or of the state.
Apparatchik	A member of the apparatus: a party (or state) functionary.
ASSR	Autonomous Soviet Socialist Republic.
AUCCTU	All-Union Central Committee of Trade Unions.
Blat	Pull, influence.
C.C.	Central Committee (of the CPSU).
CPSU	Communist Party of the Soviet Union (in Russian, KPSS).
GOELRO	State Commission for Electrification.
Gorispolkom	Executive Committee of a Town (City) Soviet.
Gorkom	Town (City) Party Committee.
KGB	Committee of State Security.
Kommunist	Theoretical journal of the C.C. of the CPSU.
Komsomol	All-Union Leninist Communist League of Youth.
Komsomolskaya Pravda	Newspaper of the *Komsomol* (abbrev. *Kom. Pravda*).
Krai	Territory: a large, relatively sparsely populated administrative region.
Kraiispolkom	Executive Committee of a Territorial Soviet.

Kraikom	Territorial Party Committee.
Literaturnaya gazeta	Weekly newspaper of the Writers' Union (abbrev. *Lit. gaz.*).
MPA	Main Political Administration (the Party propaganda and education apparatus in the Army).
Narodnoe khozyaistvo SSSR	Statistical handbook issued irregularly by the Central Statistical Administration (abbrev. *Nar. kh. SSSR*).
Nomenklatura	Appointment list controlled directly or indirectly by the Party.
Novy mir	*New World*. Monthly journal of the Writers' Union.
Oblast	Province, region.
Oblispolkom	Executive Committee of Province Soviet.
Obkom	Province Party Committee.
Partiinaya zhizn	*Party Life*. Journal of the C.C. of the CPSU.
Partiinost	Party-mindedness.
Raion	District: an administrative division within a province, territory, republic or city.
Raiispolkom	Executive Committee of a District Soviet.
Raikom	District Party Committee.
RSFSR	Russian, Soviet, Federal, Soviet Republic.
Samizdat	Unofficial press (lit. Self-Publication Press).
Sovetskoe gosudarstvo i pravo	*Soviet State and Law*. Monthly Journal of the Institute of State and Law (abbrev. *S.G.i P.*).
Sovety deputatov trudyashchikhsya	*Soviets of Workers' Deputies* (abbrev. *Sovety*). Monthly governmental journal.
Sovnarkhoz	Council of National Economy. Agencies of economic administration established on a regional and republican basis 1957–64.
Spets khran	Abbreviation for *spetsialnoe khranenie* (special safe-keeping).
Subbotnik	A Saturday working-bee.
USSR	Union of Soviet Socialist Republics (in Russian SSSR).
Vedomosti verkhovnovo Soveta SSSR	*Gazette of the USSR Supreme Soviet* (issued weekly).

Vestnik Akademii Hauk SSSR	*Herald of the Academy of Sciences of the USSR.* Monthly (abbrev. *Vest. Akad. Hauk SSSR*).
VOKS	USSR Society for Cultural Relations with Foreign Countries.
Voprosy ekonomiki	*Problems of Economics.* Journal of the Institute of Economics.
Voprosy filosofii	*Problems of Philosophy.* Journal of the Institute of Philosophy.
Voprosy istorii	*Problems of History.* Monthly academic journal.

'The Soviet intelligentsia considers that its patriotic duty is to be in the forefront of the sharp ideological struggle which has developed in the contemporary world. Our weapon in that struggle is the Leninist theoretical legacy, developed and enriched by the Communist Party of the Soviet Union, by the international communist and workers' movement.' (Academician M. V. Keldysh, President of the USSR Academy of Sciences, Moscow April 22, 1970)

'Intellectual freedom is essential to human society—freedom to obtain and distribute information, freedom for open-minded and unfearing debate and freedom from oppression by officialdom and prejudices. Such a trinity of freedom of thought is the only guarantee against an infection of people by mass myths, which, in the hands of treacherous hypocrites and demagogues, can be transformed into bloody dictatorship. Freedom of thought is the only guarantee of the feasibility of a scientific democratic approach to politics, economy, and culture.' (Academician A. D. Sakharov, 1968)

Introduction

Intelligentsia is an international word of Russian origin. As originally used in the 1860s it referred to the small minority of educated Russians who came from all sections of Russian society but mainly from the nobility and the urban bourgeoisie. Before the end of the nineteenth century the term intelligentsia was often used more narrowly to describe that section of the broad social intelligentsia which sought radical changes to the Russian social and political structure. While this radical intelligentsia was increasingly significant after 1890 it was never a majority of the intelligentsia. But its impact on Russian political history was so great that to this day many persons persist in regarding the radical minority as the essential intelligentsia. Some writers attempt to distinguish between these two groups by applying the concept 'intelligentsia' to the one and reserving the term 'intellectual' for the other group. But this is confusing since what some writers call 'the intelligentsia' other writers call 'intellectuals'. The distinction is difficult to apply in Russian since the word *intelligentsia* is simply the general abstract noun based on the noun *intelligent* or intellectual. Russians who seek to make this distinction are obliged to use the English word 'intellectual' to provide the contrast. Many Russians still use the term *intelligentsia* in its traditional nineteenth-century Russian sense and apply it only to a small minority (of perhaps half a million people) who are non-careerists, fully involved with intellectual activity of all kinds and in general are perennial critics of their own society and culture. The majority of the professionally-trained specialists are referred to as 'technocrats' or as 'intellectuals'.[1]

For my part, I make no distinction between the terms 'intellectuals' and 'intelligentsia'. The term *intelligentsia* I use in the Marxist sense. This I do not merely because it is the basis of

Soviet writing on the subject but because it provides an objective definition. Such a definition is clearly inadequate for certain aspects of the problem we are investigating, but it does at least provide a better starting point for our investigation of the social position of Soviet intellectuals than any subjective definition.

The intelligentsia in Soviet society

Definition

Soviet writers generally take a Marxist approach to the problem of the intelligentsia. They regard the intelligentsia in any modern society as a *social stratum* (or as a series of social strata) rather than as a class in itself. While writers such as Mannheim[1] and Bukharin[2] have argued that the intelligentsia is a kind of intermediate class, independent of the basic social classes, this view has never become Soviet orthodoxy. The orthodox viewpoint is that given in the official publication *Fundamentals of Marxism-Leninism*;[3]

> The development of industry, technology and culture in capitalist society results in the formation of a broad stratum, the *intelligentsia*, consisting of persons engaged in mental work (technical personnel, teachers, doctors, office employees, scientists, writers, etc.). The intelligentsia is not an independent class, but a special social group which exists by selling its mental labour. It is recruited from various strata of society, chiefly from the well-to-do classes and only partly from the ranks of the working people. As regards its material position and way of life the intelligentsia is not homogeneous. Its upper strata, the high officials, prominent lawyers and others, are closer to the capitalists, while the lower strata are closer to the working masses.

Much the same definition of the intelligentsia is found in the 1958 Soviet *Political Dictionary*:[4]

> A social stratum (*prosloika*) consisting of persons professionally employed in mental labour. Included in it are scientists and artists, engineers, technicians, agronomists, doctors, lawyers,

teachers, and the great majority of office workers. The intelligentsia is not a separate class because it does not occupy a particular place in the system of social production.

The above two statements, which could easily be multiplied by quotations from recent writings of Soviet philosophers, historians and sociologists, paraphrase the various pronouncements on the matter made by Stalin between 1936 and 1939.[5] But they represent an older tradition which goes back at least to the writings of Lenin and other Russian Marxists before the first Russian Revolution of 1905.[6]

Several problems emerge from such a definition. In the first place, the social role of the intelligentsia tends to be negatively defined—i.e. intellectuals are not a class although they are recruited from various classes. While most intellectuals receive a salary in return for the sale of their mental labour power (which surely should make them workers) we are advised that some are nearer the capitalist class. This negative or one-dimensional approach does not allow the social roles of the intelligentsia to be fully examined. Marxists outside the Soviet Union have long been aware of this problem and have sought their own solutions. Thus A. Gramsci in a stimulating essay on 'The formation of intellectuals'[7] argued that while intellectuals were a series of social strata rather than a class, their relationship to the world of production was 'mediated' by the social fabric of the social structure and by the complex of the superstructure of which they were the 'officials'. As 'officials' of the superstructure intellectuals served directly (in 'political society') or indirectly (in 'civil society'). As officials of the ruling class they exercised the subordinate functions of social hegemony and political government. The proletariat, in the process of its emergence as a class challenging the capitalist social structure, created its own intelligentsia, partly from within itself and partly by means of penetrating and absorbing elements of the existing intelligentsia. But Soviet writers have drawn small inspiration from Gramsci[8] and nothing at all from his approach to the problem of intelligentsia. Nor have Soviet writers obviously been influenced by any of the various European or American Marxist writings on the problem.

A second difficulty inherent in the Soviet approach is its

failure to adopt a clear standard for inclusion within the intelligentsia. Thus 'employed persons engaged primarily in mental labour' includes persons with various levels of professional and technical qualifications, and persons with no formal qualifications at all. But should all 'white-collar workers' be included in the intelligentsia? What are the main subdivisions of the intelligentsia? Marxist writers before the revolution sometimes drew a distinction between the *intelligentsia* proper and the *semi-intelligentsia* (*polu-intelligentsia*).[9] The former were those with a tertiary education, the latter, those with only a secondary specialist education (primary teachers, nurses, technicians, etc.). But even then allowance had to be made for self-educated specialists and intellectuals. Soviet sociologists in recent years have been worried by this problem and have taken a variety of approaches to it. Some regard the official category of 'persons employed primarily in mental labour' as too wide and make various adjustments to official figures to exclude 'white-collar workers' (*sluzhashchie*).[10] Others distinguish between intellectuals with a tertiary education and professionals with a secondary specialist education only. But the distinction is hard to maintain and is not altogether realistic.

A third problem with the Soviet definition of the intelligentsia is that it excludes some who are obviously 'intellectuals', including professionals employed in the armed forces, retired professionals, and students. These groups are excluded because the definition of the intelligentsia commonly used in the Soviet Union relates to a sector of the civilian workforce, and because most statistics used by Soviet scholars to determine the size and structure of the Soviet intelligentsia are derived from the Central Statistical Administration and are generally limited to the employed workforce at a given time.

One Soviet writer who has sought to overcome the limitations of orthodox Marxist theory on the intelligentsia is the Leningrad sociologist, P. P. Amelin. In a short book, *Intelligentsia i Sotsializm*, published in Leningrad in 1970, Amelin seeks to present a Marxist explanation which combines a functional with a historical analysis. He claims that this approach helps to bring out the specific characteristics of intellectual work and activity.

What then is the intelligentsia? The intelligentsia is a

particular, internally differentiated social group consisting of people who are highly qualified and trained in mental labour in any sphere of social-historical activity, with a profession as the only, or at least the main, source of their existence. People of this social group, serving the varied demands and interests of a particular class (or classes) of the given social system seek their livelihood primarily by means of their intellectual ability, general and special knowledge, skill, know-how and experience. Professional mental labour is not necessary for intellectuals (*intelligentov*) but it is the main sphere of their life activity. Above all their inclinations and talents are shown in this sphere, making their creative energies and social ideals, crystallizing their political and moral norms and orientations and producing their formation and self-affirmation as individuals. (p. 47)

There are many definitions of the intelligentsia and there is no single Marxist definition of the Soviet intelligentsia. My own definition has been influenced by Soviet definitions but it also differs from them. I regard the intelligentsia as consisting of *persons with a tertiary education* (whether employed or not), *tertiary students*, and *persons lacking formal tertiary qualification but who are professionally employed in jobs which normally require a tertiary qualification*.

The above definition is an objective definition in the Marxist tradition. However, it presents certain difficulties because the size of some categories of intellectuals (e.g. pensioners with a tertiary education, specialists serving in the armed forces, intellectuals lacking formal qualifications) cannot be determined very exactly from Soviet statistical sources.

In Table 1 below I set out my estimate for the size of the Soviet intelligentsia as it stood at the end of 1967, fifty years after the Bolshevik Revolution.

Although my definition is an objective one it nevertheless requires some explanation. My first category, 'gainfully employed professionals with a tertiary education', can be precisely measured on an annual basis. Some might question my exclusion of persons with secondary specialist qualifications from this group. There were 8,290,000 persons in the work force with secondary specialist education at the end of 1967. To include

6

this group would needlessly inflate the size of my category of employed professionals. Since I wanted to include tertiary students in my concept of the intelligentsia the inclusion of secondary specialists would have meant considerable double counting as many tertiary students (especially part-time and correspondence students) already have secondary specialist qualifications. Besides this there is in most professions an important distinction between jobs requiring tertiary training and those requiring secondary specialist qualifications. Like the earlier Russian Marxists I prefer to regard professionals with secondary qualifications as 'semi-intelligentsia' rather than intelligentsia.

TABLE I *An estimate of the size and composition of the Soviet intelligentsia, December 1967*

1 Gainfully employed professionals with a tertiary education	5,565,000
2 Tertiary students	4,311,000
3 Unemployed graduates	500,000
4 Military specialists with tertiary qualifications	200,000
5 Others	100,000
Total	10,676,000

(Based on information in *Narodnoe khozyaistvo SSSR v 1967 g.* and in *Soviet Union: Fifty Years*, Moscow, 1969, pp. 278, 282.)

My inclusion of tertiary students, especially part-time students, requires some justification. I have done this because no full discussion of the intelligentsia is possible without considering the problem of recruitment and virtually all employed intellectuals are recruited from graduates. To direct some attention to tertiary education, therefore, throws light on the training, orientation and recruitment processes. For certain statistical comparisons the students will be excluded as they are not yet all participating in the workforce. They are incipient professionals rather than fully-fledged professionals.

The unemployed graduate is an important segment of the

7

intelligentsia in any modern society. The actual number in this category cannot be exactly determined in the Soviet Union and my estimate of half a million is very approximate. This category includes women graduates not currently in the workforce as well as retired professionals of both sexes. It is impossible to establish the relative strength of these two groups but the first group is almost certainly smaller than the second. The unemployed woman graduate is certainly less significant in Soviet society than she is in capitalist societies.

Soviet statistics do not provide us with an accurate figure for fourth and fifth categories. Nevertheless, if we are to estimate the total size of the broad Soviet intelligentsia there seems to be no good reason to exclude either category. While there are no published figures for the number of specialists with tertiary qualifications serving in the armed forces some figures have been given for the ratio of specialists to other officers in different branches of the armed forces. In 1967, 19 per cent of mental workers in the civilian workforce had tertiary education compared with 30 per cent of military officers. It is therefore probably safe to assume a higher ratio of tertiary to secondary specialists than is to be found in the civilian workforce. That being so, our estimate of 200,000 as the number of military specialists with tertiary qualifications in 1967 cannot be far off the mark. Such specialists are mainly trained outside the regular military academies in various branches of engineering and technology but they also include journalists, historians, economists and jurists.

My figure of 100,000 for my fifth category is merely a guess. No figures of any sort are available for estimating the size of this group in the post-war period. That such 'unqualified' specialists still exist can be established from references in Soviet newspapers, periodicals and literature. Some of them have unfinished tertiary qualifications, others do not. It is certain that this group is declining in numbers and importance. Today almost all professionals are qualified specialists, holders of degrees or diplomas. There remain some thousands of elderly intellectuals, including some leading specialists in management, technology, literature and art, who are largely self-trained. They represent the thinning ranks of the first generation of Soviet specialists. As such they cause little resentment amongst more recent and more highly qualified recruits.

A group of persons numbering almost eleven million is not likely to have any high degree of homogeneity. Soviet intellectuals differ widely in their social position, in their relations to production, in their power and influence, in their outlook, in their income, material living standards and life styles. Nor does the common tertiary qualification afford much cohesion, since only a minority are university students or university graduates. Moreover the range of tertiary institutes and the numerical weight of part-time students means that Soviet professionals receive their qualifications at different stages in their careers and through different channels. What they have in common, educationally, is that they are specialists in various branches of production, in community services, in research and development, and in cultural activities. Even the students are primarily specialists in the making.

The intelligentsia as such is neither a 'ruling class' nor a 'managerial class'. Even the superior intelligentsia do not possess a private property base from which they might exert pressure on the government to defend their group interests. They are simply highly paid officials of the Party and the State or of some public organization. Like officials in any bureaucratic structure they are liable to dismissal or demotion if their service displeases the party leadership. Power and influence is not evenly distributed throughout Soviet society, but there is little evidence that heredity plays a major role in the exercise of power or in the enjoyment of wealth. The intelligentsia is well represented in the Soviet political leadership, in the party and government bureaucracy, in the managerial élite, in the military élite and in the party membership. But the intelligentsia extends beyond these élites.

General features of the intelligentsia

At this stage in my analysis it is necessary to draw attention to certain general features of the social situation of Soviet intellectuals. In the first place, the Soviet intelligentsia during the 1960s represented the most rapidly growing sector of Soviet society, expanding by over 70 per cent between January 1959 and December 1967. Second, Soviet intellectuals are mainly urban-based. In January 1959, when 52 per cent of the Soviet

9

population lived in the country, only 16.1 per cent of all tertiary graduates did so. Moreover, many Soviet intellectuals dread 'going to the periphery', and try their hardest to remain in Moscow or Leningrad. At present probably more than 60 per cent of the scientific intelligentsia live in the above two cities or in Novosibirsk. More than a quarter of Soviet writers reside in Moscow. In general, the social and political influence of the intelligentsia is greater in urban areas than it is in rural areas.

Third, the overwhelming majority of Soviet intellectuals today are post-revolutionary. This was true as early as 1940 but by 1960 there were very few pre-revolutionary intellectuals surviving. The best single index of the growth and changing structure of the Soviet intelligentsia is the output of tertiary graduates. The foundations for the modern Soviet intelligentsia were laid down during the years 1918–28. Over these eleven years 340,000 persons graduated from Soviet tertiary educational establishments. The move over to rapid industrialization in 1928–29 required a more rapid expansion of both secondary- and tertiary-trained specialists. Thus over the twelve years of pre-war economic planning (1929–40) 876,000 tertiary specialists were graduated, more than twice the number produced in the period 1918–28. The war slowed down but did not reverse the development of higher education and there were 954,000 tertiary graduates over the decade 1941–50. The decade of most rapid expansion of graduates was 1951–60. Over this decade 2,619,000 persons graduated from Soviet universities and other tertiary institutes. This expansion proceeded more slowly during the 1960s. Over the nine years 1961–9 there were 3,719,000 graduates.

Two comments are worth adding to this statistical summary of the growth of Soviet graduates. First, the entrance of women into the intelligentsia was well advanced before the war, but the war accelerated the process. Thus women constituted 32.1 per cent of persons with a tertiary education in 1939, but 48.8 per cent in 1959. Second, the statistics quoted above make it clear that four-fifths of the employed Soviet intelligentsia in 1970 had graduated since the death of Stalin in March 1953. While this new Soviet intelligentsia was drawn from all sections of Soviet society, including the industrial workers and the peasants, the intelligentsia was disproportionately represented. Today, many of the younger Soviet intellectuals are second or third generation intellectuals. At the same time education is still the main road to social mobility in the USSR. More than in most European societies, the career is open to talent. This in itself tends to make Soviet intellectuals loyal and conformist. Radical or dissident attitudes are not uncommon but they are clearly held only by a small minority. The alienation of the intelligentsia was a major problem of tsarist Russia and it survived the revolution, at least until the thirties.[11] It is less significant today, notwithstanding certain irritations and dissatisfactions over censorship and increased political supervision which has been imposed since mid-1963.

TABLE 2 *Output of tertiary graduates, 1918–69 (in thousands)*

	Total	Annual average
1918–28	340	30.9
1929–32	170	42.5
1933–7	370	74.0
1938–40	328	109.3
1941–5	302	60.4
1946–50	652	130.4
1951–5	1,121	224.3
1956–60	1,498	299.7
1961–5	1,732	346.3
1966–9	1,987	496.7

(Taken from *Nar.kh.SSSR v 1969 g.*, p. 684.)

Fourth, while all important national and cultural groups are represented in the Soviet intelligentsia today, some groups are 'over-represented'. Jews, Georgians, Armenians and Russians are over-represented in proportion to their strength in the total population. Some national groups, especially the Kirgiz, Turkmen, Tadjik, Uzbek, Kazakh and other Central Asian peoples, are under-represented. But these generalizations tend to obscure the real picture. Russian representation in the intelligentsia is declining more slowly than that of minority groups such as Jews and Georgians. On the other hand, Central Asian peoples are increasing their representation. These inequalities certainly cause some friction over educational policy on matters such as admission to universities, and teaching, research and administrative appointments. They also produce a tendency for intellectuals belonging to 'under-privileged' minority groups, such as Ukrainians, Estonians, Tartars, Azerbaidjanis, to attempt to hold their own intellectually and politically against the increasing social presence of the Russian majority. Such struggles, where they exist, are generally centred in the non-Russian areas, especially in the republican capitals. In cities like Moscow, Leningrad, Novosibirsk and Irkutsk, there are many non-Russian intellectuals holding positions of influence in administration, management, education and science, but such intellectuals are frequently more Russian than the Russians.

A fifth factor which requires emphasis is the changing professional composition of the Soviet intelligentsia. This is a consequence of a much broader regrouping of the workforce, which is one aspect of what Soviet scholars call the 'scientific and technological revolution'.[12] Amongst other things this revolution is characterized by a rapid increase in the number of people engaged in technology, scientific research and development, and in the social sciences. Between October 1955 and December 1967 the number of scientific workers* rose from 223,893 to 770,000. The proportion of scientific workers in technology rose over the same period from 27.3 per cent to 44.1 per cent, while the proportion engaged in physico-mathematical science rose from 8.8 per cent to 10.0 per cent. The proportion engaged in medical and biological sciences, chemistry, agricultural and veterinary science fell from 29.9 per cent to 19.6 per cent. The proportion engaged in social sciences at the end of 1967 (15.7 per cent) was lower than the figure for 1955, but it had been increasing since 1965. While one cannot assume that the most rapidly growing sections of the scientific workforce have increased their political influence, their improved strategic position has probably extended the scope of their political competency, i.e. it has increased the number of issues over which their advice is sought by the leadership. Changes in the location of employment are also important. The most significant change

*The term 'scientific worker' includes all grades of scientific research workers and all teachers at the tertiary level.

here over recent years is the increased proportion working in scientific research institutes, compared with the proportion working in higher educational establishments and in government departments. Whereas 53.2 per cent of all scientific workers were employed in tertiary educational institutes in 1950, only 32.5 per cent were in 1965. Conversely the percentage employed in scientific research establishments increased from 43.4 per cent to 58.7 per cent[13] over the same period. Under these conditions it would be surprising if the social prestige, influence and political weight of scientific research workers had not increased.

Finally, an important problem concerning the position of the intelligentsia in Soviet society needs to be raised, at least generally, at this point. This is the relationship between the intelligentsia and the State. The problem tends to be avoided by Soviet writers since their definition regards Soviet society as consisting of two basic friendly classes, the workers and the peasantry, and a social stratum, the intelligentsia. Because of the crucial role played by intellectuals in a society undergoing accelerated industrialization and modernization, the party leadership has generally given them preferential treatment over other sections of Soviet society. Many intellectuals enjoy higher incomes, better living standards, and greater prestige than do ordinary citizens. Intellectuals are also better represented in the Party than are either workers or peasants. Inevitably, this causes some resentment on the part of the under-privileged sections of Soviet society. Some Russian manual workers still see the basic social division as that between the 'white' and the 'dirty' hands.[14] Such a distinction tends to equate the intellectuals with the party functionaries. From this point of view, intellectuals and party officials are all 'white-handed' shirkers. But political realism prevents the popular mind from equating the intellectuals with the party leadership. It is all too obvious that the wielders of decisive power are few while the intellectuals are many, and that most intellectuals are restrained by the party machine just as the masses themselves are. Inkeles and Bauer, in their investigation in the fifties into the attitudes of Soviet displaced persons, found that all four of their classes (workers, peasants, employees and intelligentsia) shared a common resentment against party and state officials, but only a modest degree of class hostility and conflict between themselves. All four classes felt themselves to be exploited and unfairly treated by the regime. The chief difference between the intelligentsia and the employees on the one hand, and the workers and peasants on the other, was that the former two classes recorded a higher estimate of their 'non-recognition' than did the workers and the peasants.[15] Intellectuals were also more apt to hold the view that relations between these four classes were mainly harmonious.

The findings of Inkeles and Bauer are based on persons who left the USSR during the Second World War. Therefore they cannot be taken as fully valid today. My own contacts in the Soviet Union have been mainly with intellectuals and they do not enable me to question any of the findings of Inkeles and Bauer. They do however tend to confirm these findings about the attitudes of intellectuals. Most intellectuals, in certain contexts at least, still see themselves as outside of the establishment, as belonging to 'we' rather than to 'they'. This applies even to many party intellectuals. The dividing line between 'we' and 'they' seems to coincide not with 'non-party' and 'party' positions but with the non-holding or the holding of office. Most intellectuals do not hold bureaucratic positions and those who do hold mainly minor positions. Perhaps one in ten Soviet intellectuals holds some sort of official position in the Party, state, or related administrative structures. The Gramscian distinction between intellectuals serving the superstructure in 'political society' and those serving in 'civil society' is harder to make in the Soviet Union than in a capitalist society but it still has some validity. Certainly, Soviet intellectuals draw a distinction between bureaucratic and non-bureaucratic positions within the intelligentsia. Even though they might class many professors, academic secretaries and research directors as bureaucrats rather than scholars, and thus closer to party secretaries, trade union secretaries, factory managers and *Komsomol* officials, they will regard the non-office holders as reasonably independent and 'genuine' intellectuals. There is an element of false consciousness here but it is not entirely so, as any Westerner who has mixed in Soviet intellectual society will clearly recognize. The problem is a complex one and makes any easy generalizations about the intellectuals being opposed to the *apparatchiki* or the intellectuals 'capturing' the party apparatus,[16] misleading or meaningless. In a later chapter in this book I shall explore the problem in detail. Before this can be done however it will be necessary to examine more carefully the structure of the Soviet intelligentsia, its recruitment and training, its professional organizations and culture, its social roles and its political influence.

2   The social structure of the Soviet intelligentsia

My aim in this chapter is to provide a general picture of the composition and structure of the Soviet intelligentsia during the decade of the sixties. The intelligentsia, as I have defined it, grew from six and a half million to above twelve million over the decade 1960–9. By the end of the decade more than one in twenty of the total population belonged to the intelligentsia, one in ten of the adult population. This represented a higher proportion of the population than in most European countries although much lower than in the USA.

Soviet writers, especially when discussing the total society, usually bracket the intelligentsia with office workers as a social group working mainly by mental labour. The intelligentsia is not regarded as a class, as it has no special relationship to the means of production to distinguish it from manual workers in industry or in agriculture.[1]

It is only when Soviet writers are examining the structure of the intelligentsia *per se* that they find it necessary to recognize groups within the intelligentsia. The groups distinguished are of two types—*professional* groups (chemists, physicists, mathematicians, economists, historians, jurists, etc.) and *structural* or *structural-functional* groups. Some years ago the Soviet sociologist V. S. Semenov[2] distinguished three basic groups within the Soviet intelligentsia:

1 Workers in state and public organizations;
2 The technical-economic intelligentsia;
3 The scientific-cultural intelligentsia.

More recently Shyaraev and Arutyunyan recognized four main groups:[3]

1 The administrative intelligentsia;
2 The creative intelligentsia;

3 The production intelligentsia;

4 The general (*massovaya*) intelligentsia.

As long ago as 1950 Alex Inkeles[4] distinguished ten major 'social-class groups' in Soviet society. The upper three groups within Inkeles's classification cover the intelligentsia.

1 The *ruling élite*. A small group consisting of high party, government, economic and military officials, prominent scientists, and selected artists and writers.

2 The *superior intelligentsia*, consisting of the intermediate ranks of the above groups, plus certain important key technical specialists.

3 The *general intelligentsia*, incorporating most of the professional groups, the middle ranks of the bureaucracy, the managers of small enterprises, junior military officers, technical specialists, etc.

While Inkeles uses somewhat different criteria from Soviet sociologists for his analysis of the Soviet social structure, he does accept a good many of the claims made by them. Thus he writes:[5]

> Despite the fact that the range of income and special privileges available to each of the major groups was fairly distinct there was a significant degree of overlapping. Thus an appreciable number of workers and peasants had incomes on the average higher than large elements of the white collar group and in some cases equalling the incomes of many individuals in the general and even superior intelligentsia.

> On the eve of the war decade the Soviet Union possessed virtually a completely open class system, characterized by a high degree of mobility. This mobility was created predominantly by the tremendous expansion of the national economy, but was given additional impetus by the rate of natural attrition accompanying the revolutionary process, by the declassing—and in part, physical elimination—of major portions of the former upper and middle classes, and by a political system which periodically removed large numbers of people from responsible positions by means of *chistka* or purge.

Soviet writers make the same claim about Soviet society being an 'open society' but they make it with greater conviction and with less qualification. Thus a Soviet scholar, writing in the early sixties, stated that:[6]

> The differences between classes are becoming more conventional than real, more relative than essential. There is a distinct community among them. Soviet society has no class fences. There are no barriers or restrictions to prevent a citizen going from one social stratum to another. It is often hard to determine what social bracket a person belongs to. A worker innovator, for example, is at once a worker and an intellectual. The demarcation between social groups is becoming less distinct. The various groups are gradually blending into a classless association of people of labour.

Some Soviet writers have gone even further and acclaimed the 'intellectualization of society', and 'the withering away of the intelligentsia as a professional group' with the rapid rise in the general educational level of society.[7]

There can be no doubt about the improvement in the educational level of the Soviet community. The number of persons with a tertiary and secondary education rose from 433 per 1,000 in the workforce in January 1959 to 653 per 1,000 in January 1970. By the end of the sixties over 80 per cent of those completing the 8th grade were continuing to complete secondary education. However, during the sixties the number of tertiary students expanded much more slowly than the number of secondary school graduates, thus increasing the competition for places. Each year a lower percentage of school graduates was able to proceed to tertiary educational establishments. As we shall see later in the book, considerable departures from the principle of 'career open to talent' have developed.

Let us now proceed to examine the main *structural-functional* groups within the Soviet intelligentsia. These we would define, along the lines of Shyaraev and Arutyunyan, as the *administrative*, the *creative*, the *production* and the *general* intelligentsia. These have been listed in order of social prestige and influence rather than size. Almost half of the intelligentsia would be in the final category of the general intelligentsia, since this group includes the bulk of those in services such as education and health. Teachers, academics, student-teachers, doctors and medical students represent almost one third of the Soviet intelligentsia.

Slightly over one in three Soviet intellectuals are engaged in production or in preparing for professions in technology and engineering, and in agriculture. The number of intellectuals engaged in administration is difficult to establish as Soviet statistics are often contradictory on this point and usually do not indicate the proportion of administrators having tertiary qualifications. If we accept the official figure of 1,651,000 employed in all branches of civilian administration at the end of 1967, then one million would seem to be a reasonable estimate for the number of administrators with tertiary qualifications in civilian and military administration. This would represent about 10 per cent of the total intelligentsia. The proportion would be higher if students were excluded and only graduates considered. Even so not more than one in five of Soviet graduates would be found in an administrative position.

At the end of 1967 almost half (5,565,000) of the entire Soviet intelligentsia was in the civilian workforce. Of these, 1,620,500 were in engineering and technology. Most of these were working directly in industry, transport, communication, construction, or agriculture, although some were employed in administration in both party and state posts. In addition to the above 1,620,500

TABLE 3 *Distribution of Soviet professionals within the civilian workforce, December 1967*

	Number with tertiary qualifications	Percentage of total
1 Engineers*	1,620,500	29.1
2 Schoolteachers	1,043,500	18.7
3 Scientific workers & academics	770,000	14.0
4 Doctors*	556,500	10.0
5 Agricultural scientists	124,500	2.2
6 Various	1,450,000	26.0
Total	5,565,000	100.0

(Based on figures in *Nar.kh.SSSR v 1967 g.*)
*Figures adjusted to avoid double counting.

engineers, a further 340,000 with engineering qualifications worked in various scientific research institutes.

There were 1,043,500 Soviet school teachers with tertiary qualifications at the end of 1967. These were teaching mainly at the secondary level, especially over the last two or three years of the secondary school. Only 10 per cent of primary teachers (grades 1–4) had tertiary qualifications.[8] Of all teachers with tertiary qualifications, 18.5 per cent (193,580) held essentially administrative posts as principals or vice-principals in the school system.

An important functional group of the Soviet intelligentsia is that of advanced teaching and research personnel. This group numbered 770,000 in December 1967[9] and 883,400 at the end of the decade. That is to say, 14 per cent of employed intellectuals in 1967 were working at scientific research or in advanced teaching and research. The changing distribution of this scientific workforce is indicated in Table 4 below:

TABLE 4 *Distribution of scientific workers 1950–65*

	1950	1960	1965
In scientific institutes	70,500 (43.4%)	200,100 (56.5%)	390,000 (58.7%)
In tertiary educational establishments	86,500 (53.2%)	146,900 (41.3%)	221,800 (33.4%)
In ministries & departments	5,500 (3.4%)	7,200 (2.2%)	52,800 (7.9%)
Total	162,500	354,200	664,600

Thus over the entire period 1950–65 the number of scientific workers in research institutes increased relative to the number in tertiary educational establishments. This reflected government decisions taken in the early 1960s for the reorganization and strengthening of scientific research work. These decisions[10] resulted in the more rapid expansion of scientific research institutes and the restriction of the amount of research work done in tertiary educational establishments.

The distribution of the scientific workforce according to speciality, as it stood at the end of 1967, is given in Table 5 below:

TABLE 5 *Distribution of scientific workers according to speciality, December 1967*

	No. of scientific workers	%	Including	
			Dr of Science	Candidate of Science
Technology	340,303	44.2	3,755	45,324
Physics–maths	77,108	10.0	2,034	16,040
Economics	42,475	5.5	651	10,485
Philology	42,191	5.5	641	7,938
Medicine & pharmacy	41,548	5.4	3,830	22,451
Chemistry	38,984	5.1	1,056	9,900
History & Philosophy	32,257	4.2	1,150	12,726
Agric. & vet. science	31,932	4.1	1,175	11,396
Biology	31,785	4.1	2,028	13,253
Education	26,639	3.4	168	3,895
Geology & mineralogy	18,396	2.4	873	5,815
Fine arts	9,760	1.3	97	992
Geography	6,344	0.9	288	2,194
Law	3,759	0.5	239	1,917
Architecture	2,276	0.3	53	700
Others	24,256	3.1	216	4,305
Total	770,013	100.0	18,254	169,331

(Source: *Nar.kh.SSSR v 1967 g.*, p. 810.)

The above table indicates that in scientific research and advanced training technology is king. In 1967, 44.2 per cent of the scientific workforce was in technology and the percentage was increasing. On the other hand, the social sciences (including economics, philology, history, philosophy and law) accounted for only 15.7 per cent of the scientific workforce. The table also indicates the unevenness of the qualifications of scientific workers. Some professions, especially medicine, biology, physics and mathematics, and geology, had a much higher percentage of Doctors of Science than others. On the other hand, the social sciences and education trailed behind the overall average.

While the USSR Academy of Sciences acts as the main planning and co-ordinating agency for Soviet scientific research, it does not employ the majority of scientific workers. In December 1967 the USSR Academy of Sciences maintained 215 scientific research institutes employing 29,987 scientific workers, and the Academies of Sciences of the Union Republics operated 331 scientific institutes employing 30,295 scientific workers. Overall only 7.8 per cent of scientific workers were employed in institutes controlled by the Academies of Sciences.

The fourth structural group which we notice in the Soviet intelligentsia is that of doctors and medical research workers. There were 598,200 doctors in the USSR at the end of 1967, or one for every 396 inhabitants.* A minority of highly qualified doctors (41,548) are fully engaged in scientific research in various institutes linked to the Ministry of Health and to the Academy of Medical Sciences. The overwhelming majority work as physicians, surgeons, or specialists of various sorts, in the vast network of hospitals and clinics stretching throughout the USSR. While there is some unevenness in the distribution of doctors to population throughout the country, and some Union Republics have a better ratio of doctors to population than others, there is a remarkable uniformity and evenness in the medical services for such a large and diversified society. Thus in 1967 there was one doctor for every 376 inhabitants throughout the RSFSR, slightly better than the USSR average. In the Far Eastern Region the figure was 1 per 363 inhabitants, while in

*The USSR had 25.3 doctors per 10,000 population in 1967. Comparable figures were: the United Kingdom 14.5 (1964), the USA 18.9 (1965), and West Germany 19.3 (1965).

Eastern Siberia it was 1 doctor to 492 inhabitants and 1 to 208 inhabitants in the Central Region. The figures for the Central Asian republics were poorer, but still very good by international standards. Thus Turkmenia had 1 doctor per 461 inhabitants, Uzbekistan 1 per 542 inhabitants and Kirgizia 1 per 516 inhabitants.[11] Overall there were fewer doctors in rural than in urban areas, and there was a heavy concentration of more highly trained specialists and research workers in Moscow and Leningrad.

Our fifth group of Soviet intellectuals is that of agricultural scientists. Agricultural scientists of various specialities with tertiary qualifications numbered about 170,000, or almost 3 per cent of all intellectuals in the workforce. The majority of these (124,500) were employed as agronomists, zootechnicians (specialists in animal husbandry), and veterinary scientists. Most of these specialists worked in the field, as employees of state farms and field research stations, or as members of collective farms. Others worked in urban-based agricultural research institutes, or were employed in administrative positions in the agricultural ministries.

Our group of unclassified intellectuals, estimated at 1,450,000, includes most of the creative intelligentsia (writers, artists, actors, film producers, etc.), and most of the specialists employed in mass communications, such as journalists and television personnel. I have also put into this unclassified group the large number (perhaps as many as 750,000) of Soviet graduates working in civilian administration. Intellectuals are to be found at all levels of the party apparatus from the Politburo to the *raikom*, and in the state administration from the USSR Council of Ministers down to the *raiispolkom* and even the village Soviet. Other intellectuals are serving in senior positions at all levels in the parallel administrative structures of trade unions, co-operatives, *Komsomol*, and social organizations.

In all the above sections of the Soviet intelligentsia the lower professional positions tend to be held by persons with secondary specialist qualifications. In technology, agricultural science, health, and teaching, tertiary trained specialists are still in a minority.

The growing importance of the intelligentsia as a whole is clear enough. It is the most rapidly growing section of the workforce. Thus while the workforce increased by 28.5 per cent over the years 1960–6, the number of tertiary graduates in the workforce increased by 47.3 per cent. Engineers increased by 57.6 per cent, scientific workers by 101.1 per cent, and scientific workers in technology increased by 140 per cent.[12]

The rural intelligentsia

At the time of the 1959 census only 608,000 tertiary graduates, or 16.1 per cent of the total, lived in rural areas. While there were 32 persons per 1,000 population with tertiary education in the USSR there were only 5.6 per 1,000 in the country.[13] By the end of the sixties probably less than 15 per cent of Soviet intellectuals lived in the country but the gap between the educational level of urban and rural areas was somewhat less.

The rural intelligentsia is not only less numerous than the urban intelligentsia, it is less diverse. Its most important groups are the rural doctors, teachers and other cultural workers, agronomists and other agricultural specialists, economic managers, local administrators and party officials, and military officers. Generally speaking, qualifications are lower in the rural areas. In 1959 persons with secondary specialist qualifications outnumbered persons with tertiary qualifications by more than three to one, while they were less than two to one throughout the entire economy. Outside of the district centres the rural intelligentsia is spread very thinly. In 1965 there were only 17–18 specialists (including those with secondary specialist qualifications) per state farm.[14] Even in 1969 only about 3 per cent of all workers in agriculture were specialists, and only a minority of these had tertiary qualifications.[15]

The weakness of the rural intelligentsia cannot be easily corrected. Although the number of both tertiary and secondary specialists increases steadily, the intelligentsia, even more than other sections of rural society, experience the limitations of rural life and the strong pull of the cities. Not only do rural intellectuals have to contend with isolation and the lack of cultural facilities, but their salaries and living conditions are often inferior to those of their city cousins. The salaries of specialists employed on collective farms vary in accordance with the productivity of the farm. Thus at the end of the sixties collective farms in Belorussia were divided into ten groups. The monthly salary of a farm chairman in the first group was 270–300 rubles, whereas the monthly salary for a farm chairman in the tenth group was only 140 rubles. Agronomists, engineers, veterinary scientists and zootechnicians received 100–120 rubles a month if they worked on a farm in the first group, but only 95 rubles if they were unlucky enough to work on a farm belonging to the tenth group.[16]

Housing entitlements of rural intellectuals vary according to the profession. Teachers, doctors and medical workers, and qualified cultural workers, are entitled to receive rent-free flats, which are provided out of the village or district budget. But specialists employed in collective and state farms do not receive this treatment and often have inferior housing. Rural specialists are often permitted to own individual plots and cows. However, the subsidiary household economy holds small joy for the majority of rural professionals, especially the more highly qualified ones. Thus a recent survey of the household economy of specialists employed in state and collective farms, agricultural stations, rural schools and hospitals, in five Belorussian provinces showed that only 684 out of 1,455 specialists kept cows. The only groups where a majority of specialists kept cows were specialists employed on collective farms, lower grade medical workers, and cultural workers. On the other hand, only 2.2 per cent of scientific workers, 19 per cent of doctors, and 38 per cent of school teachers and kindergarten workers, kept cows.[17]

Because of the poverty of rural life many professions are under-staffed. Thus rural schools are forced to a greater extent than urban schools to rely on untrained teachers, and medical services are sometimes operated on a skeleton staff of doctors filled out by lower qualified medical assistants. An investigation in Belorussia in 1967 showed that 12 per cent of teachers in rural schools in the Mogilev *oblast* had no teacher training as against 7 per cent of teachers in the urban areas of the same *oblast*. In Gomel *oblast* the figures were 15.6 per cent and 6.6 per cent respectively.[18] Rural medical services were worse off than rural education. Thus, although there were on average 23 doctors for every 10,000 inhabitants in the republic, in some outlying districts one doctor, assisted by three to five lower level medical workers, had to look after 7–8,000 inhabitants. In Kirov district in Mogilev province there were positions for 48 doctors but only 29 of them were filled. In the Rogachev district, Gomel province, only 64 out of 112 doctor's positions were filled.[19]

In some ways Belorussia is untypical of the USSR. The republic was heavily hit by the war and during the fifties and sixties there was a good deal of emigration from Belorussia to Kazakhstan and other rapidly developing areas. Consequently the under-supply of specialists could well be worse in Belorussia than in most other areas.

One of the greatest problems confronting rural authorities in the Soviet Union over recent decades has been to ensure that a reasonable proportion of rural youth remain in the country after they have qualified as professionals. The task has been a difficult one as the range of jobs in the countryside is generally much less than that offering in the cities. Rural youth tend to follow the professional opportunities offering, and these often draw them away from the villages. At the present time more youth aspire to tertiary education than can realize it. But in some areas at least, the rise in agricultural productivity, and in living and cultural standards, has led to an increase in professional opportunities. In such areas more rural youth are planning to remain in the country. This was shown in two investigations into the level of job expectancy and job realization carried out in 1964 and 1970 into school leavers in Pochinok district in Smolensk province. The first survey[20] was based on 430 interviews with pupils in the graduate classes (two schools were eight-year schools, three were ten-year schools) from five village schools. In 1970,[21] a follow-up interview of 401 of these pupils showed considerable differences between their aspirations and their realizations. This was particularly so in the case of those aspiring to a non-technical tertiary education. Whereas 28.8 per cent of the respondents in 1964 sought to enter a non-technical tertiary educational establishment (category 5 in Table 6), only 12.6 per cent of the 401 persons in the follow-up interviews had realized this ambition. On the other hand, three times as many as had expected to had ended up in industry. The 1970 survey of 458 graduate pupils in the same five village schools showed interesting variations in the pattern of job expectancy. The proportion expecting to go on to non-technical tertiary education had risen to 37 per cent. A higher proportion

—41.9 per cent in 1970 as against 30.5 per cent in 1964—indicated a desire to stay on in the villages either working on the farms or as some kind of rural specialist.

The under-supply of rural intellectuals is thus a product of a dual development pattern. Urban intellectuals do not occupy all the available professional positions in the country because conditions there are worse than they are in the urban areas, because authorities in the rural areas are often unable to meet the norms laid down by the profession and, consequently, professionals find it easy to locate excuses for moving back to the cities. Second, those rural youth who do gain secondary specialist or tertiary qualifications are usually urbanized in the process of education so that they are apt to emulate their more urbanized colleagues and stay in the cities. Until the material and cultural levels in the countryside reach those of the city this dual under-supply of intellectuals is likely to continue. While Soviet leaders may aim at abolishing the distinction between town and country they have not yet realized it.

Women intellectuals

In no country in the modern world have women held such a prominent place in economic life as in the Soviet Union. Because of the loss of male workers in both World Wars and in the Civil War, and because of the greater opportunities for female employment provided under socialism, women have moved into most occupations in considerable numbers, and today provide the major portion of several professional groups. Women constituted 47 per cent of all workers and employees in 1959 and 50 per cent in 1967. In 1967 women constituted 47 per cent of all workers and employees in industry, 28 per cent in construction, 44 per cent in state farms and dependent agricultural industries, and 24 per cent of workers in transport. In several professions with a high concentration of graduates women represented even higher proportions of the workforce. Thus women constituted 52 per cent of professional workers with a tertiary education in 1967, including 30 per cent of engineers, 40 per cent of agronomists, zootechnicians and veterinary scientists, 63 per cent of economists, 72 per cent of doctors, and 68 per cent of teachers, librarians, cultural and educational workers,[22] 38 per

TABLE 6 *Village youth—hopes and realization*

| | Graduates of 1964 | | Graduates of 1970 |
	Plans	Realized (1970)	Plans
1 Stay at work on the *Kolkhoz*	27	27	47
2 Go to agricultural school, agric. technicum or agric. college	56	50	61
3 Go to work in industry	31	93	54
4 Enter technical tertiary establishment *or* a technicum	102	51	57
5 Enter university, pedagogical, medical, or other tertiary educational establishment	124	51	169
6 Continue studies but speciality as yet undecided	90	129	70
Total	430	401	458

(Source: A. Aleksandrov, M. Garin, N. Shtanko, *Izvestia*, 12 November 1964, p. 2.
M. Garin, A. Druzenko, *Izvestia*, 12 July 1970, p. 3.)

cent of scientific workers,[23] and 45 per cent of tertiary students.[24]

Despite the prevalence of women in the professional workforce they tend to be under-represented in the highest scientific, educational, administrative and managerial positions. Thus women constituted only 12 per cent of Doctors of Science and 27 per cent of Candidates of Science in 1967, but 38 per cent of all scientific workers. While 70 per cent of teachers were women in 1967, only 22 per cent of principals of secondary schools, and 25 per cent of principals of eight-year schools were women.

Ethnic inequalities in the Soviet intelligentsia

Until the January 1970 census material has all been published there will remain some uncertainties about the extent of the educational and employment opportunities afforded to various national groups throughout the USSR. However, the general picture seems clear enough and enables some conclusions to be drawn.

In the first place, the educational levels and opportunities offering were still very uneven as between advanced and less developed national groups in the USSR at the time of the 1926 census. The period between the 1926 and the 1939 censuses saw the establishment of a uniform network of primary and in-complete (i.e. seven-year) secondary schools throughout the USSR but universal education to this level was still not achieved. The period between the censuses of 1939 and 1959 was complicated by the war losses (84,000 schools and other educational establishments were destroyed), but there was nevertheless a steady expansion of education, especially in the formerly backward regions, so that by 1970 universal ten-year schooling was within reach.

Second, despite the evening up of educational standards throughout the USSR some considerable differences still remain between the larger cities and the rural areas, and between more advanced and less advanced national groups. Third, the very process of evening up means the reduction of the earlier differential advantages of certain groups such as Jews and Georgians. Fourth, the rising educational level of the USSR, while at first producing an increase in the number of written languages in use has, over the past two decades at least, been tending towards the predominance of the major language within each republic and, overall, the dominance of the Russian language.[25] National minorities are becoming steadily Russianized,* and conse-

*Russification is the process of national erosion by conscious identification with the majority Russian group. Russianization proceeds through education

quently, the percentage of Russians in the population, notwith-standing lower birth-rates, is declining only slowly. Between 1959 and 1970 it fell from 54.9 to 53.4 per cent. This dual process of Russianization and Russification[26] is most rapid amongst Jews, Poles, Germans, Belorussians, Ukrainians and Armenians; and less pronounced amongst Georgians, Kazakhs, Uzbeks, Azerbaidjanis, Tadjiks, Tartars and the Baltic peoples.

Fifth, since facility in spoken and written Russian is virtually a prerequisite for admission into the Soviet intelligentsia, the entire intelligentsia is to some extent Russianized, and because of this, the intelligentsia is the most mobile section of Soviet society.[27] However, some national groups are more scattered than others, and this probably holds good for intellectuals as well as for other members of the group. Russians and other Slavs are widely dispersed, while Baltic peoples and Central Asians are more concentrated. The most dispersed groups are the Jews and the Armenians, the least dispersed of the major national groups, the Georgians.[28] Local nationalism (in the Soviet con-text, 'bourgeois nationalism'), has been most pronounced over recent years amongst the Baltic peoples, Georgian and some Central Asian national groups, Ukrainians and Tartars. It is probably weaker amongst the more dispersed groups such as Jews and Armenians, although even here it seems to have in-creased somewhat during the sixties. Armenian nationalism is quite strong in the Armenian Republic, although it is less noticeable amongst Armenians living outside Armenia. The up-surge of Tartar nationalism since 1964 has been directly related to the refusal of the Soviet government to consider the restor-ation of the Crimean ASSR. The rise of Ukrainian nationalism, especially amongst some sections of Ukrainian students and writers, represents a smouldering resentment at the swamping of Ukrainian culture by Russian culture,[29] fanned by the strength-ening of national communism in Eastern Europe.[30]

The Table below provides a summary of the inequalities between the main national groups as they stood at the census in 1959. During the decade of the sixties, Jews, Armenians and

---

in Russian language. Both processes are facilitated by the law which allows some discretion to the individual when he registers his nationality at the age of sixteen. This is particularly so in the case of children of mixed marriages.

TABLE 7 *Inequalities in the ethnic composition of professionals with tertiary qualifications, January 1959*

Rank order	Nationality	% of total population	Nationality	No. of professionals (thousands)	%
1	Russians	54.9	Russians	1,077.2	58.1
2	Ukrainians	17.7	Ukrainians	471.1	14.6
3	Belorussians	3.6	Jews	(275.0)*	8.5
4	Uzbeks	2.9	Belorussians	87.9	2.6
5	Tartars	2.8	Georgians	83.6	2.6
6	Kazakhs	1.7	Armenians	69.0	2.1
7	Azerbaidjanis	1.4	Tartars	46.4	1.4
8	Armenians	1.4	Azerbaidjanis	44.1	1.4
9	Georgians	1.2	Uzbeks	42.2	1.3
10	Lithuanians	1.1	Kazakhs	31.5	0.9
11	Jews	1.1	Lithuanians	26.9	0.8
12	Moldavians	1.1	Latvians	22.8	0.7
13†	Chuvashis	0.7	Estonians	17.9	0.5
14	Latvians	0.7	Chuvashis	13.1	0.4
15	Tadjiks	0.7	Tadjiks	10.2	0.3
16	Turkmen	0.5	Moldavians	9.9	0.3
17	Estonians	0.5	Turkmen	8.8	0.3
18	Kirgiz	0.5	Kirgiz	8.6	0.3
	USSR Total†	100.0		3,235.7	100.0

*Estimate only. No figures were published for Jewish professionals in the 1959 census. In December 1957 there were 260,900 Jewish professionals, 9.3 per cent of the total. In December 1962 there were 310,600, 7.9 per cent of the total. In November 1964 there were 322,700, 7.1 per cent of the total.
†Some groups are omitted after no. 12.
(Based on the Table in N. de Witt (1961) p. 531, and on Tables in *Chislennost, sostav i razmeshchenie naselenia SSSR*, 1961, p. 25.)

Georgians, suffered less through deliberate exclusion than through the consequences of a policy which gave preferential treatment to under-privileged national groups. The position in the smaller republics varies. It is clear that indigenous, 'administratively recognized' peoples, receive preferential treatment in admissions to universities and other tertiary establishments. Thus Moldavians receive preferential treatment in Moldavia, Belorussians in Belorussia, Tadjiks in Tadjikistan, and Uzbeks in Uzbekistan. Tartars receive preferential treatment in the Tartar ASSR, but not elsewhere. Jews are especially affected by this policy since there are few Jews and no tertiary establishments in the Hebrew Autonomous *Oblast*. But Central Asian Jews, who have been settled in Uzbekistan for centuries, are not considered indigenous and get less generous treatment than do native Turkic peoples.[31] Similarly, in old Jewish areas such as Moldavia and Odessa Jews get no special privileges and are negatively discriminated against. Jewish students in tertiary institutes in Odessa in 1969 were said to represent only 3 per cent of students, yet Jews formed almost one quarter of the population of the city.[32] In other regions a disproportionate percentage of Jewish students were studying part-time or doing courses by correspondence, a fact which probably indicates restriction of the number of full-time places going to Jews.[33] While little is known about the selection process operating in strategic educational institutes, such as those leading to the diplomatic service and senior government posts, it seems clear that Jewish applicants are discriminated against.[34] On the other hand, Jews are still 'over-represented' in law, medicine, economics, mathematics, philosophy, sociology, art, literature and music. Jews still form over 7 per cent of all scientific workers in the USSR and are the third largest group in the ranks of scientific workers. Only Russians and Ukrainians supply more scientists and the Jewish representation is relatively much greater than the Russian or the Ukrainian.

If more information were available about the representation of various national groups in particular professions, we would perhaps find that many nations show a preference for particular occupations. Such preferences are partly historical and cultural, although they are also influenced by current administrative practices. Jews represented only 1.9 per cent of the population of Belorussia in January 1959 and the percentage was less in 1970. However, Jews formed 5.1 per cent of tertiary students in Belorussia in 1960–1,[35] and 3.5 per cent of medical students in 1969–70.[36] Jews formed 12.1 per cent of the cultural intelligentsia of Belorussia in 1970 as against 45.2 per cent Belo-

TABLE 8 *Ethnic composition of scientific workers*

Nationality	1950 No.	1950 %	1960 No.	1960 %	1969 No.	1969 %
Russians	98,948	67.0	229,547	64.8	583,564	66.1
Ukrainians	14,692	9.0	35,426	10.0	95,079	10.8
Jews	25,125	15.4	33,529	9.5	63,661	7.2
Armenians	3,864	2.4	8,001	2.3	18,708	2.1
Belorussians	2,713	1.7	6,358	1.9	17,850	2.0
Georgians	4,263	2.6	8,306	2.3	17,100	2.0
Azerbaidjanis	1,932	1.2	4,972	1.4	12,396	1.4
Uzbeks	845	0.5	3,748	1.1	11,254	1.3
Tartars	1,297	0.8	3,691	1.0	10,899	1.2
Lithuanians	1,213	0.7	2,959	0.8	7,482	0.8
Kazakhs	739	0.5	2,290	0.6	7,132	0.8
Latvians	1,468	0.9	2,662	0.8	5,758	0.7
Estonians	1,235	0.8	2,048	0.6	4,539	0.5
Moldavians	126	0.08	590	0.2	2,213	0.3
Tadjiks	168	0.1	866	0.2	1,949	0.2
Turkmen	128	0.08	707	0.2	1,704	0.2
Chuvashis	301	0.2	606	0.2	1,650	0.2
Kirgiz	94	0.06	586	0.2	1,640	0.2
Others	13,857		7,266		30,850	

(Source: *Nar.kh.SSSR v 1969 g.*, p. 696.)

russians and 29.2 per cent Russians.[37] On the other hand, Jews provided only 3.05 per cent of directors of secondary schools and 5.5 per cent of directors of schools for workers and peasant youth.[38] But of 18,678 scientific workers and academics in Belorussia in 1969, the Belorussians provided 48 per cent, the Russians 35.5 per cent, the Jews 7.8 per cent, and other nationalities 2.7 per cent.[39]

Jews, Georgians, and to a lesser extent, Armenians and Russians, seem to have suffered from the preferential treatment afforded to applicants for admission to higher educational establishments with industrial or other work experience. This policy, the result of the Khrushchev educational reform, was operated strictly between 1958 and 1964, and less strictly after August

1964. These groups were affected because they already had achieved 'over-representation' in education, a situation which encourages a high demand for tertiary education on the part of the younger generation. Jews and Russians were also over-urbanized in terms of the USSR average, and with a consequent higher level of professional employment. The percentage of Jewish tertiary students fell from 3.2 per cent in 1960–1 to 2.7 per cent in 1962–3, and to 2.4 per cent in 1969–70.[40] The percentage of tertiary students who were Russian fell more slowly to reach 61.3 per cent in 1962–3 and 59.7 per cent in 1969–70, while the Ukrainian percentage fell from 14.2 per cent to 13.6 over the same period. The percentage of Georgian students dropped from slightly over 2 per cent in 1960–1 to 1.9 per cent in 1969–70, while the Armenian percentage sank to 1.5 per cent in 1962–3 but had risen to almost 1.8 per cent by 1969–70. Over the same period, Kirgiz, Tadjiks, Turkmen, Uzbeks, Azerbaidjanis, Moldavians and Belorussians, increased their representation in the student population. The inequalities are sharper amongst scientific workers. Thus in 1967, 66.2 per cent of all scientific workers were Russians, 10.6 per cent Ukrainians, and 7.7 per cent Jews.[41]

Despite the inequalities between national groups within the Soviet intelligentsia the main trend over the entire period since 1917 has been towards the raising and equalizing of opportunities. Cultural lags have sometimes acted to retard this process. Thus the low prestige of professions such as engineering and technology in Central Asia has restricted the influx of native intellectuals into these professions. On the other hand, the opposite has been the case with revered professions such as medicine and administration. But the drive to develop a unified socialist economy and Soviet civilization, combined with the use of Russian as the *lingua franca* of intellectuals, has had a remarkably homogenizing effect on the intelligentsia. The process has been stimulated by the practice of centralized decision-making in appointments which has meant that industries and research establishments, schools and advanced educational institutes, clinics and hospitals, are mainly controlled by centralized ministries which allocate specialists to available jobs on the basis of qualifications rather than nationality.[42] Hence any large hospital, research institute, school or industrial enterprise, commonly has a mixture of nationalities on its staff. This is especially true of Moscow, Leningrad and Novosibirsk. The position in the non-Russian areas is far from uniform. It seems likely that indigenous specialists receive preferential treatment in appointments to universities and other teaching establishments, to hospitals and to public administration. In old centres such as Riga, Vilnius, Tartu, Kharkov, Kiev and Tbilisi, Russians are probably in the minority. In like manner, student populations are always international, especially those in Moscow and Leningrad. The same is true of smaller universities and colleges, even when selection policy favours the indigenous population.

3 Recruitment and training of the intelligentsia

Intellectuals require special training over a long period of time. No one is born into the intelligentsia but children of intellectuals have at least a three-to-one[1] advantage over the children of industrial workers in gaining entry into the intelligentsia. At the present time applicants for admission to Soviet tertiary educational establishments (*vuzy*) must have completed secondary school and be between eighteen and thirty-five years of age. All tertiary establishments have many more applicants than places, so often only one in three applicants or even one in ten will gain admission. A range of written and oral exams, references and recommendations from schools, *Komsomol*, Party or Trade Union Committee, are used to select students. The examinations vary not only as between universities and colleges but as between faculties within the same establishment. The written examination commonly includes a test in Russian language and this gives some advantage to Russian children or at least to graduates of Russian schools. Formal discrimination against particular ethnic groups or against women does not exist. However, some universities in non-Russian areas give preference to nationals and this acts to counter the differential advantage possessed by better-educated, widely dispersed groups such as Russians, Jews and Armenians. Some institutions closely linked to the Ministries of Foreign Affairs and Foreign Trade are reputed to discriminate against Jews and women. For all that it can still be stated that the majority of places in Soviet tertiary establishments are filled on the basis of merit. *Blat* (pull or influence) operates 'legally' through the fact that certain references are weighted more than others. Influential parents often try to exert pressure on the selectors and in certain prestige institutes in Moscow this is systematized to the extent that lists of candidates appear before the selection board with certain names already asterisked. Such marked candidates are guaranteed acceptance. The 'strategically placed' phone call is so common in many Moscow institutes that students consider it almost a part of the entrance procedure. On rare occasions examiners have been known to accept bribes from wealthy students.

While a high degree of social mobility existed in the Soviet Union throughout the 1960s it was probably declining. The main factor here was the slower rate of expansion of tertiary education compared with secondary education. Thus in the eight years 1960–1 to 1967–8 the number of tertiary students increased by 79 per cent but the number of pupils in the last two years of the secondary school increased by 167 per cent.[2] In 1969 the number of tertiary students increased by 2 per cent over the previous year but the number of school pupils rose by 16 per cent.[3] Throughout the 1960s probably not more than one in ten or one in eight of the university age group (eighteen to twenty-five years) succeeded in gaining a higher education.[4] And yet before the end of this decade Soviet sociologists had shown that between 45 and 97 per cent of pupils in the final year at school wanted to go on to higher education.[5] Clearly, such a contradiction between opportunities and expectations must produce personal strain and intensified competition for the available places. In these circumstances the children of intellectuals have a clear advantage over others. Soviet sociological investigations in Chelyabinsk, Novosibirsk, Moscow, Leningrad and Riga have shown that the children of professionals are much more likely to choose a professional career than are the children of workers or peasants.[6] Children of workers and peasants think of mobility in more limited steps—from a collective farmer to a mechanic, from a mechanic employed in the collective farm to a position as a skilled worker in some urban industrial plant, from a skilled tradesman to a clerical worker. Some aspire to positions in the semi-intelligentsia through rural teachers' colleges or agricultural colleges.

The situation towards the end of the 1950s was such that Khrushchev claimed in 1958 that 70 per cent of university students in Moscow were the children of intellectuals or white collar workers. One of the main objectives of the Educational

Act of December 1958 was to reverse this trend. For some years after 1958 only a minority of places in tertiary institutes were open to school leavers, the majority being reserved for those with two or more years experience in industry, agriculture, construction or in the armed forces. However, resistance from parents and educational authorities effectively sabotaged this reform. Even before it was revised in August 1964[7] many of those with work experience entering universities were not workers or peasants in the strict sense of the term but merely high school graduates who had been diverted into unskilled or semi-skilled industrial, construction, agricultural or service posts. By the end of the sixties most Soviet universities and other tertiary institutes were operating on a double-quota system. One quota (about 70–80 per cent of places) was open for competition to school graduates. The other quota (only 20–30 per cent of places) was reserved for deserving industrial and agricultural workers and for ex-servicemen. There was no competition between the two streams and many of the latter group would certainly not have gained a place under conditions of open competition. The poor quality of many candidates offering themselves for special selection in this way caused most universities and other tertiary institutes to provide special courses to assist rural and working-class applicants. About the same time city high schools began to run special two-month courses to prepare rural candidates for higher educational establishment entrance exams. In 1969 the Central Committee of the CPSU and the USSR Council of Ministers issued a joint decision which required all tertiary institutes to organize preparatory courses of eight to ten months for rural and working-class students. Students doing these courses are paid the same scholarships as first-year tertiary students.[8] Such measures will undoubtedly tend to check the trend towards a hereditary intelligentsia. It is probable however, that the city-based intelligentsia will continue to dominate the tertiary educational network. The only exceptions will be in certain 'low prestige' tertiary and secondary specialist institutes where rural youth enjoy a certain natural advantage over city youth. These include agricultural colleges, provincial teachers' colleges, and economics faculties and institutes. Graduates of such institutes tend to move into the rural rather than into the urban intelligentsia.[9]

Higher educational institutions

Higher educational institutions are widely scattered in the USSR. In the 1967–8 academic year there were 785 tertiary institutions, of which 422 were in the RSFSR, 136 in the Ukraine, and the remainder scattered throughout the thirteen smaller Union Republics. Each Union Republic has at least one university and several other tertiary institutions. Tertiary institutions exist in 250 cities and towns. The accelerated educational development of the sixties has led to some redistribution of tertiary institutions. Thus over the eight years 1960–1 to 1967–8 the total number of tertiary institutions in the Russian federation rose from 430 to 442 while in the five central Asian republics it rose from 68 to 102. Over the same period there was a 112 per cent increase in the number of tertiary students in Central Asia and the Central Asian proportion of total students rose from 9.1 to 11.2 per cent.[10]

There is a wide range of types of tertiary educational institutes, but there are four basic types—universities, technical institutes, factory-based technical institutes, and specialized professional institutes.

Universities vary greatly in size and range of courses offered, from Moscow State University (with fourteen faculties, two campuses, over 200 departments and research centres and upwards of 40,000 students) to universities of only a few thousand students with a limited range of faculties and departments. Even a major discipline such as law is not offered at every university but only at Moscow, Leningrad, Tbilisi and Erevan, and, of course, at several specialized tertiary institutes. Two new universities established during the 1960s were the Patrice Lumumba Friendship University at Moscow and a university in the Yakut ASSR in Siberia. The Lumumba University was established as a training centre for students from the developing countries. In 1970,[11] ten years after its foundation, it had an enrolment of 4,061 students of whom 969 were Soviet, 834 Africans, 964 Latin Americans, 770 from Arab countries and 524 from South-East Asia. There were 44 universities with 317,700 students in 1967–8.

Higher technical institutes exist in most large cities. The general or polytechnical institutes offer courses in various branches of technology, mathematics, physics, radio-electronics, economics, etc. Branch institutes are usually more specialized and give diplomas in one or a few related specialities. Some higher educational institutes are linked to particular ministries such as the Ministry of Finance, the Ministry of Agriculture, the Ministry of Foreign Trade, or various industrial ministries. Some large industrial plants, such as the Likhahev Plant in Moscow, the Leningrad Metalworking Plant, and the Rostov Agricultural Machinery Works operate their own tertiary institutes. Students at these factory-based institutes study full-time for the first half of each academic year and do practical work for the second half. They receive stipends which are higher than those received by students in ordinary technical institutes and most students are employed by the firm when they graduate. Finally, there are several hundred tertiary educational establishments giving training for particular professions, teachers' colleges, medical institutes, agricultural colleges, economics institutes, law institutes, fine arts institutes, and physical culture institutes.

Courses in all tertiary institutes are of four to five years duration for full-time students and they are invariably intensive courses which provide for a combination of political instruction, foreign language instruction, basic and advanced theoretical training, and practical work. Practical work begins earlier than in most Western universities so that medical students will be assisting in operations and other hospital duties from the second year of their course and teacher trainees start intensive teaching practice rounds in the third year of their course.

Higher education in the USSR means primarily advanced specialist training. Thus the Regulations on Higher Educational Establishments of the USSR, 22 January 1969, state the aims of tertiary education as follows;

> To prepare highly qualified specialists with deep theoretical and necessary practical knowledge according to specialty, possessed with Marxist-Leninist theory and the latest developments of domestic and foreign science and technology, educated in the spirit of high communist consciousness, of Soviet patriotism, of friendship of peoples and proletarian internationalism, possessing skills for organizing mass-political and educational work.

University students receive a slightly broader education than do other tertiary students, but it is still highly specialized. As the rector of Leningrad University stated recently: 'Our goal is to create specialists with a deep understanding of their specialty, and to do it with a maximum of efficiency and a minimum of time.'[12] Students consequently find that thirty-five to forty-five hours a week are spent in attending lectures, seminars, or laboratory classes, especially in the first two years of their course. Since progress is determined by a process of continuous examination homework is heavy and steady. In so far as the universities provide a 'liberal education', it is expected to come mainly through the compulsory political and social studies courses and through extra-curricula activities. All students do a minimum of three ideological courses (usually one a year over the first three years of a course). The three basic courses were changed early in 1962 to the following: historical materialism, fundamentals of scientific Communism, and, Soviet construction. Students in social science will normally do additional compulsory courses on dialectical materialism and the history of the CPSU. They may also do advanced courses on Marxist methodology as it applies to their speciality. These ideological courses are handled by special departments. In larger institutes separate ideological departments exist in the history of the CPSU, philosophy, political economy, and scientific Communism. In smaller institutes all courses are controlled by a single Department of Marxism-Leninism.[13] While these compulsory courses do provide a kind of compulsory broadening of narrow specialist training they are frequently criticized by students as being too rigid and dogmatic. Consequently they make a minimal impact on the general student body.

Streams in education

While minor differences exist between the above types of higher educational institutes, they are less significant than the differences between three types of students—full-time or day students, evening students, and correspondence students. Although no distinction exists between these three groups as to final qualifications received, they do represent distinct streams which receive their tertiary education under very different conditions. In

1967–8 there were 1,890,000 full-time tertiary students, 652,000 students attending evening classes and 1,769,000 students doing courses by correspondence. Thus only a minority of students were full-time students. Throughout the sixties the percentage of part-time and correspondence students increased, rising from 52 per cent of the total in 1960–1 to 55 per cent in 1967–8.[14] Most full-time students receive stipends[15] although many receive financial support from home or hold part-time jobs to supplement their stipends. Full-time students are mainly in the eighteen to twenty-five age group. Evening and correspondence students hold full-time jobs and do their courses over a longer period and often under greater difficulties than do full-time students. They are often older and finish their diplomas later. The drop-out rate is higher. Consequently, from the point of view of efficiency, the full-time student body is the most productive source of specialists. Thus in 1967 while full-time students constituted 45 per cent of all students they provided 52 per cent of graduates.[16] Notwithstanding this slight differential Soviet evening and correspondence courses do account for almost half of the annual output of graduates, a surprisingly high proportion. That this is so is a consequence of decades of effort on the part of the Party and the government.

By 1967 there were thirty independent correspondence and evening faculties at regular institutes.[17] Correspondence institutes usually arranged for students to spend several weeks each year in residence at the institute doing intensive courses of lectures and seminars. For example, the All-Union Legal Correspondence Institute in Moscow was founded in 1932. It had graduated 40,000 students up to 1968. In 1968, 43,000 out of 65,000 law students in the country were studying by correspondence, 15,000 at the Moscow Institute. The Institute provides general training in legal sciences, civil and criminal law, administrative law, labour law, agrarian law, etc., and it prepares specialists for all legal occupations, including posts in the Soviet administrative apparatus. The Institute maintains regional groups of lecturers and operates tutorial courses for its students at various centres. Students receive printed lecture notes and books and journals which are sent out from the central Institute. Students are brought in to the central Institute at various stages during their course to attend lectures and seminars, and to have consultations with lecturers and other experts.[18]

Even though Soviet sociologists have not so far examined in detail the differences between the three streams of students it is clear that evening and correspondence courses are used mainly by workers seeking to become specialists. Consequently they must provide the main avenues through which the children of workers and peasants enter the intelligentsia.

While evening classes and correspondence training give special benefit to workers and peasants seeking to become specialists, the Soviet Army offers additional opportunities. Many conscripts, especially rural youth, complete their secondary schooling in the army. Many also receive secondary specialist qualifications and so enter the ranks of the semi-intelligentsia when they leave the army. Others remain in the army and gain higher education through various military academies. Such academies train not only staff officers but engineers, scientists, military historians, and other highly qualified specialists.

Higher Party Schools

While the overwhelming majority of Soviet intellectuals are recruited via the formal tertiary institutes a small number of more mature recruits come via the Higher Party Schools. The present network of Higher Party Schools was established by a decision of the Central Committee of the CPSU on 2 August 1946. The schools originally provided a three-year course and shorter nine-month retraining courses for senior party and government officials. In 1947 the older system of Party Correspondence Schools was absorbed into the Higher Party Schools. Shorter two-year schools were organized under City, Territory and Province Party Committees for training local officials. By 1953 there were seventy-five of these Province-City Party Schools. In 1953 the two-year course was extended to a three-year course, thus bringing it into line with the courses provided in the Higher Party Schools. Advanced post-graduate 'in-training' was provided by the Academy of Social Sciences under the Central Committee of the CPSU, established in August 1946. This academy is concerned with the training of research and theoretical workers for the central party apparatus and for republican, provincial and city establishments. Courses in this academy normally last three to four years.

By a decision of 26 June 1956 the Central Committee established four-year Higher Party Schools in thirty cities throughout the country. This modification was designed to give senior *apparatchiki* a higher Marxist education and also to increase general training in technology, agricultural economics, production principles, etc. At the same time the courses at the Higher Party Schools under the Central Committee were reduced from three to two years because the higher general level of students made this possible. At the same time the Correspondence Departments were reorganized into Higher Party Correspondence Schools offering a four-year course. Between 1955 and 1957, fifty-two Soviet Party Schools were organized in the provinces, territories and republics. These offered a three-year course designed for training chairmen of collective farms, secretaries of rural party committees, chairmen of village Soviets, and departmental officers of party and Soviet district committees. In all, over the years 1946 to 1957, 3,500 persons graduated from Higher Party Schools under the Central Committee, 9,193 from Higher Party Correspondence Schools, and 65,628 from provincial, territorial and city schools. The majority of these graduates were party cadres but there were also thousands of Soviet workers,[19] newspaper workers and *Komsomol* officials. Over the years 1946 to 1966 there were 160,448 graduates from Higher Party Schools, from regional Party Schools and from Soviet-Party Schools.[20]

National representation in the Soviet intelligentsia

The object of Soviet educational policy since the Revolution has been to promote a unified Soviet intelligentsia. But since some groups were more advanced at the outset the process of equalizing educational opportunities has inevitably meant some restrictions on the rate of expansion of the more advanced groups. The Table below indicates clearly enough the progress of this 'levelling-up' process during recent years. The main 'over-represented' groups among the students at the end of the sixties were Jews, Georgians, Armenians, Russians, Kazakhs, Azerbaidjanis. The Baltic peoples were slightly under-represented

TABLE 9 *Ethnic composition of tertiary students*

		Percentage of USSR population of national groups January		Numbers in thousands and percentage of tertiary students from particular national groups					
		1959	1970	1962–3		1967–8		1969–70	
1	Russians	54.9	53.4	1,803.8	61.3	2,599.5	60.3	2,716.3	59.8
2	Ukrainians	17.7	16.8	426.9	14.5	600.1	13.9	620.4	13.6
3	Belo-russians	3.6	3.7	85.0	2.9	125.6	2.9	129.2	2.8
4	Uzbeks	2.9	3.8	70.1	2.4	126.3	2.9	147.5	3.2
5	Tartars	2.8	2.4	57.1	1.9	76.6	1.8	83.7	1.8
6	Kazakhs	1.7	2.2	51.8	1.7	85.3	1.9	98.2	2.2
7	Azer-baidjanis	1.4	1.8	36.6	1.2	72.5	1.7	85.7	1.8
8	Armenians	1.4	1.5	44.6	1.5	73.4	1.7	80.0	1.7
9	Georgians	1.2	1.4	58.5	2.0	82.4	1.9	87.6	1.9
10	Lithuan-ians	1.1	1.1	31.8	1.0	47.4	1.1	48.9	1.1
11	Jews	1.1	0.9	79.3	2.7	110.0	2.5	110.1	2.4
12	Moldav-ians	1.1	1.1	15.9	0.5	29.0	0.7	30.7	0.7
13	Chuvashis	0.7	0.7	11.5	0.4	15.5	0.36	15.7	0.3
14	Latvians	0.7	0.6	19.8	0.7	22.3	0.52	22.2	0.5
15	Tadjiks	0.7	0.9	13.5	0.46	22.9	0.53	27.3	0.6
16	Turkmen	0.5	0.6	11.8	0.41	19.2	0.45	22.7	0.5
17	Estonians	0.5	0.4	15.4	0.52	19.4	0.45	18.4	0.4
18	Kirgiz	0.5	0.6	11.9	0.40	20.0	0.46	24.4	0.5
	Others (not estimated)								

(1959 population figures from *Chislennost, sostav i razmeshchenie naselenia SSSR*, Moscow, 1961. 1970 figures from the statement of the Central Statistical Administration, *Pravda*, 17 April 1971. Other figures taken from tables in various editions of *Nar.kh.SSSR*.)

but not so much as were the Moldavians, Belorussians, and Ukrainians. Central Asian peoples, Uzbeks, Tadjiks, Kirgiz and Turkmen, were approaching parity. Of the larger minority groups the worst represented seem to be the Tartars and the Chuvashis. While the majority of places in tertiary institutes in the smaller republics are no doubt intended for the main national group in that republic, some national groups seem to gain less than their fair share of places even in their own republics. Thus it can be calculated that Latvian students comprised less than 60 per cent of tertiary students in Latvia in 1967–8, while Uzbeks represented less than 61 per cent and Moldavians less than 67 per cent of tertiary students in their respective republics. Armenian students in the USSR however measured 151 per cent of the tertiary students in Armenia in 1967–8. Once again the dispersed urban peoples such as Russians, Jews and Armenians got certain differential advantages over other nationalities in admission to tertiary educational institutes.

Main professional groupings

More than in most industrial societies the output of professional cadres in the USSR is geared to the development of the national economy. Thus while there is some sociological evidence that upwards of 30 per cent of Soviet students are interested in the social sciences,[21] the economy demands that first priority go to technology and engineering and that the social sciences be afforded only limited opportunities for expansion. Despite the great development of sociological research during the sixties there was still no undergraduate training in sociology in 1970.

The largest group of Soviet students—45.2 per cent in 1967–8 —were training to become specialists in technology, in industry, construction, transport and communications. Over 30 per cent of students were training to become teachers, about 10 per cent were students of agriculture, 7.1 per cent were in economics or law, 6.4 per cent in medicine, less than 1 per cent in fine arts and cinematography. The same professional groups dominate the output of tertiary graduates. Thus in 1967 there were 479,500 graduates of higher educational institutions of whom 38.2 per cent were in technology, 35.4 per cent were in education, 8.2 per cent in agriculture, 8 per cent in economics and law, 7 per cent in medicine and physical education and 1.1 per cent in fine arts and cinematography. University graduates represented less than 8 per cent of all tertiary graduates in 1967.

Postgraduate students

If the tertiary degree or diploma is the normal entrance certificate to the general Soviet intelligentsia the postgraduate degree is increasingly a prerequisite for admission to the superior intelligentsia, to controlling positions in the administration of scientific research and education. At the end of 1968 there were 20,000 doctors of science, 186,400 candidates of science and 98,139 aspirants in the USSR. Thus only 4.6 per cent of all graduates had postgraduate degrees or were aspiring to secure them.

It is not easy to commence postgraduate research in the Soviet Union. Persons seeking admission to aspirant courses must be under thirty-five years of age (unless they intend doing the course part-time without leaving their employment when they may be up to forty-five years of age) and have completed at least two years postgraduate employment. Brilliant students may be admitted as aspirants immediately after graduation. Before admission to the aspirant's course students must pass an entrance examination in a given specialty, in the history of the CPSU, and a foreign language.

Aspirants attend special lectures and do other course work over one academic year. At the end of this they must pass the aspirant's examination in a speciality, a foreign language and dialectical and historical materialism. They then commence work on a candidate's thesis which may take two or more years full-time or part-time research. Persons starting on a full-time aspirant's course are guaranteed a stipend at least equal to the salary they were receiving at their previous place of employment. The aspirant's course may also be done on a part-time basis over a period of three years. Students who make unsatisfactory progress during the course or subsequently may be excluded.[22] Notwithstanding this many theses are not completed in the specified time or are not completed at all. From what has been said above it is clear that the Soviet degree of Candidate of Science is a senior research degree, nearer to an American doctorate than to an English master's degree. The senior Soviet degree of Doctor of Science is of a much higher standard and is normally achieved by only a minority of scholars, and usually not till middle age. There are very few doctors of science in their early thirties.

The above description makes it clear that only a small percentage of Soviet intellectuals achieve postgraduate qualifications.

However, many more do short-term retraining or advanced courses in order to improve their qualifications. Professionals doing courses to raise their qualifications receive special stipends so that their earnings will not be less than they would have been had they stayed at work. Such courses are organized in most, if not in all professions, including medicine, school teaching and lecturing. Thus lecturers in social sciences are provided for by special courses organized by the USSR Ministry of Higher and Secondary Specialist Education at the Universities of Leningrad, the Urals, Rostov-on-Don, and Tashkent. These courses last five months and provide for 800 places. The USSR Academy of Pedagogical Sciences organizes four-month courses to raise the qualifications of lecturers employed in teachers' colleges and universities.[23]

TABLE 10 *Distribution of aspirants according to discipline, December 1968*

	In tertiary educ. est.	In scientific institutes	Total	%
Technology	21,047	18,069	39,116	39.8
Physics–maths	7,505	3,927	11,432	10.6
Economics	5,649	3,313	8,962	9.1
Agric. & vet. science	3,223	3,914	7,137	7.3
Biological science	2,541	3,496	6,037	6.2
Chemistry	3,052	2,506	5,558	5.6
Medicine	3,637	1,705	5,342	5.5
History & philosophy	3,618	1,016	4,634	4.7
Geology	1,154	1,582	2,736	2.8
Philology	1,883	456	2,339	2.4
Education	1,231	566	1,797	1.8
Fine arts	657	222	879	0.9
Law	602	222	824	0.8
Geography	498	315	813	0.8
Architecture	248	285	533	0.6
Total—all aspirants	56,545	41,594	98,139	

(Source: *Nar.kh.SSSR v 1968 g.*, p. 701.)

Administration of universities and higher educational institutes

Tertiary educational institutes in the Soviet Union are all under the general supervision of the USSR Ministry of Higher and

Secondary Specialist Education and the Union Republican Ministries of Higher and Secondary Specialist Education. This means that the actual administration of higher education is handled at the Union Republican level. Some particular institutes are administered by other central or republican ministries but these also are subject to general supervision by the Ministry of Higher and Secondary Specialist Education.

Educational institutes, like most other administrative units in the USSR, combine the principles of one-man management and collective leadership. Each institution is headed by a rector and pro-rector who are appointed by the appropriate ministry. There is also an academic council (*ucheny sovet*) representing the staff of the various faculties and departments, the Party, the *Komsomol*, and the trade union organizations in the particular institution. The academic council is the main administrative agency in the institute and is chaired by the rector. The academic council is also responsible for planning the teaching and research work carried out by the institute, for the appointment of junior staff and for promotions.

Each institute is subdivided into a number of faculties and departments, each with its own dean and chairman and academic council. Departments may be further divided into sectors (or sections), each sector instituting a small collective for promoting the teaching and research work of its members. For most university and college teachers the department or faculty is the boundary of their academic world. Party or *Komsomol* activities may occasionally carry them beyond the limits of the department.

Teaching appointments in universities and colleges are made primarily on the basis of qualifications and experience. Senior administrative positions, such as rector and pro-rector, are certainly influenced by the Party and are probably on a party *nomenklatura*. All appointments are temporary and in principle terminate every five years. In practice, most appointments are renewed. Lecturers and senior lecturers who have not demonstrated sufficient zeal for research are sometimes 'banished' to provincial universities or colleges. This is regarded as a hardship since teaching, research and publication opportunities are often worse for provincial scholars than for those in the larger cities. In addition to many hundreds of specialist and scientific journals in the USSR on a central or republican basis, each university or large institute publishes its own research reports, usually in the form of a bi-monthly bulletin. Even so there are often complaints from younger scholars about the difficulty of getting articles published either in the specialist journals or in the daily newspapers.

Students play only a very minor role in the administration of Soviet universities and colleges. The *Komsomol*, to which more than half of Soviet students belong, has official representation in the main academic council of every university or college and sometimes on faculty academic councils. But the *Komsomol* is not an organization which fully reflects student opinion. Even more than Students Representative Councils in most British universities the *Komsomol* Committee represents a minority of politically minded and ambitious students. Many *Komsomol* secretaries in universities and colleges are already paid functionaries of the organization. Students are directly represented on faculty and departmental councils and seem to play an important role in criticizing courses and teaching arrangements. Larger issues, including domestic and international politics are taken up through general meetings of the Party or *Komsomol*.[24] Very few undergraduate students belong to the Party and only junior staff (assistants and lecturers) will be members of the *Komsomol*.[25] Outside of the *Komsomol* there are many sporting, cultural and scientific student clubs and societies. These provide reasonable scope for student activity.

The Soviet student population during the sixties was not uninterested in general social and political questions but it was quiescent, even dormant, by international standards. There were some issues (such as the writers' trials from February 1966 onwards, the Polish and Czech crises in 1968, and the Middle East situation) which caused deep unrest but even here there were no massive revolts. Student dissidence is probably growing but so far it has not provided a serious challenge to universities or to the government. Students are often taxed by the discomforts and hardships of their lives but in general they accept them because they are spurred on by the competition for a tertiary qualification, for a certificate or a degree which is the necessary ticket for admission into the intelligentsia, and into a land of opportunity, of service, of achievement, material rewards and honour.

Graduation problems

Graduation is a tremendous strain for most Soviet students. The final examination involves a combination of written and oral tests and also a dissertation (a thesis or project) done in the final year and embodying independent research. But once graduated the Soviet intellectual has fewer worries than his counterpart in most Western countries. He is assured of a job and usually can choose between several. In his final year lists of suitable positions with conditions of salary, bonuses, etc., are posted at his institute. He may also be visited and briefed by 'talent scouts' sent out from the ministries, research institutes and firms. With few exceptions graduates are required to work in an assigned position for three years after graduation. Most students accept this obligation willingly enough and count it as a contribution to society in return for their training. In practice, students are normally offered a choice of positions. Besides this there are many ways to escape an unattractive assignment, including family obligations and health reasons. Even professions which are dependent on the majority or a large minority of graduates accepting country posts (such as agricultural science, medicine, teaching) find it difficult to control their graduates and many country positions are unfilled or are only temporarily filled.

The direction of intellectual workers into suitable positions is a tremendous task when there are half a million tertiary graduates and almost a million graduates with secondary specialist qualifications each year. The complexity of the bureaucracy is such that graduates often receive posts to a distant factory or office only to find on arrival that no position is available for a person with their qualifications, or, if a post exists, it is really redundant and their training is not utilized.[26] Country teachers arrive at a rural school but are unable to find suitable housing, even though the local authorities are obliged to give them high priority. Not unnaturally, the wastage is accelerated.[27] In other cases highly qualified specialists discover on arrival at their first job that their job is not quite what they thought it was. One solution is to look for an early transfer to a similar job in a better establishment. Another is to use one's qualifications to get a different job or even to start to 'retool', to requalify as something else. The process is officially discouraged, yet tens of thousands of intellectuals are nevertheless practising it with considerable success. Thus a country physician might switch to research, a language teacher to translating or interpreting, an agricultural scientist to engineering, a university lecturer to journalism or some specialist post in the party *apparat*. Professions from which there is normally considerable wastage provide special advantages for those wishing to change their occupation. Thus graduates without a teaching qualification may go directly into the fourth year of the course at any Pedagogical Institute.[28]

The problem is best tackled earlier. Sociological research in recent years and newspaper controversy have drawn attention to some notable gaps in the Soviet system of professional training. Thus, while transference from one tertiary institute to another is fairly easy in the Soviet system during the first two years of a course in order to work for a different diploma, high school graduates lack sufficient knowledge about the range of jobs available for graduates, or even about the range of qualifications being provided at the institute to which they are seeking admission. The intensity of the competition for places in tertiary institutions causes many applicants to try for several, sometimes as many as a score of institutes. Consequently they frequently gain admission to institutes about which they know very little and which are not high on their preference list. Applications are determined partly by preference but also by knowledge of the law of supply and demand, so that students whose results are not good enough to gain admission to preferred institutions will try to get in where the pressure is less and the entrance standard somewhat lower. Few Soviet schools have proper facilities for pupil guidance. Few parents can fill the gap. Hence already by the end of the sixties some Soviet cities had established municipal guidance centres offering advice on institutes, courses, and future job opportunities to school leavers.[29] While an expansion of these facilities will certainly ease the situation it will not solve it. The problem is more fundamental and can only be resolved by a several-fold expansion of tertiary education. This is not an immediate possibility even in an advanced socialist society such as the USSR.

4 The intellectual culture

It is doubtful if intellectuals in any modern community possess a distinctive life style which marks them off from the rest of the population. In all modern and developing societies intellectuals will be more urbanized, better educated, more cosmopolitan, more 'civilized' than the population at large. Many, and in some societies, most intellectuals, will enjoy higher living standards than their non-intellectual neighbours. But in any advanced society the size and complexity of the intelligentsia and the unevenness of rewards for particular occupations and positions will mean that there will be a wide range of income and general living standards amongst intellectuals. Some few will be rich, more will be quite well off, but many will live in poverty or near poverty. This is certainly true of the Soviet Union.

Attempts have been made to define intellectuals in terms of the characteristics of their training and the requirements of their discipline. Sharp and White[1] distinguish between the 'creative intelligentsia' and the 'intellectually trained'. While the former are primarily engaged in developing scientific and intellectual skills (university teachers, basic research scientists, etc.), the latter are mainly engaged in applying their skills, technique and generalizations to particular situations. The intellectually trained apply 'intellectual technique', which is derived from the 'intellectual culture' rather than from practice. This intellectual technique is applied to production and to all spheres of non-productive labour. It differs from the 'material technique' of the craftsman and the production worker in that it is primarily concerned with applying generalizations and rests on a highly conscious grasp of abstract generalizations and their relationship to particular situations. The alienation of intellectually trained persons arises largely from a conflict between the ethics of their intellectual training and the objectives of their work which are not set by themselves but by their employers.

Because of the values implicit in intellectual work through its ties with the intellectual culture a collision tends to arise between two ideologies. On the one hand there is the rational, universalist, humane and autonomous outlook of the intellectual culture. On the other hand there is the sectional, 'materialistic' and purely instrumental approach of the owners and controllers.

Such a conceptualization is very difficult to apply to the Soviet Union. The utilitarian emphasis in all higher educational establishments is such that teachers and students, research workers and graduates, generally accept their role as 'specialists', as instruments for the furthering of the economic, social and cultural objectives of the regime. Education is so specialized and intensive that students are not encouraged during training or during subsequent employment to generalize about the role of intellectuals in society. The basic ethical attitude of the Soviet intellectual is that of the highly trained specialist. His skills are rarer than those of the skilled worker so he receives higher material rewards. His idealism is the limited idealism of the specialist. His alienation is also likely to be limited—limited to the perennial frustrations of intellectual specialists who can never get the ideal conditions necessary to produce the ideal results. But while he can continue to work as an intellectual and to produce less than perfect solutions, or less than perfect articles or books, and to receive better than average income and facilities, then the intellectual will continue to work without open rebellion. He will even do this when major elements in his working environment change for the worse. This is so not because the intellectual is passive or cowardly but because the very fact that he is highly specialized gives him unusual determination to continue to operate as an intellectual specialist come what may. The strains which arise from bad working or living conditions, inadequate material resources, staff shortages, range of work demands, bureaucratization of work situations, etc., are much more likely to be seen as unavoidable frustrations than as basic contradictions requiring a revolutionary solution.

What I have written above applies to most but not all of Soviet intellectuals. During the 1960s the number of 'alienated intellectuals' was certainly increasing. Many writers, artists, actors, and scholars, found an increasing conflict between their professional obligations and the rules and practices of the regime. Thus increasing numbers of intellectuals have been brought into opposition with the party leadership on questions of censorship and basic civil rights. Senior scientists have been driven by their scientific ethic to protest against pollution, economic waste and the fetishism of technology. Such people have moved beyond a narrow professionalism and are reasserting the traditional role of the intelligentsia as 'the conscience of humanity'.

Is the Soviet intellectual specialist only marginally different from any other specialist, from a skilled industrial or agricultural worker? Soviet writers, in their effort to stress the 'unity of Soviet society' naturally argue that no basic differences exist between various sections of the workforce. Thus the Leningrad sociologist, P. P. Amelin, writes:[2]

> Intellectual culture (*intelligentnost*)—the totality of inspired, intellectual, cultural, civic and ethical qualities of the individual, is not necessarily connected with his social and professional membership of the intelligentsia. The term 'intellectual culture', in my opinion, includes two aspects; one of them fixes the spiritual quality of leading Soviet persons developed in the process of building socialism and communism and reflecting the contemporary level of socialism and spiritual development of socialist society; the other is connected with the aims and perspectives of socialist society, with the transformation of the 'intellectual culture' into the property and possession of all members of society. Interpreted in this sense the concept of 'intellectual culture' is larger in volume and richer in content than the concept of the 'intelligentsia'. The quality of the 'intellectual culture' is already inherent not only in the majority of professional workers of mental labour, but in the leading representatives of other large and small social groups.

While it may well be true that the qualities of the intellectual culture do not depend only on professional qualifications, they are at present more likely to be found amongst intellectuals than amongst others.

Soviet intellectuals are not clearly demarcated from other

townsfolk in terms of housing, dress, cultural amenities or eating habits. The things which separate intellectuals from others stem from differences in training and in work situation. The training of the Soviet intellectual may be more specialized (or more professionalized) than is the case with many Western intellectuals, but it is still very much an intellectual training, a training on the basis of lectures and seminars, set laboratory drill and individual study. Direct production or field experience plays a relatively small part in this training. While most graduates are employed in production they are mostly not working directly on the production line. Thus the peculiar qualities of intellectual labour acquired as a student are carried through to the factory and to the farm. The engineer works in the engineers' office, the scientist in the research laboratory, the economist as a teacher or as a research officer in a scientific research institute or in a planning office. By and large the intellectual wears a suit and keeps his hands clean. He works with books and other printed material, with ideas for new equipment, with solving production problems, or management and research problems. Much more than the industrial worker or the farm worker his work involves him in direct person to person situations. Though these situations are seldom 'pure', and are very much complicated by power and status factors, they differ fundamentally from situations dependent on machines and material production. To this extent the 'intellectual culture' or a rather imperfect equivalent of it, operates in the Soviet Union as in other advanced countries. Certainly there are fewer 'free professionals' in the USSR than there are in advanced capitalist countries. Virtually all doctors, teachers, lawyers, architects, even writers, are dependent on the Party, government, or other large organizations. In this respect the Soviet Union is merely in advance of most countries since the trend in all advanced countries is towards the decline of the free professionals. And while the eclipse of the free professionals might tend to bureaucratize relations amongst professionals[3] it is counterbalanced by the elimination or near elimination of motives of private gain from professional employment. Soviet professionals, especially doctors, dentists, pharmacists, teachers and lawyers, are expected to give unselfish service to the general community irrespective of the income level of their clients. Moreover, Soviet professionals are not particularly restricted in their jobs because they are all or mainly government employees. There is a great deal of movement within a profession from one institute or agency to another. There is also a great deal of mobility between professions. Very many graduates change their speciality once or even twice within ten years of graduation. This is caused partly by the rapid expansion of Soviet science and technology[4] which creates new opportunities and new disciplines quicker than new courses can be organized to train new experts. It is also accelerated by persons moving from one post to another in the hope of gaining better conditions, higher salaries and more freedom from the irritations of bureaucratic control.

To a far greater extent than the general Soviet public or even than the higher party and Soviet officials, Soviet intellectuals are a part of the international community of the intelligentsia. That is to say, the restrictions which operate to limit the contacts between ordinary Soviet citizens and foreigners are less rigid or less effective in regard to intellectuals. Intellectuals find it easier to travel and easier to make contacts with foreign specialists. Soviet specialists participate regularly in international scientific conferences and institutes engage in a wide range of exchange agreements with Communist and non-Communist countries. Such exchanges are closely controlled by the government. This means that many eligible scientists are excluded from Soviet scientific delegations and even if they are included they are closely disciplined and seldom speak as individuals. The Soviet delegation at an international conference is likely to be 'culture bound' and less successful in its contacts with Westerners than are delegations from East European Communist states. This is particularly true in the social sciences, as was shown by Soviet participation in international sociological and political science conferences during the 1960s.

A measure of this increase in international scientific exchange is shown by the following figures. Whereas 1,600 foreign scientists visited the USSR in 1959 as guests of the USSR Academy of Sciences, 9,000 did so in 1966. In the latter year over 3,500 Soviet scientists made foreign trips, including 1,648 to socialist countries and almost 2,000 to 53 capitalist and developing countries. In 1966 the USSR Academy of Sciences participated in over 130 international scientific congresses and conferences to which 865 Soviet delegates went. Exchanges of scientific material are steadily growing. Thus in 1966 the Fundamental Library of the Social Sciences in Moscow, operated exchange agreements with some 1,300 organizations in 70 foreign countries and exchanged 220,000 books and magazines.[5]

Despite close control over international contacts Soviet intellectuals are often surprisingly well informed about international developments in their own and allied fields. Students and graduates alike listen regularly to foreign news broadcasts, including the BBC and The Voice of America and even Radio Free Europe.[6] To meet the interest of Soviet intellectuals in overseas news the Union of Soviet Journalists was forced to establish a special weekly paper, *Za rubezhom* (Abroad), consisting mainly of translations from foreign newspapers. This paper has a circulation of almost a million and is always quickly sold out. The gap in overseas papers and journals is made up partly by overseas Communist publications and the U.S. journal, *Amerika*, which comes out in a limited edition. But intellectuals, especially graduates, employed in research institutes have access to all manner of foreign periodicals, newspapers and books in their institute libraries, or in special libraries such as the Fundamental Library of the Social Sciences in Moscow. Certain sources may only be used with special permission and in special reading rooms. Consequently Soviet scholars are avid for exchange agreements with foreign scholars they happen to meet. Such agreements work to the advantage of both parties. Soviet intellectuals, because they are more likely to know one or more foreign languages are more likely to meet visiting scholars than are ordinary Russians. Many of these meetings will take place in work places and while polite and friendly they are likely to remain somewhat stiff and formal. But increasingly during the sixties as restraints on foreign contacts were relaxed and as housing conditions improved, foreign intellectuals have been able to visit their Soviet counterparts in private homes and to talk freely over a wide range of subjects. Notwithstanding the remarkable increase in the 5th Department of the KGB[7] during the last few years, especially since March 1968, foreign visitors to the USSR have continued to find a steady improvement in their personal contacts with Soviet citizens.

Soviet intellectuals are not only more international than other

Soviet citizens, they are usually more Sovietized. Soviet scholars are first of all conscious of the fact that they are Soviet intellectuals, only secondly of the fact that they are Russians, Georgians, Armenians, Jews, Latvians, etc. To a far greater extent than is the case with industrial workers or rural workers, their professional and social contacts are truly trans-national, truly country-wide. Intermarriage between Russians and non-Russians is quite common among intellectuals, almost certainly more common than among the population generally.

The fuller understanding of the 'intellectual culture' of the USSR requires a consideration of the professional organizations of intellectuals, of their professional life and also of the life styles of individual intellectuals. The remainder of this chapter and the following chapter will be concerned with these matters.

Professional organizations

In one sense Soviet intellectuals are more integrated into the general community than are intellectuals in other countries. Thus amongst students and younger graduates the main youth organization, as amongst workers and collective farmers, is the *Komsomol*. More than half of Soviet students belong to the *Komsomol* and these associations continue into adult life. Even after he has graduated from the *Komsomol* at twenty-eight, a Soviet intellectual, if he is not a member of the Party, will retain some *Komsomol* contacts for years. He will, for example, be quite likely to participate in *Komsomol* public service (e.g. in 'agitation groups' during elections or in *subbotniks*). Like the individual worker, intellectuals belong to trade unions. All employees, professional and non-professional, in a given enterprise, hospital, school or institute, will belong to the same trade union. But trade union activity is less relevant to the intellectual than it is to the industrial worker. In most research and teaching institutes, for example, the trade union is less important than the party organization or the *Komsomol* group. In an institute in which I worked in 1965 the trade union work seemed to fall mainly onto the clerical and office staff. Most research workers belonged to the trade union but they found little time or enthusiasm for its activities.

The party organization or group is the main non-professional organization in any teaching, research or industrial enterprise. The party organization not only controls activities such as the 'wall newspaper' but extramural or extension lectures, and general participation in public organizations and party campaigns. It is also responsible for the party education of members and sympathizers, for the ideological work of intellectuals in the given institute, and even in assisting in formulating and fulfilling research programmes.[8] Party organizations in schools and universities keep teaching courses closely under survey. In production enterprises party organizations work closely with both management and trade unions and form an essential part of the 'directing triangle'. Throughout the 1960s party primary organizations exercised the right of control over the work of administration in 'research institutes directly related to production' (Art. 59, Rules of the CPSU, October 1961). However this right was not possessed by party primaries operating in Academy of Sciences institutes. In the months after April 1968 it was evident that the role of party organizations in academy institutes was being expanded and this was formally recognized at the 24th Congress in April 1971 when party primary organizations in all research institutes were given control over administration.

Not only are the basic organizations the same for the intellectuals as they are for the workers but the basic forms of work organization are very similar. Thus the basic groupings within the collective farm or workshop are the work brigade or team and the smaller 'link'. These collectives are held together by socialist competition with other collectives and by the knowledge that individual rewards depend on the ability of the collective to fulfil and to over-fulfil the production plan. In like manner the basic group within the research institute is the sector (or laboratory), a group of seven to twenty-five or more scholars working in the same or related fields. Such a sector will have no formal organization other than an honorary chairman who is responsible for calling meetings of the sector for discussing joint and individual research programmes, hearing and discussing papers, and mutually assisting each other. Because of this emphasis on collective labour much more of Soviet scientific and literary research is group research than is the case in Britain, Canada, Australia or even the United States.

Despite the similarities described above there remain many features of the work organization of Soviet intellectuals which distinguish them from the rest of society. The sector, like the work brigade, produces a close face-to-face relationship between its members. Such basic units establish egalitarian attitudes between their members, even though qualifications, status, experience and income differences continue to operate. But in the case of this intellectual collective work relationships operate outside the enterprise, in libraries, in homes, and in social contacts. Friendship circles amongst Soviet intellectuals are often closely related to past or present intellectual collectives.[9] Friendships begun in one institute or in one sector of an institute are often carried on even when some members have transferred to other institutes. Such friendship ties often prove fruitful in establishing new institutes. A key scientist appointed to head an important department in a new institute will recruit his team from amongst his former colleagues now working in various institutes. It is doubtful if such continuity and development occurs on the basis of work brigades in collective farms or in the factories.

Above the sector of a research institute is the department. A major research institute might have four or more departments and a dozen or more sectors. All these organizational levels are part of the formal structure of the institute but the administrative structure is minimal. Thus even departmental heads are usually held by senior associates or professors who combine administrative duties with research duties. Departments are sometimes headed by deputy-directors of the institute. The director and one or more deputy-directors hold mainly administrative posts. Even the director of a research institute is expected to do scientific research, although many directors are so taken up with administration that their research falls away. This is partly because research institutes of all kinds are grossly understaffed in terms of office personnel. The usual practice is for only the director and the deputy-directors to have full-time secretaries. Other administrative posts such as editors of journals, academic secretaries, etc., will be held by scientists. Typing pools are virtually non-existent.

The main administrative and controlling body in a research institute is the academic council (*ucheny sovet*). The academic council is quite a small body, usually of fifteen to twenty persons, although on some occasions it could be up to forty. The size is directly related to the size, complexity, and geographical distribution of the institute. The academic council is responsible for the general administration of the institute; for determining salaries (within centrally determined norms) and for supervising post-graduate research work. It is also responsible for planning the research work of the institute as a whole and for controlling its publications. Beyond this it is also concerned with arranging meetings and conferences. The academic council will also be ultimately responsible for the research programmes of sectors and individuals, although in practice there is a good deal of decentralization in the operation of research and other scientific programmes. Individual members of an institute are required to submit regular monthly work plans which indicate the range of work planned for the coming month. Again, in practice, there is a good deal of flexibility in the way such requirements are met. Most scientific research institutes have long since abandoned planning for planning's sake.

One requirement for creative intellectual activity is direct personal contact across institutions and universities. This is managed fairly well in the Soviet Union. In the first place, the mobility of Soviet teachers and research workers means that many scientists retain associations with former institutes. These links include co-operation with former colleagues on particular publications, consultation, participation in conferences, etc. Second, many senior Soviet scholars have part-time appointments in one or more institutes in addition to their main institute. Thus one scholar of my acquaintance, a senior staff member of the Institute of Eastern Studies in Moscow, had part-time posts at the Moscow State University and the Higher Diplomatic School (under the Ministry of Foreign Affairs). Another divides his time between a senior post in the Institute of State and Law and a Military Academy. Several members of the Institute of State and Law simultaneously hold teaching posts in the Law Faculty of the Moscow State University. Third, there are frequent conferences organized by university faculties, by Academy of Sciences Institutes, by other research institutes and by higher educational establishments and Higher Party Schools. Such conferences draw together scholars from several institutes, universities, cities and even countries to listen to papers and to discuss particular topics within a given field. These conferences are necessary because there is a good deal of overlap between the research work being carried out by particular centres and the conferences serve to keep scholars up to date with work being done in other centres and also to prevent unnecessary duplication. Over recent years, with the growth of particular professional associations, conferences have also been organized by professional associations, the Soviet Association of Political Science and the Soviet Sociological Association both organized several major conferences during the sixties. Fourth, the setting-up of scientific councils (*nauchnye sovety*) under the main divisions of the USSR Academy of Sciences in the early 1960s greatly influenced co-operation between scholars working over fairly large research fields. Such councils are primarily concerned with the co-ordination of research being done at different centres in different institutions. One scientific council I investigated in April 1969 was based mainly on the Institute of Eastern Studies. It had about seventy members, mostly belonging to the Institute and its various regional branches. About 20 per cent of its members belonged to other institutes, including several representatives from other senior Moscow institutes such as the Institute of World Economics and International Relations. In addition to the scientific councils of the USSR Academy of Sciences there are also scientific councils linked to USSR and Union-Republican Ministries.[10] These are particularly important in Education, Public Health, Culture, and in industrial Ministries. In these advisory scientific councils there are many representatives of institutes other than those controlled by the particular Ministry.

Professional associations in the narrow sense of the term, i.e. associations representing particular professional groups within the intelligentsia, are relatively unimportant in the Soviet Union. Many professions, including engineers, doctors and lawyers, are without any distinctive professional organization. Professional organizations which survived the 1917 Revolution were mostly eliminated during the years 1929–31.[11] The existing professional organizations fall into two broad groups—those organized directly by the Party in order to increase its ideological control over strategic sections of the intelligentsia such as writers, artists, journalists and film workers; and organizations of particular segments of intellectuals where a professional organization is almost a condition of representation in international professional associations and participation in international conferences. Thus Soviet philosophers participated in the International Sociological Congress as early as 1956 but from June 1958 this participation has been through the Soviet Sociological Association. This Association was in existence several years before a central Institute of Concrete Social Research was established in the USSR late in 1968. Similarly, Soviet participation in the International Political Science Association (from the 3rd Congress in 1955) was at first handled through the legal section of VOKS. In 1960 a Soviet Association of Political (Governmental) Sciences was established,[12] with members drawn from the Institute of State and Law and from other institutes and universities. But even as late as 1970 there was no Institute of Political Science in the Soviet Union nor was political science taught as an academic discipline in any Soviet university. Only a few of the members of the Association were interested in developing political science as an academic discipline.

Associations like the above do not have any real life, although there are some signs of the Soviet Sociological Association becoming more effective as an organizer of conferences and liaison between its members. Its present membership is reported to be well over a thousand, at least thrice that of the Soviet Association of Political Science. Neither of the above associations has a journal or even a regular newsletter. Nor is there any likelihood of this situation changing in the immediate future. Under such conditions strictly professional associations can have only a token existence.

While conferences organized by specific professional associations are still a rarity, large centrally organized conferences of particular professions are very frequent, perhaps too frequent.

Major conferences held during the sixties included the following:

The All-Union Conference of Soviet Medicine (December 1960)

The All-Union Conference of Scientific Personnel (June 1961)

The All-Union Conference of Higher School Personnel (July 1961, February 1967)

The All-Union Conference of Heads of Departments of Social Sciences of Higher Educational Institutes (February 1962, June 1968)

The All-Union Conference of Historians (December 1962)

The All-Union Creative Conference of Publicists (June 1964)

The All-Union Economic Conference (May 1968)

The All-Russian Conference of Cultural Workers (January 1968)

The above conferences were in addition to the 'trade union type' congresses of various professional unions—architects, teachers, artists, film workers, and writers, which were held at fixed intervals throughout the decade. Such conferences normally lasted four to five days and included speeches by party, government and *Komsomol* leaders, as well as by educators, scientists and various kinds of specialists. Such conferences are clearly multi-purpose conferences designed to put particular groups of specialists more closely in touch with central policy-making agencies in their area and to allow for some cross-fertilization of ideas concerning new developments and old problems. They are public rather than narrowly professional conferences.

The 'creative intelligentsia', or key sections of it, are effectively organized into professional trade unions. Some of these go back many years but most were established during the late fifties or early sixties. The oldest of these, the Union of Soviet Writers, was established in 1932 and held its 1st Congress in 1935. At the time of the 4th Writers' Congress in May 1967 there were 6,608 members, almost a quarter of whom lived in Moscow. The Writers' Union is a privileged association with its own press, newspapers, journals, club rooms in various cities, apartments and rest homes, and an independent income, the Writers' Fund, derived from a tax on book sales. Since a number of publications (varying according to the type of writing) is required to join the Writers' Union, only established or successful writers may belong to the Union.[13] Exclusion from the Union enormously increases a writer's difficulties, deprives him of the Union's facilities, and reduces his living standard. Notwithstanding this, the Writers' Union has been more involved in political struggle than most Soviet professional associations and over several years in the 1960s, the Moscow Branch of the Union was under liberal control, while the Union leadership was conservative. While Writers' Congresses are occasions for public re-dedication of the writers to the Party and the people[14] they are also opportunities for the open voicing of sectional demands.[15]

The Union of Architects was founded in the same year as the Writers' Union, 1932. It held its 3rd All-Union Congress in May 1961. In 1966 there were over 10,000 members of the Union of Architects. The Union publishes the magazines *Arkhitektura SSSR* and *Sovetskaya Arkhitektura* and runs the Architects' Club in Moscow.[16]

The Union of Composers was also established in 1932. This is a small union of only 1,500 members (in 1965), organized along similar lines to the Writers' Union. It runs two musical magazines and the Composers' Club in Moscow.

The Union of Artists is an association of professional artists and art critics. Formed in 1939 it held its 2nd All-Union Congress in April 1963. By June 1967 the membership of the Artists' Union had reached 11,400 and it published three magazines and ran an Artists' Club and display galleries in Moscow. The importance of the ideological role of Soviet artists is illustrated by the 2nd All-Union Congress of Soviet Artists in April 1963. This Congress was attended by several party leaders including Brezhnev, Kirilenko, Kozlov, Mikoyan, Polyansky, Suslov and Ponomarev. The main report, delivered by the Secretary of the Board of the Artists' Union, G. V. Gerasimov, was marked by bitter condemnation of the work of contemporary artists, E. Neizvestny, A. Andropov, P. Nikonov and A. Pologova.[17] Neizvestny was repeatedly attacked throughout the 1960s but despite this he survived and in the early seventies his reputation and success were rising steadily.

The Union of Cinema Workers was founded in 1957 and it includes film directors, producers, camera men, script writers and film actors. It had over 4,000 members in 1966. It publishes two magazines and runs the Cinema Workers' Club in Moscow. The Union held its 1st All-Union Congress in November 1965. Attended by over 600 delegates and 1,000 guests it lasted a full week. Party leaders attending the Congress included

Brezhnev, Kirilenko, Kosygin, Mazurov, Podgorny, Suslov, Demichev and Andropov.[18] The Congress elected a Board to replace the organizing committee which had run the Union until then.

The Union of Journalists, an association of professional journalists, including radio and T.V. newsmen, was formed in 1959. The political importance of the organization was indicated at the outset when N. S. Khrushchev, then First Secretary of the Party and Chairman of the USSR Council of Ministers attended and addressed the 1st Congress of the Union in November 1959.[19] This Congress, like all similar Congresses, sent a message of warm support to the Central Committee of the CPSU.[20]

The Union of Journalists is certainly the most rapidly growing association of creative intellectuals in the USSR. Its membership had topped 40,000 by 1966. Among its journals is the weekly, *Za rubezhom* (*Abroad*), a popular Russian language review of the foreign press. The Union operates the Journalists' Club in Moscow as well as a Photography Studio. It is the main agency behind the semi-official Soviet newsagency, Novosti Press Agency (APN), established in 1961.[21] Today Novosti publishes more than forty magazines and newspapers, including the popular *Sputnik* which is published in several languages.

Intellectuals in public organizations

Mainly because of the fact that Soviet intellectuals are qualified specialists they are unusually active in a wide range of cultural, sporting and scientific organizations of national and local significance. Such organizations form a sort of extension of the exclusively professional organizations we have been discussing hitherto. In 1966 there were 54,000 scientific and technical organizations (NTO) linked to the All-Union Council of Soviet Trade Unions. Intellectuals played a considerable role in these organizations. Besides this there were many scientific and technical associations based on universities and research institutes. In 1966 there were twenty-one scientific and technical societies and more than twenty medical research societies of all-Union importance.[22]

Probably the most important organization for extending the intellectual culture is *Znanie*, or the Knowledge Society. Founded in 1947, the All-Union Society for the Dissemination of Popular and Scientific Knowledge achieved a membership of 40,000 within its first two years, including many leading scientists, scholars, artists and writers. Its importance increased after 1957 when the job of organizing political and scientific propaganda lectures throughout the countryside was transferred from the USSR Ministry of Culture to the Knowledge Society. By 1958 the society had grown to 781,600 members,[23] and to 1,460,820 members by January 1965. Its membership was almost two million by 1970. The society organizes public lectures by various kinds of specialists throughout the cities and villages of the country. In addition to the Knowledge Society, the Party operates through the Higher Party Schools, Universities of Marxism-Leninism which draw many party intellectuals into one aspect or another of adult education.

The Union of Soviet Societies of Friendship and Cultural Relations with Foreign Countries, while not entirely intellectual in its membership, draws its members mainly from the ranks of the intelligentsia, from students, scientists, academics and other professional people. The Union links together about forty national friendship societies and maintains contacts with over 120 foreign countries. The popularity of this Union with students and intellectuals is enhanced by the fact that membership of one of the affiliated societies confers the privilege of using the excellent club rooms and restaurant services of Friendship House in Kalinin Street, Moscow. But the society also attracts intellectuals because it offers access to various foreign delegations visiting the USSR and also opportunities for reading foreign literature and for language practice with visitors. Working in a near-by institute in 1965 I could not fail to notice the frequency with which Friendship House activities were publicized on the institute's notice board.

Other societies founded or extended during the sixties in which intellectuals have been heavily involved include the All-Union Society of Inventors and Rationalizers (formed in 1959 it had over 45,000 primary organizations and four million members by 1965), the All-Union Society for the Preservation of Historical and Cultural Monuments (formed 1965)[24] and the

All-Russian Society For the Preservation of Nature (with 9.5 million members by 1965).[25]

The political significance of such public or social organizations is not being examined here. The creation of new organizations and the activization and expansion of existing organizations was always done on the basis of decisions taken at the highest party level. At times a good deal of moral pressure was brought to bear on different categories of intellectuals to persuade them that it was their civic duty to become active in particular societies. Thus cases were reported in the Soviet press in 1966 of entire school staffs being obliged to take out membership cards in the All-Union Society for the Preservation of Historical and Cultural Monuments. But at the same time the Party and government seemed genuinely concerned with extending the scope and usefulness of such organizations. Thus on 17 October 1962, the USSR Council of Ministers issued a decision 'Concerning the Increased Use in the National Economy of Recommendations and Proposals of Scientific-Technical Societies', which obliged ministries and government departments to apply these recommendations. The same objective was behind the setting up of scientific councils within the ministries in July 1967, the Statute on the Standing Commissions of the USSR Supreme Soviet of 12 October 1967,[26] and the decision of the Presidium of the USSR Supreme Soviet, 'Concerning the Arrangements for Examining Proposals, Communications and Complaints of Citizens' of 12 April 1968.

As we shall see later in this study Soviet intellectuals have not been slow to take up this challenge and have already played a major role in shaping public policy in many fields, especially those concerning economic reform, education, health, scientific research and technology, preservation of natural resources and struggle against water and air pollution.

5   Intellectual life styles

The life styles of individuals in any society are determined partly by personal preference and choice but mainly by class and status situations. Class, at least in the Marxist sense, would seem to be totally unimportant in the Soviet Union. Almost all members of the intelligentsia own no capital and are dependent for their income on the sale of their labour power. Differences in living standards and styles of living between the intelligentsia and the rest of society, or for that matter, within the intelligentsia, are the result of status and power differences rather than class differences. Uneven distribution of power, privilege, income and prestige within Soviet society is closely related to the status position held by individuals. And each important status group tends to produce its own particular ethic, sense of honour and even life style.[1]

Status groups within the intelligentsia

Both Western and Soviet investigations of the question of status groups within the intelligentsia are unsatisfactory. As a rule they recognize only a few groups distinguished by their power position or general professional situation. Thus Inkeles recognizes three groups—the ruling élite, the superior intelligentsia, and the general intelligentsia.[2] V. S. Semenov also recognizes three groupings within the intelligentsia—the government officials, the technical-economic intelligentsia, and the scientific-cultural intelligentsia.[3] While Soviet writers sometimes break these large groups down into smaller groups they mainly use unsuitable census categories for the purpose. Thus Rutkevich and Semenov both use the category 'leaders of organs of government administration and social organizations and their structural divisions'. This entire group numbered 392,100 in 1959. But this group is neither a status group nor a power group since it includes administrative heads at all levels in the governmental, party and other hierarchies from the central down to the district level. Likewise the group of 'leaders of enterprises', numbering 955,200 in 1959, included the leaders of all forms of economic enterprise and their main departments. But clearly there would not be much in common between the leader of a large city based trust and the chairman of a backward collective farm.

The main differential in status (and often power) determination in the USSR would seem to be *position within a formal hierarchically organized power structure*. Since such official hierarchies overlap and are clearly interdependent at all levels, each administrative level tends to produce its own status or status-power system. Thus at the centre, members of the Politburo, Secretariat, and departmental heads of Central Committee departments, form the leadership of the party apparatus. While these people clearly hold more power than people in top state positions (Ministers, Chairmen of State Committees, officials of the Presidium of the Supreme Soviet, heads of main departments, etc.), they are outnumbered by this second group and enjoy no obvious superiority in living standards or life styles. Leaders of other central structures would also need to be included in the central 'leadership group'—secretaries of the *Komsomol*, the AUCCTU, Knowledge Society, and the Presidium of the USSR Academy of Sciences. The same situation operates at republican, city, provincial and district levels. Thus at the district level the leadership group would include *raikom* secretaries, the chairman and secretary of the *raiispolkom*, some key *raiispolkom* officials, directors of local industries, directors of state farms and chairmen of collective farms, district police chiefs and district newspaper editors, the first secretary of the District Committee of the *Komsomol*, and some others. At the district level at least such groups are distinguished by a general similarity in living standards and life styles which mark them off fairly clearly from the surrounding peasants and workers. They often have larger or better situated apartments or houses. They may have an official car. They enjoy incomes which are 50–200 per cent above the district average. They are often members of the leading political bodies of the district, of the *raikom* or the *raiispolkom* or both. Official, business and professional associations often extend to 'friendship circles' so that members of this leading group frequently exchange home visits, attend the same cultural gatherings, and even go on holidays together. While these linkages between different leadership circles have not to my knowledge been studied by Soviet sociologists, there is a wealth of illustrative material in Soviet literature of the fifties and sixties.

The Polish sociologist, Leszek Kolakowski, has pointed out that social stratification in the Communist societies of Eastern Europe, 'is based not on a quantitative inequality of wealth but on a qualitative inequality of privilege'.[4] This is even truer in the USSR where wealth without privilege is wealth without power. There is no class of property owners capable of exerting pressure on the government to promote, influence or check policy. In such a society inequalities in wealth flow from positions achieved and from posts held by individuals. Nowhere is this clearer than in the power relations which operate in the Soviet countryside. The formal structure of government places considerable power in the hands of the village Soviets, but in reality there is often an enormous gap between the village officials and the district officials. While district officials are subject to direction and control from the higher provincial level this is usually limited to re-enforcing the authority of district officials. Members of Village Soviet Executive Committees, who are often drawn from the rural intelligentsia and are important persons in the village community, are repeatedly brought to recognize their powerlessness in the face of higher officialdom. I recently came across a letter in a Soviet journal with the pathetic title, 'Nobody authorized that!' The letter was a saga of the impotence of village officials in the face of district officials. I include the whole letter[5] as the case it describes is not untypical although rather an extreme example of the situation normally found in the Soviet countryside.

Dear Editor,
    I have already worked for four years as chairman of the Sharlyk Village Soviet. Before that I worked as bookkeeper. Having recently read in your journal the letter by

the chairman of the Dyuryulin Village Soviet Executive
Committee (Bashkir ASSR), cde. Federova, I burned with
the desire to justify myself. I write, not because I am
anxious to write and complain, but only out of necessity
and devotion to duty.

I have often thought in recent times, 'It's only until the
next election and if I am again recommended to that post
I will firmly refuse.' Why? I write on the most important
reasons.

I have studied the new Statute on Village Soviets and
I know their rights and duties. But all the time I saw and
felt that I didn't carry them out fully. And not through
any fault of mine. I swallowed my conscience to receive
payment for particularly serious irregularities in the work
of the Soviet. I will give some examples.

Arising out of one of the articles in the new Statute
our Village Soviet took a decision at its session in January
this year to direct supplementary resources arising from
the overfulfilment of the budget to the extent of 10,600
rubles for the following urgent needs—on repairs to
kindergarten No. 1—five thousand rubles; on village
public services—three thousand rubles; on repairs to
Karmal Eight-Year School—one thousand; on materials
for monuments and museums—six hundred rubles; and on
the acquisition of equipment for the Executive Committee
of the Village Soviet—one thousand rubles.

This decision was taken by the deputies after a lively
discussion and a unanimous recommendation from the
Executive Committee for its adoption. And what
happened?

Shortly after the session the chairman of the *raiispolkom*,
cde. A. M. Ilichev, summoned me and the vice-chairman
of the Executive Committee of the Village Soviet,
N. Ya. Ryakhovsky, and the book-keeper of the village
Soviet, N. I. Borobina, and said:
'We will construct a new building for the Village Soviet.
You have the money in the shape of supplementary
revenue received at the end of the year for overfulfilling
the income side of the Village Budget. Transfer this to the
Orenburg Brick Works for bricks and transport costs.'

The book-keeper and I attempted to argue that this decision was illegal since it conflicted with a decision already taken by the Village Soviet. We knew that the Village Soviet had no immediate need for a new building. We occupied three rooms in premises constructed in 1968 with the painful participation of the village Soviet. However, the chairman of the *raiispolkom* was not impressed. Then I said that the decision of the *raiispolkom* had to be formalized by a written order of the chairman.

On that I received the following answer:
'So you want to show me which order to write! It's been given, now get to and fulfil it!'

And so we went against our will and the will of the Soviet and fulfilled the verbal order of the chairman of the *raiispolkom*. We spent 5,623 rubles on the purchase of bricks and 764 rubles to pay for the plan of the new Village Soviet building.

And what for? They brought the bricks and they are lying there and heaven knows how much longer they will lie there. Most of our supplementary funds were spent on them. And what happened to the decision of the Village Soviet? After these happenings how will I be able to look the deputies in the eyes and make the decision known to the directors of the kindergarten and the school?

And do you think that this is an exceptional happening? In 1968, by such a verbal order from the chairman of the *raiispolkom* the resources of the Village Soviet were used to buy tables for the Raion Soviet and the C.S.B., sheeting for covering the garage of the *raiispolkom* and other things. Besides that, out of the Village Soviet resources we paid half of the wages of the stokers and drivers employed by the *raiispolkom*.

Our Village Soviet is situated in the district centre in the same courtyard as the *raiispolkom*. Despite this, over the four years of my work I can't recall the occasion when somebody from the leadership of the Raion Soviet has dropped in on us to find out how we were working. At the end of January this year in the session of the *raiispolkom* they examined the report on the activities of our Village Soviet. But nobody came from the *raiispolkom* to verify our work. In place of that we received questions and we gave written answers to those questions.

Is that proper? The Village Soviet could speed up its work by better management with the practical help of the *raiispolkom*. Not only have we received no help from them but they have put a spoke in our wheel, acting outside of the law.

	M. Kharlamova,
Sharlyk raion,	Chairman *ispolkom*,
Orenburg oblast.	Sharlyk Village Soviet.

Power depends on position within a formal hierarchy but it also depends on the relative importance of the particular hierarchy to the Soviet system as a whole. Village Soviet officials are weak because they are at the very bottom of the Soviet hierarchy, which in itself is less important than the party hierarchy. The director of a factory or state farm is more powerful than the chairman of a village Soviet because he is higher up the hierarchical structure (being usually supervised by a district or town Soviet), because he is in control of a productive enterprise and not of a purely administrative agency, and because he has a greater chance of checking decisions of the supervising Soviet which he dislikes by appeal to his ministry or to higher party agencies.

Prestige and prestige rating

Intellectuals have always enjoyed considerable prestige in Soviet society, especially since the period of rapid industrialization in the 1930s. However, popular prestige ratings vary considerably from official ratings. This has been clearly established by the work carried out by the economist, V. N. Shubkin, and a research group from the Institute of Economics of the Siberian Division of the USSR Academy of Sciences. A survey of 289 school leavers in Novosibirsk city and district and in the town of Kyzyl (Tuva ASSR) in 1962 showed that most sons of graduate fathers wanted to choose professional careers in technology or in physics and mathematics. Girls showed a weaker tendency to move in this direction. Thus, while no sons of fathers occupied in natural science and humanities sought to specialize in these fields, 23 per cent of girls of fathers who were natural scientists and 61 per cent of girls whose fathers were in humanities, wanted to work in the same field as their father. Amongst the children of fathers working in technology and physico-mathematical science, 8 per cent of sons and 33 per cent of daughters wanted to move into the humanities.

In reporting these findings, Shubkin drew attention to the fact that:[6]

the humanities and natural sciences are falling more and more to the share of women, while men choose professions demanding physico-mathematical training. The prospect of such a division of labour according to sex is hardly satisfactory. An interest in the humanities and natural sciences evidently must be aroused among boys and a liking for physico-mathematical subjects developed in girls.

While Shubkin does not discuss the reasons for this difference they clearly include both sociological and psychological factors. The direction of economic development, coupled with the official stress on physical science and technology, attract the boys more strongly than the girls because girls find occupations in natural science and the humanities more congenial and easier to combine with their family and domestic responsibilities. On the other hand, the only boys in the survey wanting to move into the humanities were the sons of fathers who were in technology and physico-mathematical science. Such patterns in horizontal mobility are not peculiar to the Soviet Union and are not to be explained purely in economic terms. In Shubkin's survey only 2 per cent of respondents claimed that it was money which attracted them towards a particular profession, compared with 25 per cent who said it was 'the importance of the profession for the national economy'.

A different approach to the question of prestige of professional occupations was undertaken in the Novosibirsk district in 1963 by Shubkin and his associates. On this occasion a larger sample of about 3,000 school leavers were asked to rank occupations according to general attractiveness, not according to their own professional aspirations. This survey revealed

TABLE 11 *Fathers' social status and children's inclinations*

| Groups to which parents belong | Children want to be: | | | | Total |
	Indust. & building workers	Agric. workers in kolkhozes	Public service workers	Intelligentsia	
Industrial and Building workers	35	—	5	60	100
Agric. workers and collective farmers	87	13	—	—	100
Public service workers	56	4	4	36	100
Intelligentsia	25	1	3	71	100

(Source: V. N. Shubkin (1966), p. 93.)

that both boys and girls ranked specialists in education, health and culture ahead of engineers in terms of attractiveness of occupation. The girls placed scientists ahead of engineers while the boys gave construction-engineers second place but placed scientists ahead of all other types of engineers. In the ranking of individual professions there were several differences between girls and boys, but in each case eight of the first ten choices were 'intellectual' professions, i.e. requiring tertiary education.

Not only was there a difference between the high rating for mathematics and physics and medicine and the lower rating of social sciences, but there were also marked differences between the sexes and between rural and urban respondents. Rural respondents, perhaps because of lower expectations and less information, gave lower ratings to prestige scientific occupations. Similar studies made at Chelyabinsk produced similar attitudes, although with local variations. Soviet studies of school graduates show that between one half and three quarters of school graduates seek to enter teaching, medicine, engineering, or scientific research. Studies of parents' preferences for occupations for their children show a similar, although less spectacular, preference for the high prestige intellectual professions.

As Yanowitch and Dodge point out in their detailed discussion of the Novosibirsk investigation: 'The popularity of intelligentsia occupations as a group coexists with relatively low esteem for individual intelligentsia positions, depending upon the particular sector of the economy or branch of science with which these positions are associated.'[7]

While school leavers are attracted by professional careers they do not all share the same level of expectancy. Thus Shubkin's Novosibirsk-Kyzyl survey showed that 60 per cent of children of industrial workers, 36 per cent of children of public service workers and 71 per cent of children of intellectuals aspired to become intellectuals, whereas no children of agricultural workers and collective farmers had this ambition (Table 11). The majority of the children of both public service workers and agricultural workers and collective farmers preferred a job in industry or construction to a professional job. Such lower aspirations evidently reflect reality. As things stand now not all who seek professional jobs can secure them.

TABLE 12 *Ranking order of individual occupations, Novosibirsk, 1963*

Girls	Boys
1 Medical scientist	1 Radio engineer
2 Physician	2 Radio technician
3 Pilot	3 Physicist
4 Literary personnel	4 Engineer: geologist
5 Mathematician	5 Pilot
6 Physicist	6 Electrical engineer
7 Chemist	7 Mathematician
8 Academic (tertiary teacher)	8 Engineer in machine building
9 Radio technician	9 Engineer in communications
10 Engineer in chemical industry	10 Mining engineer

TABLE 13 *Ranking order of attractiveness of sciences, Novosibirsk, 1963*

Girls	Boys
1 Medicine	1 Physics
2 Mathematics	2 Mathematics
3 Physics	3 Geology
4 Chemistry	4 Chemistry

Girls	Boys
5 Philology	5 History
6 Geology	6 Mathematical econs
7 Mathematical econs	7 Medicine
8 Philosophy	8 Philosophy
9 History	9 Biology
10 Biology	10 Philology

Living standards

There is no exact correlation between the prestige rating and living standards of various professional groups. In 1967, when the lowest legal wage was 60 rubles a month, and when the average wage of all workers in the national economy was 105.4 rubles a month, the salaries paid to intellectuals ranged from 80 rubles to over 500 rubles a month. Very many intellectuals, including most of the highly rated doctors and teachers, received less than 140 rubles a month. Most scientific research workers received between 135 and 250 rubles a month. Many lower officials received between 80 and 120 rubles a month. Only a very few, including top party and state officials, directors of large industrial establishments, directors and senior staff of scientific research institutes, top university administrators, etc., received as much as 500 rubles a month. In 1967 the average income of industrial workers (including managerial personnel) was 108.9 rubles a month, but the average for sectors of the economy with a heavy concentration of intellectuals, showed only slightly higher, or even lower earnings. Thus, while the average monthly income for officials was 112.7 rubles and for scientific workers 122.1 rubles, it was only 96.4 rubles for employees in education and 92.2 rubles for employees in health.[8]

Soviet living standards vary according to variations in income levels but the variations are less than they are in capitalist societies.[9] Public housing and public allocation of housing lead to a surprising uniformity in housing. Differences between intellectuals and others are marginal. While some Moscow intellectuals live in 'privileged' locations such as close to the Academy of Sciences network in Leninsky Prospect, the majority are scattered throughout the older and newer suburbs, as are white-collar workers, factory workers, construction workers, pensioners, and service personnel. Standards vary according to the age of the building. In Moscow many older intellectuals are living in pre-revolutionary or pre-war buildings under crowded and rather dilapidated conditions. Those who live in the newer post-1957 suburbs are more comfortably housed. Some prefer to live in settlements on the outskirts of the city or even in the country, but most will live within seven miles of the city centre. Intellectuals, like most other citizens, use public transport to get to and from work. For the most part intellectuals do not live in special areas or apartments. Since 1957 almost all public housing has been allocated by municipal housing agencies known as ZhEK.[10] These are organized on the basis of the micro-*raion* or sub-district. Each ZhEK controls the housing allocation for between two and eight thousand people. While intellectuals sometimes seek to exert *blat* in order to improve their housing, the ZhEK agencies responsible to the Executive Committees of the District Soviets, have a reputation for fairness and impartiality in the distribution of housing.[11]

Intellectuals sometimes secure special advantages in housing allocation. During the 1960s these were of two main sorts. In the first place, some housing (as much as 10 or 15 per cent in some cities) is constructed and controlled by economic enterprises or research institutes. Such agencies allocate this accommodation only to their own staff and on a special priority system which tends to follow status lines so that leading intellectuals, such as senior engineers, directors, departmental heads, senior research staff, etc., get first preference. Second, some intellectuals, because of higher incomes, have better chances than ordinary workers of joining housing co-operatives and consequently, of receiving quicker improvement to their housing position. Since as much as 30 per cent of housing construction in Moscow and Leningrad is now handled by housing co-operatives, this is an important advantage to upper income groups.

Living standards of intellectuals are generally above the average for the community. While there is not much difference between an industrial worker's flat and an intellectual's flat in terms of size, basic fittings and consumer durables, there will often be higher quality (new or imported) furniture, more books (especially on general subjects), and more radios, record players and tape recorders. Other intellectual tools of trade such as reading lamps, drawing boards and typewriters are also more common.

Life styles of intellectuals

It is more difficult to generalize about the life styles of intellectuals than about the life styles of other individuals. While the life style of most people is closely dependent on their class, race, sex, and social status, that of the intellectual is much more dependent on his professional training. Since professional training is increasingly differentiated intellectual creativity is also becoming more differentiated. Increased division of labour is of course also characteristic of modern industrial and agricultural work but the division of intellectual labour has been less effectively routinized.

Intellectual life styles, like other life styles, can be portrayed by means of individual life portraits. This was attempted, with considerable success, by Raymond Bauer some years ago in *Nine Soviet Portraits*.[12] These were composite portraits based on several hundreds of interviews of Soviet displaced persons. It would be difficult, if not impossible, to repeat such an operation today. An alternative method would be to select case studies either from Soviet literature and press stories or from one's personal experience. However, such biographies could hardly be considered typical or representative of particular categories of intellectuals. What I shall attempt over the next few pages is to suggest how the variables affecting individual life styles in the Soviet Union apply to intellectuals.

Class origin is given considerable emphasis in Soviet statistics on the intelligentsia. Class position certainly influences the chances of individuals entering certain professions but it does not seem to be a major factor influencing the life styles of established intellectuals. A factory manager who 'rose from the ranks' is not likely to model his life on that of his workers, although he might still retain some remnants of pride in his working-class origin. A first generation intellectual might also experience greater uncertainty in his role than that of a second or third generation intellectual, although this does not necessarily follow.

Race is not supposed to be a major factor in Soviet life experience. The educational system actively promotes the advance of backward peoples. The socialist economy offers equality of job opportunity and equality of income, housing and services. The legal system provides guarantees against racial discrimination. Yet despite this there is considerable evidence that racial feeling was increasing in the Soviet Union during the sixties. The increasing pressure on admission to tertiary educational institutions has meant that a scattered and highly educated nationality, the Jewish nationality, is seriously restricted in its educational opportunities. Other 'advanced nations', Russians, Armenians and Georgians, have not been affected by the equalizing trend in Soviet education to the same extent as the Jews. Jewish intellectuals are virtually excluded from certain occupations. On the other hand they represent a major grouping within some other professions. No study exists of how far Jewish intellectuals are discriminated against in securing positions and promotions. Certainly Jews are very much under-represented in senior administrative posts, although they are probably 'over-represented' within the party membership.[13] While the Jewishness of an intellectual is not likely to affect his material position or professional advancement, except in a small number of cases, it will probably affect his job security and self confidence in many situations. Where a significant number of Soviet intellectuals disassociate themselves from party politics (as in the writers' trials of 1966–8, or the invasion of Czechoslovakia in August 1968) Jews are more likely to lose their positions than non-Jews. In non-Russian republics, where there is increasing pressure on professional jobs from the Russian minority, the native intellectuals are quite likely to become associated with moves to preserve native culture. This has been the case in Kiev and other Ukrainian centres since 1959, and in Latvia, Lithuania, Azerbaidjan and other republics. On the other hand, non-Russians who have established themselves in important positions within the intelligentsia in Russian cities such as Moscow and Leningrad are quite likely to be 'more Russian than the Russians'.

Sex equality is much emphasized in the Soviet Union and a large measure of equality has been achieved in broad terms. However, sex continues to restrict the entry of women into certain professions and especially into senior administrative positions. Women are forced to interrupt their professional careers to have children and the care of the home places much greater demands on Soviet women than on men. The burden of shopping and supply hunting[14] no doubt helps to explain the preference of women for low-level professional and office jobs with a fixed working day. While no statistics are available it is certain that the average income of a Soviet woman graduate is much below that of a male graduate. This is because of the high concentration of women in lower-paid professions such as teaching, medicine and cultural work, and the fact that in all professional occupations relatively few women hold senior and better-paid positions. Job mobility is also more likely to be affected by family responsibilities. Thus a single woman of my acquaintance gave up secondary teaching after five years to take up a more highly-paid job as a translator for an industrial firm. Such a transfer was not likely to raise her professional standing but it did give her more income, shorter hours, less responsibility and more time for social and cultural activities. Another woman teacher, separated from her husband, gave up school teaching for a less regular job as an Intourist guide and interpreter, mainly because it gave her more time to look after her small daughter. All other things being equal, women without children can compete more equally with men in their professional careers. While no statistical evidence is available about the movement of professionals from one city to another in the course of promotion, it is probable that men use this type of mobility more than women. Such moves often cause the break-up of marriage but if the partners stay together the wife follows the husband more often than the husband follows the wife. In many cases such a move will result in a poorer job for the wife than the one she left.

Age differences influence Soviet intellectual life styles in various ways. Older intellectuals, those above fifty in 1970, would have reached maturity and received their early professional experience in the Stalin period. They represent the generation which bore the brunt of the war. The war brought disruption to their professional careers, physical hardship and suffering, and the loss of close relations and friends. For many the disruption of the war years was followed without a break by long years spent in labour camps and in exile. For some, entrance into the professions was the direct result of their war service. This generation has a disproportionate number of men in it and women outnumber men by ten to six. Members of this generation are likely to hold senior, responsible and well-paid positions in their professions. Consequently they are apt to be conservative and somewhat circumspect in their behaviour. They steer clear of newer fashions in dress and in taste. They are small supporters of jazz or modern poetry and plays; they prefer classical music, Russian popular music and the productions of the Moscow Art Theatre. They are cautious in their interest in foreign productions. They may well be less idealist and more realist than their children and younger colleagues. Some will be hardened cynics but more will be conformist and establishment-minded. Quite a few will have retained their youthful idealism through thick and thin. One such, well known to me, is a woman professor of philosophy in Moscow. Now in her fifties she has always sought to serve the Party and the people throughout her life. She still recalls the impact Ostrovsky's novel, *How the Steel Was Tempered,* made on her youthful mind, and she still finds the hero of that novel, Pavel Korchagin, an ideal model for today's young Communists.

Intellectuals of the younger generation, those under thirty-five in 1970, would have received their entire tertiary education and professional training in the post-Stalin period. They are old enough to have understood some of the restrictions and liabilities of the Stalin era but they have benefited by the slow thawing of intellectual life in the years since 1953. They are likely to be more critical and independent in their thinking than their parents. They are less concerned than their parents with keeping their national purity and quite openly admit their interest in Western music, dress, films, literature and scientific theories. They are also careerist but their careerism is often less individually-centred and is more likely to be influenced by the ethics of their professions. In this respect they are not unlike the younger intellectuals of Western countries. While many of them, especially if they are already above thirty, will be party members, they are less prepared to direct their energies into the full range of party activities, striving all the time to preserve their status as intellectual experts.

Occupation has traditionally been a main determinant of life styles in every society. Occupation has also been closely associated with social status. This is certainly the case in the Soviet Union. Certain occupations are regarded by the regime as more crucial, at least for the existing stage of social development, than others. Hence senior party positions, state administrative positions, managerial positions, senior scientific and academic positions are much better paid than the general run of positions in teaching, medicine and the civil service. Particularly high rewards and other privileges go to outstanding members of the 'creative intelligentsia', to successful musicians, artists, dancers, singers and actors. Social status varies according to income, position in an official hierarchy, power, official and community prestige ratings. The factors I have discussed so far operate for all sections of society, not merely for the intelligentsia. There remain, however, some factors which affect intellectuals in a special way, at least as far as the determination of intellectual life styles is concerned. The first special factor I would mention is the relation of the intellectual to the production process. Intellectuals, like all white-collar workers, are often separated from the production process. Yet some important categories of intellectuals are not so separated. Thus industrial managers, directors and engineers working on construction projects, chairmen of collective farms, agricultural engineers and agricultural scientists working in farms are much more closely associated with the actual process of production than are their counterparts working in government departments and ministries or in scientific research institutes. While both groups of intellectuals will be forced to gear their activities to the economic plan, the pressure of plan fulfilment is always more stringent in productive enterprises than it is in universities and scientific research institutes. Research conducted in industry, agriculture or construction is, generally speaking, 'applied science'. Research conducted in scientific research institutes attached to the Academies of Sciences and in the universities is much more likely to be general and theoretical. Again, the industrial or agricultural enterprise imposes its own peculiar discipline on the professionals working in it. The discipline imposed on and the opportunities available to the individual academic or scientific research worker are different.[15]

85

Professional occupations such as medicine or school teaching produce greater pressures to routinize intellectual work than do university teaching or research work, but even here the direct contact with individuals, the person-to-person relationship, produces a very different work environment to that met with on the farm or in the factory.

A second variable which affects the life styles of the intellectual in a very special way is distance from or closeness to the centres of the intellectual culture. It is difficult for Soviet intellectuals to operate as intellectuals if they are isolated in some small settlement hundreds or even thousands of miles from Moscow. Other intellectuals are few or non-existent in the locality and the low cultural level of the local population tends to force intellectuals to become narrow specialists. Hence the determination shown by Soviet intellectuals to avoid 'going to the periphery' is not merely due to narrow selfishness but to the desire to maintain professional standards. Generally speaking, it is much easier to be an intellectual in Moscow or Leningrad than it is in the remote outback.

The third special variable I would like to mention is that of administrative position. Intellectuals who hold administrative positions in the party, in the state structure, or even in related structures such as trade unions, co-operatives or professional associations, invariably become closely identified with the party *apparat*. Such individuals, even though they might have high professional qualifications, soon tend to function as administrators rather than as intellectuals in the full sense of the term. Moreover they generally lose touch with their professional colleagues. Tension between the 'true professional' and the 'administrator' is very noticeable in universities and scientific research institutes. Inevitably, seniority and promotion mean increased encroachment on research by administrative activity. But the ideal academic or scientist for the younger Soviet intellectual is the one who escapes administrative responsibility, or, if he has to accept it, still manages to operate as a scholar and to hold a leading position in his field. Those few intellectuals who accept postings out of the intellectual establishment into the party or state apparatus are likely to be soundly condemned. In terms of life styles and occupational activities the full-time administrator tends to diverge from the rest of the intelligentsia. His career begins to resemble that of the party functionary or the civil servant and his associations increasingly change from professional colleagues to members of the *apparat*.

My fourth variable which especially concerns the life style of the intellectual is the relative importance of the *nomenklatura* system in his career. More than farmers or ordinary workers, the intellectual is likely to be directed to positions on the basis of the party-controlled job list. The likelihood of an intellectual being affected by this system increases with age and seniority. In some agencies between one-third and two-thirds of positions held by intellectuals will be on the *nomenklatura* of the Party.

No attempt has been made here to discuss intellectual life styles in terms of cultural and intellectual interests and activities. These are important aspects of the problem but they are difficult to generalize about. Nor does the variety encountered lend itself to easy classification. Even distinctions which might be drawn along generational lines are far from rigid. Thus a theatre such as *Sovremenik* (The Contemporary) draws its support mainly from those under thirty-five but it has many older intellectuals among its supporters. Participation in unofficial performances of tapes, poetry and short story reading is very much a pastime of students and younger intellectuals but many older writers also participae.t[16]

The generalizations suggested may sound trite, but accurate generalization about particular professions or other groups is difficult while we have so little sociological research into the problem. One experimental study of young research workers in the 350 scientific research institutes in Moscow was conducted by the newspaper *Komsomolskaya Pravda* in 1967.[17] The survey found that half the city's scientific workers were under thirty years of age, the majority holding positions as junior research officers and receiving 135 rubles a month salary. Of all young scientists 18.7 per cent claimed that they loved their work and regarded their salaries as unimportant, 65.8 per cent believed that salary was important but work the main thing. Only 12.9 per cent admitted that pay was foremost in their minds. Of all research work being undertaken by junior research workers only 20.5 per cent was independent research, while the remainder was group, co-operative or general research. Publication was given a central place in almost all research institutes and 42.9 per cent of all young scientists had published one paper over the past three years, 27.9 per cent two or three papers, and 29.2 per cent four or more papers. Most young scientists seemed fairly well satisfied with their work. Only 6 per cent regretted their decision to become research workers, and 24 per cent expected promotion within a year. Status factors seemed less worrying than they had been in the fifties.[18]

Perhaps in the next decade further concrete research studies will be made by Soviet sociologists into various groups of Soviet intellectuals to extend the recent studies into school graduates, tertiary students and young scientists. Until such time we will have to be content with imprecise generalizations or with impressionistic sketches squeezed from individual contacts and from the pages of Soviet literature.

6 Social roles of the Soviet intelligentsia

Basic role

In any society intellectuals perform a variety of social functions —criticism, education, planning and administration, health protection, social engineering, legal services, religious maintenance, research and development, etc. In all contemporary societies there is bound to be considerable similarity between the roles of various categories of intellectuals. This is so if only because of the basic similarity between urban industrial societies in terms of resources, technique, organization and services. The sharpest contrasts are between developed and under-developed societies, between North America, Japan, Western Europe and the USSR on the one hand, and the countries of Asia, Africa and South America on the other. The contrast between advanced societies, especially between capitalist and socialist societies, is nevertheless considerable, even fundamental.

It has been argued that the social system which 'maximises the conditions for the emergence, proliferation and functioning of the intellectual, is capitalism'.[1] Communist societies such as the USSR have largely replaced the intellectual by the *apparatchik*. Since the Party maintains such close control over intellectual activity, there is little opportunity for individual intellectual critique, which is said to be the main social function of the intellectual. From an opposite position, Soviet writers have asserted that the intelligentsia can reach its full development only under socialism. These different viewpoints reflect different images of the role of intellectuals in modern society, but they share a concern at making the most of differences between capitalist and socialist systems. My purpose in this chapter is not to discuss the role of intellectuals in general, as they operate in all modern societies, but simply to explore the role of intellectuals in a single socialist society, the USSR, during the decade of the sixties. How far the specific roles we discern in the Soviet Union might be true of other socialist systems or even of capitalist systems, will not be discussed. I would suggest however that the fundamental difference between a socialist and a capitalist intelligentsia rests less on differences in class origins than on the fact that socialist intellectuals in all their roles are set clear social obligations and purposes by the political culture to which they belong.

The basic role of the Soviet intelligentsia is to provide high-level specialists for all branches of human endeavour, including government and administration.

All Soviet statements on the intelligentsia emphasize the fact that they are specialists of high degree, primarily specialists with tertiary qualifications. Since virtually all graduates have received free primary, secondary and tertiary education, they are expected to render the account by a lifelong service to the people. The government requires all graduates to serve for three years after graduation in an assigned position. In a situation of continued shortage of skilled and professional labour the success of the economic plan clearly requires this minimal direction of graduates. But while the contractual obligation to serve in an assigned position ends after the first three years, Soviet society assumes that the basic obligation of the intellectual will continue. Almost 30 per cent of all graduates are party members[2] and these have a special personal obligation to serve where the Party directs them. But all intellectuals are subject to frequent appeals to serve the community interest as the Party sees it—writers to strengthen *partiinost* (party-mindedness), social scientists to assist the improvement of the state and society, economists, engineers, and managers to rationalize production and reduce labour costs, agricultural scientists to develop and apply new agricultural techniques, teachers to raise educational standards and to hasten the process of training the youth in communist morals. Such calls are issued in various ways, through editorials in daily newspapers, through professional journals, through party journals, through speeches by party leaders delivered at congresses and conferences of intellectuals, and through special resolutions of the Central Committee. Thus over the decade 1959–68 more than twenty major decisions directed at various sections of the intelligentsia were taken by the Central Committee or by the Central Committee and the USSR Council of Ministers. These decisions included directions on history teaching in secondary schools,[3] directions on improving the quality of postgraduate theses,[4] on improving the selection and training of scientific personnel,[5] on measures for improving biological science,[6] on improving the work of the USSR Academy of Sciences and the Academies of Sciences of the Union Republics,[7] on the improvement of legal training,[8] on the development of the social sciences,[9] and on improving health services.[10]

Soviet intellectuals are expected not only to serve the Party and the people by contributing their special abilities and skills to the task of social improvement and Communist construction, but, as the most educated section of Soviet society, they are expected to give special assistance to the Party in fields such as enlightenment, propaganda, ideological struggle against 'bourgeois ideas'.[11] Intellectuals thus tend, more than the community at large, to become involved in the life of the Party and to become party members. Within the Party they will be disproportionately represented in Conferences and Congresses, and also on Party Committees. The proportion of intellectuals in the Party throughout the sixties was at least twice[12] what it was in the general population. The proportion of intellectuals amongst the delegates to the 22nd and 23rd Congresses was three or four times their proportion in the total population.[13] Similarly, intellectuals enjoy 'over-representation' in all Soviets from the village level right up to the USSR Supreme Soviet, in Executive Committees of Soviets, in the People's Courts, and in many of the main social organizations operating in Soviet society. Thus the percentage of deputies of local Soviets with higher education rose from 14.8 per cent in 1965 to 16.3 per cent in 1967, and to 16.8 per cent in 1969.[14] The percentage of graduates among deputies rose with the importance of the Soviet. Thus in 1969 it was 11.6 for village Soviets, 13.9 for settlement Soviets, 26.4 for town Soviets, 29.3 for rural district Soviets, 30.9 for city district Soviets, and 42.9 per cent for territorial and provincial Soviets. Executive Committees were even more dominated by intellectuals. Thus 24.2 per cent of all members of Executive Committees of local Soviets in 1969 had tertiary education, while in town

Soviets 48.6 per cent of members of Executive Committees had tertiary education. In district, city district, and territorial-provincial Soviet Executive Committees the percentages were higher—60.9, 68.1, and 84.6 per cent respectively. The main factor in this steady trend towards greater use of intellectuals in local government is the increased complexity of administrative tasks, and the recognition that the intelligentsia, through ability, training, and, in some cases, greater leisure, can contribute a disproportionate number of activists. This trend has been examined by Soviet sociologists in several places in recent years, including Estonia,[15] Kazakhstan,[16] and Armenia.[17] In every investigation it was found that persons with tertiary qualifications contributed above average to local Soviet work, to work of Executive Committees, Standing Commissions of Soviets, control activities, and social organizations generally.

The basic role of the intelligentsia, to provide the high-level specialists for Soviet society, is really a specialized leadership role. For this reason the Party, which claims the main leadership role in Soviet society, must recruit extensively amongst intellectuals and so keep the subordinate but specialized leadership under firm party control. The percentage of party members amongst particular groups of intellectuals varies considerably depending on the strategic position of the group concerned. Rigby estimates that 25 per cent of Soviet teachers in 1964 were party members compared with 22 per cent of doctors, 42 per cent of engineers, and 44 per cent of agricultural specialists.[18] In 1963 it was reported that 48 per cent of the staff in tertiary institutes were party members.[19] In 1967, 43 per cent of scientific research workers in the USSR Academy of Sciences were party members.[20] At the same time over the entire graduate population only 27 per cent were party members. If we include the students as part of the intelligentsia the figure falls to 21–2 per cent. Amongst tertiary students in 1967 only about 4.6 per cent were party members. There was no great increase in the percentage of party members amongst Soviet intellectuals during the sixties, indeed there was probably a slight decline.[21] Rigby considers that party membership amongst intellectuals had reached close to 'saturation point' by the mid-1960s. Any further increase would soon convert the leadership into a majority in some professions. In view of this degree of interpenetration of

Party and intelligentsia it is perhaps not misplaced enthusiasm which led one Soviet writer to claim that:[22]

> The Soviet intelligentsia, under the leadership of the Communist Party, travels together with all the people the glorious path of struggle and achievement. Shoulder to shoulder with the working class and the peasantry it labours selflessly in order to increase the material and spiritual strength of the Soviet state and to transform it into an indestructible stronghold of socialism.

The role of intellectuals in Soviet and other societies has been subjected to functional analysis by different writers. Thus Antonio Gramsci divided the intelligentsia into the 'technical-directive intelligentsia' and the 'organizers of culture'.[23] The Soviet sociologist, Amelin,[24] recognized four main functions of professionals in socialist societies—participation in the development of the productive forces, theorizing and generalizing social experience, playing the dominant role in communications, and the improvement and further development of forms of scientific management of society and politics. I have used Amelin's classification for the following analysis, although I have modified it somewhat in the light of American functional theory.

In summary form I would suggest the following main social functions of the Soviet intelligentsia:

(1) *Organization and development of the productive process*
    (a) Production and preservation of human resources—education, public health, social welfare.
    (b) Research and development.
    (c) Scientific organization of labour.

(2) *Organization of culture*
    (a) Management of communications.
    (b) Propaganda and enlightenment.
    (c) Promotion of art and literature.

(3) *To theorize and to generalize social experience*
    (a) Criticism and policy review.
    (b) Social critique.

(4) *System maintenance and system adaptation*
    (a) Political socialization.
    (b) Political recruitment.
    (c) Political legitimation.

Intellectuals as organizers and developers of the productive process

One of the main social roles of any modern intelligentsia is the education and training of future intellectuals. If educators at all levels from the kindergarten to the postgraduate level were to be counted more than one-fifth of all Soviet intellectuals and semi-intellectuals would be found to be included. But the educational role of Soviet intellectuals is not confined to professional teachers. All intellectuals are expected to assist in the promotion of culture and scientific and political knowledge. Thus hundreds of thousands of intellectuals engage in extracurricular educational activity through such agencies as the Knowledge Society, scientific and technical societies, Universities of Marxism-Leninism, and People's Universities.

Soviet writers, artists and actors, make frequent visits to factories, farms, offices and institutes, to present their art and their views on art to the people. By such methods experts are forced to assist in the general party objective of raising society to the level of the intelligentsia.[25] Prominent writers, scientists and scholars are encouraged to write articles for the Soviet press. These are sometimes over-general and jargonized, but some, including many popular scientific and technical as well as historical and political articles, are clear, concise and informed. To supplement such contributions Soviet magazines and newspapers make frequent use of interviews with prominent intellectuals in order to bring intellectual life before the public. This is particularly so when new trends are emerging and issues have been clouded by political opposition or academic in-fighting. Thus, for example, the issue of Soviet sociology was afforded special coverage in *Pravda, Izvestia, Komsomolskaya Pravda* and *Literaturnaya Gazeta* over the years 1965–8. Sometimes the party leadership promotes discussion on difficult issues concerning scientific activities. Thus early in 1965 the Party sponsored a discussion through *Pravda* of the question 'Should there be a political science in the Soviet Union?'.[26]

The educational role of the Soviet intellectual was given added emphasis by the 22nd Party Congress and the adoption of a new programme late in 1961. The report by the First Secretary of the Party, N. S. Khrushchev, and the programme itself, placed special emphasis on the education of a new Soviet man, the development of a new Communist morality to match the construction of the material basis of Communism. This new emphasis resulted in the introduction of a new compulsory course on social studies into the final year of secondary school in 1963. While the teaching of this course was primarily the responsibility of the history teachers in the schools, the Party sought to involve other intellectuals and the public generally in the venture. Similarly in tertiary education and in party education within the Party, new courses, new books and discussions were organized on the subject of Communist construction.

The Party has made health a major objective since the early 1920s. In 1968 there were 617,800 doctors (not counting military doctors) in the Soviet Union, 29.5 doctors and 104 hospital beds for every 10,000 inhabitants. There were 4,931 sanatoria and rest homes with 803,000 beds. There were 4,747,000 persons (including specialists) employed in public health and physical culture in the Soviet Union in 1968.[27]

Most specialists in public health are employed in operating the network of health services, hospitals, clinics, sanatoria, rest homes, ambulances and nurseries. Only a minority work in research institutes or in administration. Outside of their professional employment doctors and other health specialists, and for that matter, other intellectuals, are expected to play the leading role in health campaigns and in preventative medicine. Doctors, health workers and teachers seem to provide the core of the thousands of Standing Commissions on Public Health attached to local Soviets. In the early 1960s the drive to reduce the costs and complexity of local government administration often meant that either the Standing Commission on Health or the hospital board replaced the Health Department of the local Soviet.[28] This meant that doctors were being forced to add the administration of health services generally to hospital administration in the narrower sense.

The Soviet government believes that science is the key to progress and that the competition between social systems both now and in the future is to be measured in terms of the rate of scientific expansion. Thus by 1967 it was claimed that one out of four scientific workers was in the Soviet Union. The scientific workforce is the most rapidly expanding sector of the Soviet workforce—it expanded 23.9 per cent over the four years 1965–8.[29]

The number of engineers and technologists is expanding more slowly. This emphasis on science and technology goes back many years, at least to 1920 with the establishment of GOELRO. But for many years the material resources limited the rate of scientific progress. The First Five Year Plan required that Soviet science should be closely co-ordinated and so the Party reorganized the USSR Academy of Sciences over the years 1929–32.[30] The recognition that science was playing a new, qualitatively different role in Soviet society was made by the Party early in the sixties. It led to reorganizations of the Academy of Sciences in 1959, 1961 and 1963,[31] to a rapid expansion of new scientific centres, and to the upgrading of what were regarded as key sectors in the scientific and technological revolution, namely, mathematics, physics, electronics, cybernetics, computer science, mathematical economics and social sciences.

The achievements of Soviet science, especially in aviation, rocketry and space exploration, have fired the imagination of Soviet youth. Soviet scientists, who gained considerable prestige for their inventions and achievements during the war, entered a new phase of rising popularity in October 1957 with the launching of the first sputnik. During the 1960s each year seemed to bring new triumphs for Soviet science. Science and technology were kept continually before the people through articles in newspapers, scientific and popular science magazines, special exhibitions, films and T.V., and massive monuments to science which ranged from the Pavilion of Science (opened in 1957) in the Permanent Industrial Exhibition in Moscow, to the monument to the cosmonauts outside the exhibition, to an entire new city complex, Akademgorodok near Novosibirsk, to house the rapidly growing Siberian Division of the Academy of Sciences. To a far greater extent than in the past, Soviet scientists became trailblazers in the full light of the public. Academicians such as Nesmeyanov, Keldysh, Lavrentiev, Kapitsa, Sakharov, and others, became very well known for their advocacy of science in general and of particular scientific projects. Some of them also established a reputation for going beyond the existing official plans for scientific expansion or reorganization. Some even went far beyond the limits of party policy in their advocacy of greater freedom for science, more attention to problems such as pollution and the distribution of natural resources and aid to under-developed countries.[32]

An excellent example of the efforts of scientists to raise the prestige of Soviet science is the establishment of the scientific olympiad at Akademgorodok and in Moscow. Every year the Academy of Sciences publishes ten to fifteen questions in chemistry, mathematics, and physics to be solved in a two-month period. Anyone between fourteen and eighteen may take part. Almost 10,000 entries are received each year. Those who reach a certain standard in their answers are called to twenty different centres throughout the country. Contestants go to the nearest centre for oral and written examinations under the supervision of senior Academy scientists. Those who pass the second stage, about 700, are invited to Akademgorodok for a month. They spend the time in seminars, lectures, laboratory work, and in visiting research institutes. The final exams come at the end of the month. Those who do best—about 250—are accepted for an intensive preparatory course at the physico-mathematical school, covering the 8th, 9th, and 10th grades. On graduation they move on to tertiary study in Akademgorodok. During their tertiary courses students at Akademgorodok work under the guidance of Academy scientists from the third year on.[33] The Chairman of the Siberian Branch of the Academy, Michael Lavrentiev, was mainly responsible for suggesting this experiment. More recently he has proposed an even more fundamental change in the Soviet school system. Lavrentiev proposed that the schools should continue teaching the same general syllabus up to the 8th grade but then with a 'definite bias' in the direction of physics, mathematics, biology, agronomy, technical science, history and philosophy. 'Our schools would then provide early training in a given field and promote thinking along the lines of that field.'[34] Some Soviet schools have already adjusted their teaching along these lines.

Soviet scientists are particularly concerned with research and development. They are also increasingly concerned with government efforts to rationalize the economy, to develop the scientific organization of labour*, and to further scientific management in industry, agriculture, construction, transport, services and government administration. Thus reports on research into attitudes to work, labour management, the relative efficiency of

*Referred to as NOT—*nauchnaya organizatsia truda.*

97

organizational forms, and division of labour within the civil service, the rational delineation of administrative divisions in rural government, are becoming much more frequent in Soviet journals.

Intellectuals as organizers of culture

The Communist Party maintains that its world view, Marxism-Leninism, is 'the science of the laws of development of nature and society'. Consequently, Soviet intellectuals are expected to co-operate fully in the work of Communist propaganda. This is regarded as a service to the Party and to the community because the gospel they are spreading is the truth, or at least the nearest approximation to the truth that the collective wisdom of the Party has so far managed to achieve. There is therefore nothing dishonest in this activity. In doing so they quote Lenin as their mentor and party resolutions as their guide.[35]

Party and state propaganda agencies rely heavily on intellectuals. The heads of the central propaganda and agitation agencies and the agencies on science, education and culture, are all highly qualified intellectuals, often men who have held scientific or academic positions. The same applies to the editors of *Pravda*, *Izvestia*, and other main newspapers and journals. Thus academician F. V. Konstantinov has been a specialist in Marxism-Leninism since he graduated from the Institute of Red Professors in 1932. Since then he has been lecturer, propaganda worker, professor, associate of the Institute of Philosophy in the USSR Academy of Sciencies, rector of the Academy of Social Sciencies under the Central Committee of the CPSU, head of the Department of Agitation and Propaganda of the Central Committee (1955–8), chief editor of *Voprosy filosofii* (1952–4) and of *Kommunist* (1958–62). He has been a full member of the USSR Academy of Sciences since 1962. Likewise, academician P. N. Fedoseev, Doctor of Philosophical Science and Vice-President of the USSR Academy of Sciences since 1962, is a graduate of the Gorky Pedagogical Institute (1930). Between 1930 and 1936 he lectured at the above institute and then transferred to the Institute of Philosophy of the USSR Academy of Sciences where he worked until 1941. Between 1941 and 1947 he worked for the Central Committee apparatus and was chief editor of the party journal *Bolshevik*, 1946–9. He later served as chief editor of *Partiinaya zhizn* (1950–5) and of *Voprosy filosofii* (1955–9). Between 1959 and 1962 he was director of the Institute of Philosophy, USSR Academy of Sciences. He became a full member of the USSR Academy of Sciences in 1960. Academician A. Rumyantsev, one of the co-directors of the recently established Institute of Concrete Social Research, is a Doctor of Economic Science. He has worked variously in scientific research, lecturing, and party work. He has been a member of the Central Committee of the CPSU since 1952. From 1952 to 1956 he was head of the Department of Science and Culture of the Central Committee. He became chief editor of the party journal *Kommunist* in 1958 and simultaneously (until 1964) the chief editor of the international journal *Problems of Peace and Socialism* (Prague). He was *Pravda* editor 1964–5 and Chairman of the USSR Union of Journalists in 1965.[36] Such men move freely between scientific posts, leading apparatus posts and editorial posts. They belong to a special group of intellectual-*apparatchiks*, but they symbolize the closeness of the connection between intellectual activity and ideological work.

Party members amongst the intelligentsia are kept in close contact with current ideological demands of the Party through the Propaganda departments and the Cultural departments of City Party Committees.[37] Special efforts are made to persuade party intellectuals to actively participate in party education, especially through the Universities of Marxism-Leninism. At the highest level, the USSR Academy of Sciences and the other main research networks receive directions on ideological matters through the Department of Science and Educational Institutes of the Central Committee, or through the Department on Propaganda and Agitation. For a brief period in the sixties (between 1963 and 1965) the most active directing agency was the Ideological Commission of the Central Committee, headed by L. F. Ilichev. Even within the Academy structure itself there are agencies specially concerned with ideological struggle. Thus the Presidium of the USSR Academy of Sciences established a scientific council for the study of problems of foreign ideological trends late in 1966. Of special concern for this council was the study and analysis of trends which were either hostile, revisionist, or reformist. A major effort was to be made to study foreign, especially American, 'Sovietology' and to work out counter-measures in terms of counter-propaganda.[38] Since that date a large, well-researched book has been published on the subject of American Sovietology.[39] There have also been several scientific conferences held on themes such as anti-Soviet propaganda, and the bourgeois theory of the convergence of capitalism and socialism.

Party pressure on intellectuals to produce active acceptance of foreign policy decisions and their ideological justification was increased during 1968 with rising tensions over Poland and Czechoslovakia. During 1968 the President of the USSR Academy of Sciences, M. Keldysh, threatened scientists with loss of employment if they continued to support sides or individuals the Party was opposing.[40] Even such relatively progressive intellectuals as academician Yuri Frantsev,[41] Professor T. Timofeev (Director of the Institute of the International Workers Movement),[42] and academician Nesmeyanov[43] lent their support to the Warsaw Pact invasion of Czechoslovakia. Thus Timofeev wrote that:

> The historical mission of the working class of socialist countries, fulfilling its international duty before the world proletariat, consists above all in strengthening the structure of socialism and communism, in the strengthening of the position of socialism in the international arena. This corresponds to the correct class interest of the workers of all countries. Life itself, so to speak, contradicts the views of those foreign authors who patently went against the interests of the USSR and the interests of the working class movement in capitalist countries, over the role taken by the Soviet Union and other socialist governments in the struggle against contemporary imperialism.

Soviet scientists were less effective in supporting their government over Czechoslovakia than were Soviet journalists. Journalists and correspondents such as Yuri Zhukov and several Prague correspondents, read the official line into the unfolding events in Czechoslovakia. Soviet journalists rallied to produce the 'unofficial' official white book issued in Moscow late in 1968 to justify the invasion.[44] *Literaturnaya gazeta*, no. 43, 1968, published an open letter signed by thirty-nine writers and members of the USSR Writers' Union supporting the invasion of Czechoslovakia. The signatories included Fedin, Tikhonov and Polevoi, but not Tvardovsky, Leonov or Simonov. Notwithstanding the special party meetings called throughout educational and research institutes in the autumn of 1968 for the purpose of 'putting intellectuals back on the line', many intellectuals continued in silent opposition and a few were expelled over the issue.

From early 1969 through to April 1970 there was an official party campaign to celebrate the hundredth anniversary of Lenin's birth. All research institutes and teaching establishments without exception organized special conferences or seminars on the issue. Theatres, film workers, journalists, artists, and other groups of intellectuals were required to organize special productions, films, plays, and art shows around the life of Lenin. Although Lenin is almost universally popular among Soviet intellectuals there was nevertheless some resentment at the massive and somewhat heavy-handed official ceremonies. On this issue, as on some other recent anniversary celebrations, there is evidence of a growing tension between the intensified official propaganda and a more sincere and critical approach to ideology on the part of some of the intelligentsia.

Intellectuals in any society are especially concerned with communication. As specialists in both the written and the spoken word they are forced to rely primarily on their ability to communicate, to persuade and convince through skilful use of words and symbols.[45] Soviet intellectuals are actively engaged in the process of communication, in communication with their peers, with their disciples and opponents, as well as with handling the elaborate network of communication between party and government officials on the one hand, and the Soviet public on the other. The scale of this network of communication is evident in the basic statistics for 1968. In that year there were 8,754 newspapers of different types with a daily output of 126 million copies being printed in the Soviet Union. There were in addition 5,108 different journals and periodicals with an issue of 2,314 million copies. There were 75,700 books printed in 1968 with 1,383 million copies in 61 of the USSR languages and 37 foreign languages. The radio network covers the entire country and the T.V. network is fast approaching this position. There were about 1,000 T.V. stations, including 243 major ones, in the USSR in 1968.[46]

A minority of Soviet intellectuals are full-time professionals in communications, employed as journalists, as political commentators, or in radio and television. This section of the intelligentsia is given special responsibility as a go-between between the Party and the public, to transmit party policy to the public. It is expected to encourage criticism and to register popular disquiet. As an article in a recent *Kommunist* stated;[47]

> The workers of the Soviet press consider it their paramount duty actively to help the Party in the education of the masses in positive examples of construction, in advanced experience on the development of business-like and principled criticism and self-criticism, and by the disclosure of all that is obsolete and unfit and hinders progress. Naturally this criticism of the mistakes and shortcomings in work hasn't anything in common with overstatement, with narrow-minded philistinism, with deliberate sensationalism.

Twice during the 1960s,[48] special decisions were taken by the Central Committee directed towards improving the general or particular responsibilities of the Soviet press.

The Soviet regime has always prided itself on its success in promoting art and literature. The cultural or 'creative intelligentsia' has therefore enjoyed high status and high remuneration, even in times of political persecution. The professional associations of the creative intelligentsia, such as the Writers' Union and the Artists' Union, have an enormous prestige and considerable influence in Soviet society. While they work under close party supervision they are entrusted with running their own affairs in most matters. They also control admissions to their membership even though expulsions may be the direct result of pressure coming from the party organization.

The objective of a cultured public has been actively pursued by the creative intelligentsia. There is an immense network of amateur theatres, literary circles, film circles, art circles, dance groups, etc., outside of the professional unions and theatres. These are actively assisted by professional artists and writers. In like manner the direct influence of the creative intelligentsia extends down to school children through special theatres (such as the Central Children's Theatre in Moscow) and by visits to art, music and literary circles in the schools.

Intellectuals as theorists and generalizers of social experience

Intellectuals in the Soviet Union have an accepted role of growing importance as critics. This criticism is mainly concerned with the detailed review of important fields of domestic and foreign policy. Criticism of this sort is officially encouraged and it oftens runs in advance of party policy on particular matters. Thus an active debate developed in Soviet journals and newspapers over several years prior to the decisions on economic reform which were taken at the highest level in September–October 1965. The performance of the Soviet economy, of Soviet agriculture, the operation of the legal system, the shortcomings of the Soviets and ministries, have all been subjected to frequent 'criticism from below' over recent years. As will be demonstrated in the next chapter, intellectuals are unusually active in this process of public criticism. Some policy fields which require criticism are not open to debate and others are open only to a limited criticism. But such 'reserved questions' are of lessening importance. The importance attached by the government to competent professional criticism is clear from such decisions as, 'Concerning the Increased Use in the National Economy of Recommendations and Proposals of Scientific and Technical Societies' (17 October 1962), which obliged ministries and government departments to apply these recommendations.

The function of social critique, a function of the traditional Russian intelligentsia, is not given open official encouragement in the Soviet Union today. Nevertheless the function persists and is certainly growing. Its practitioners are to be found mainly in the ranks of the creative intelligentsia—artists, writers and poets —but they are also to be found amongst social scientists and other scientists. Academician A. D. Sakharov clearly belongs to this tradition. The exercise of this function presents great difficulties to the Soviet intellectual for it necessitates a considerable detachment from the immediate policies of the Party and a willingness to run the risk of political pressure and social ostracism. Thus it is not easy to urge drastic reduction in defence spending, in the exploitation of natural resources, massive increases in economic aid to under-developed countries, at the expense of a slower rise in domestic living standards. Nor is it easy to suggest a complete re-examination of the Soviet educational system or of such basic institutions as collective farms, Soviets, and the political hegemony of the Communist Party. Yet Soviet intellectuals, including prominent and leading intellectuals, have raised and are raising such questions with increasing frequency and fervour. Such Soviet intellectuals are demanding a role for themselves that is larger and more fundamental than serving as organizers of technological progress.

System maintenance and system adaptation

Soviet intellectuals play a major role in the process of political socialization. The main socialization agencies in the Soviet Union, besides the family, are the youth organizations, educational institutions, trade unions, the *Komsomol* and the Party. Intellectuals are over-represented in most of these agencies. Intellectuals play a special role in reinforcing the more general process of political socialization. Through professional training which incorporates a high degree of political and ideological content, universities and other tertiary institutions and scientific research institutes are continuously involved in producing not merely skilled professionals but 'Soviet specialists'; Soviet engineers, Soviet scientists, Soviet jurists, Soviet economists, Soviet historians, Soviet doctors, etc. The measure of their success is shown by the fact that the vast majority of Soviet intellectuals are dedicated servants of their socialist society, far less self-centred than the intellectuals of most capitalist societies.

Political recruitment is the process by which persons in a given political culture are enlisted into special roles within that society. In this sense, recruitment is but an extension of political socialization. This process is more structured in Communist political systems than in most others. Thus in the Soviet Union the Communist Party and its dependent youth organizations serve as the major agencies of political recruitment. But while intellectuals play a major role in the Party and the *Komsomol* they are particularly concerned with the political recruitment of specialists. That is to say, intellectuals are concerned at reproducing their own types within the social and political system. Consequently, the undergraduate and postgraduate training of Soviet intellectuals places considerable stress on the role of specific professional groups in the Soviet system. Such professional codes overlap[49] but they do contain important differences which stem from the different objective roles of specific professional groups as well as from differences in their perceived roles.

Thus the rules or statutes governing various professional unions in the USSR all stress the dependent role of the particular group, its obligation to work under party direction and to assist the Party. But each constitution produces a special evaluation of its professional role and professional duty within the Soviet system. This applies also to broad organizations of different types of intellectuals such as the USSR Academy of Sciences. Thus the decision of the Central Committee of the CPSU and the USSR Council of Ministers, 'On Means for Improving the Co-ordination of Scientific Research Work in the Country and the Activities of the USSR Academy of Sciences' (12 April 1961) declares that:[50]

> The USSR Academy of Sciences must:
> Provide scientific and systematic leadership in the carrying out of research in the natural (physics, mathematics, chemistry, biology, astronomy and earth science) sciences and social sciences, with the aim of using the results of scientific research work accomplished for the development of the national economy and culture;
> Render greater help to the Academies of Sciences of the Union Republics in the pursuit of scientific research and carry out the co-ordination of the activities of subordinate scientific research institutes, scientific establishments of the Academies of Sciences of the Union Republics and higher educational establishments on the theoretical problems of natural and social science;
> Maintain scientific liaison with scientific establishments in foreign countries;
> Carry out the training of scientific cadres.

Soviet intellectuals play an important role in the general process of political legitimation. In earlier decades this was done chiefly through their role as 'ideology makers',[51] but during the fifties and sixties it was more through their role as assistants to the Party in its objective of perfecting (*sovershenstvovania*) the State and social structure. The strengthening of social sciences after 1964 was directly related to this objective. Since then jurists, economists and sociologists have been encouraged to place far more attention on the systematic study of Soviet and party administration and management. New research sections on business management and public administration have been developed in several institutes and research teams have been required to present specific recommendations for reform. Thus the 1968 survey by the Institute of State and Law into the state of administration in Armenia resulted in a series of recommendations which were submitted to the Presidium of the Armenian Supreme Soviet and provided the basis for special legislation enacted in 1968.[52]

The emphasis on the utilitarian role of the specialist was underlined by Professor A. Rumyantsev in an article in *Pravda* in October 1967. Rumyantsev wrote that:[53]

> Economic science in our days has taken an advanced position in Soviet social studies. The full Leninist understanding of the role of economic science is exclusively, beneficially, the result of this importance. The decisions of the October (1964), March and September (1965) plenums of the C.C. of the CPSU and the 23rd Congress of the Party, provided the definite ending of voluntarism and arbitrary decisions in economic policy, and firmly placed them on a proper scientific basis.
>
> But it would be premature in our opinion to say that the economists use to the fullest extent the beneficial situation for deepening and widening their theoretical and practical activities. The Central Committee of the Party in its decision 'On the means for Further Development of the Social Sciences' summons the economists to tackle deep and complex theoretical questions of the political economy of socialism, to raise the effectiveness of social production, and the application of economic policy at this present stage.

Official recognition and rewards

The importance of the diversified social role of the intelligentsia is given frequent official recognition. Thus important congresses of intellectuals receive messages from the Central Committee of the Party and are attended by high party officials. Congresses of specific groups of intellectuals are often the occasion for announcements of special awards. Thus the 4th Writers' Congress in May 1967 was the occasion for the awarding of the Order of Lenin to the Writers' Union. On the occasion of the Teachers' Congress in July 1968 seventy Soviet teachers were given the award of Hero of Socialist Labour.[54] An even larger number of Soviet doctors received this award on the occasion of the Medical Workers' Conference in February 1969.[55] Frequently awards are made to particular scientific institutes. Thus in April 1967 twelve Academy of Science Institutes received the Order of Lenin and a further fifteen institutes received the Order of the Red Banner of Labour.[56] Amongst the awards to scientists announced in *Pravda* on 14 March 1969 were Orders of Lenin awarded to the Institute of Automation and Telemechanics and to the Institute of Cybernetics (Ukrainian Academy of Sciences), and Orders of the Red Banner of Labour to thirty-one other institutes.

Individual artists, writers and scientists receive Lenin Prizes and other annual awards such as 'People's Artist'. Top scientists vie with party officials and military leaders for numbers of the most coveted award, the Order of Lenin.[57] Such official recognition of the worth of artists, scientists, and other intellectuals, is a measure of their official rating although not of their political influence. The political influence of Soviet intellectuals will be examined in our next chapter.

7   The intelligentsia and politics

No question is more difficult to assess than the political influence of the Soviet intelligentsia. Perhaps because of this Western writers have either dodged the question altogether or obscured the problem by over-confident generalizations. Thus writers such as Fainsod, Schapiro and Scott attach small importance to the role of intellectuals, while Alfred Meyer dodges the question altogether.[1] On the other hand, John H. Kautsky equates Russian communism with the revolt of the intelligentsia.[2] John N. Hazard, in *The Soviet System of Government* (1957), argued that the rising educational level within the Communist Party, and especially within the leadership, indicated that the political role of the intelligentsia was increasing, and that: 'This influx of educated persons into the ranks of the party has prepared the way for the greatest challenge yet faced by the small group of party leaders presently sitting in the Presidium of the Central Committee', and further, to predict that intellectuals 'will eventually demand a real share in the determination of policy within the party'.[3] In the third edition of *The Soviet System of Government* (1964) Hazard refers to the 'quiet revolution' by which the intellectuals had largely displaced the earlier proletarian *apparatchiki* in the leadership of the CPSU—most leaders of the party by 1961 (Kozlov, Kosygin, Brezhnev, etc.) were 'university men'.[4]

The same evidence has led other writers to argue that the Soviet intelligentsia is already the ruling class or a major part of it, and that it will soon challenge the party bureaucracy and thus fulfil the role of the 'Gravedigger of Communism'.[5]

On the other hand, many American specialists consider that the intelligentsia has been brought into political debate and struggle largely through divisions within the party leadership.

According to this view, what determines the activity of intellectuals and the policies they advocate is the existence of major policy differences between rival factions within the party leadership. Under such circumstances each faction seeks to broaden its support amongst intellectuals and other sections of society. But intellectual argument has no autonomy. Intellectuals merely reflect the views of the leaders. Consequently, the greater the unity of the leaders the weaker the role of the intellectuals.[6]

While most Western scholars of the Soviet system no longer argue that the intelligentsia is a class or a united political force, they are far from certain about the role of specific professional groups. Most writers assume that there is some degree of cohesion within professional groups[7] although much of the available evidence would seem to contradict the assumption. Thus on many occasions not only have professional groups been divided into two or more factions but this has also happened within individual institutes or editorial boards. On some occasions this dissent has been evident in the opposing positions being argued under the signatures of the editor and the associate editor.[8]

As long ago as August 1961 I argued that Soviet intellectuals were becoming increasingly active and important in decision-making in the Soviet Union.[9] This estimate was based on little more than an impression of the evidence of increased debate of political questions among Soviet intellectuals as reflected in the Soviet press and in Soviet specialist journals. Since then a number of more detailed and more sophisticated examinations have been made which argue the same case. Thus Milton C. Lodge has established through quantitative analysis of a number of Soviet journals over the years 1953–65 that various specialist groups (the party *apparat*, the economic élite, the military, the legal profession, and the literary élite) all recognize the growing importance of professional groups in the decision-making process and that evidence suggests 'party-specialist élite interdependence, not *apparatchiki* dominance'.[10] In a very detailed and careful study of the repeal of the Khrushchev educational programme in August 1964, Philip D. Stewart[11] argues three hypotheses:

(1) That in the arena of educational policy, interest groups form primarily (a) among individuals, and (b) on the basis of similarity of viewpoints on one or more issues. These groupings

may be found either within a single bureaucratic structure or cutting across organizational lines.

(2) Operating within a broad consensus about the conservation of the system as a whole, interest groupings openly formulate, build public support for, and urge the adoption of their specific proposals by the party leadership. Both party leaders and participants in the discussion consider that this activity is legitimate.

(3) Interest groupings may exercise influence and share power in Soviet policy-making. That is, interest groups may initiate discussion and make suggestions prior to the entry of party leadership into the process.

In the particular decision examined by Stewart, the discussion had gone on for two years before the decision was taken jointly by the Central Committee and the Council of Ministers (on 13 August 1964) to reduce the period of secondary education beyond the 8th grade to two years, thus ending Khrushchev's 1958 policy of a minimum of one year's work in industry or agriculture. The opponents of the 1958 Education Act included educationalists, teachers, prominent scientists, editors, and *Sovnarkhoz* administrators. Supporters of the 1958 Act included leading members of the Institute of Production (under the Institute of Pedagogical Science), party specialists, the editor of *Uchitelskaya gazeta* and officials of the RSFSR Ministry of Education. The final submission on which the Central Committee and the Council of Ministers based their August 1964 decision was prepared by a special commission of representatives of the Academy of Pedagogical Science and the RSFSR Education Ministry, working under the direction of the Central Committee.

Stewart's analysis supports the theses advanced by Professor Franklyn Griffiths[12] in 1968 that political dividing lines in the Soviet Union coincide with policy differences rather than with professional groups as such. Around particular policies loose coalitions of groupings emerge. In this sense temporary interest groups may be identified within a given organization, but they will seldom coincide with any organization: 'there exists a wide range of legitimate political activity in which Soviet interest groupings can and do engage.'[13]

My own examination of the role of intellectuals in Soviet

political debate and in decision-making over the years 1957–70 largely supports the thesis advanced by Griffiths and Stewart. In the following pages I shall produce further evidence in support of this thesis. But throughout this analysis my main object will be to analyse the relations between the party *apparat* and the intelligentsia.

Avenues of political influence of the intelligentsia

Avenues of political influence are widely distributed within the Soviet political system. The extent to which intellectuals can use these avenues depends on at least four variables—the status and prestige of the individual or group concerned, whether the individual is an ordinary citizen or an office-holder in a recognized organization, the administrative level of the *apparat* which the individual is seeking to influence, and the level of political conflict within the party leadership. As a general rule the higher the reputation and prestige of a given group of intellectuals, the greater its capacity to influence political debate and decision. Thus writers generally have a greater political potential than do ballet dancers or librarians, nuclear physicists than foreign language teachers, mathematical economists than history teachers. To hold an official position whether in the Party or in the government, in a scientific establishment or in a professional organization, is almost (but not quite) a prerequisite for representation at the points at which maximum influence is available for intellectuals. Thus the Central Committee elected in April 1966 had a clear majority of graduates, but only seven of the 195 full members or 3.6 per cent were intellectuals without any office in the Party, State or related social organizations. Even these seven represented intellectual bureaucracies, five from the USSR Academy of Sciences and two from the Writers' Union. Avenues of influence vary according to the administrative level concerned—they are likely to be more personal, more direct and less elaborate at the district level than they are at the all-Union level. As many writers have noticed, the involvement of public groups (including intellectuals) in the political process varies in accordance with the degree of unity in the leadership. A divided leadership normally results in greater activity by main interest groups. But this factor should not be over-emphasized, as even in years when the leadership has been most united—as from late 1957 to 1962—the leadership found it necessary on many policy matters to seek the active assistance of expert advisers. However, the removal of Khrushchev in October 1964 allowed the creation of a more delicately balanced collective leadership.[14] Such a collective encouraged the regularizing of bureaucratic processes and the creation of an environment which maximized the influence of specialists, both those in official positions and those serving as non-official advisers. My assumption here is not that the Soviet Union became more democratic after October 1964 but merely that the top political leadership became more bureaucratized and the bureaucracy became more regular, more restrained, and more rational. Consequently the political role of intellectuals increased.

I want now to describe in some detail the main avenues of political influence available to Soviet intellectuals during the 1960s. I would describe these as follows.

(1) Intellectuals have greater opportunities than others to operate in Soviet politics through their membership of the Party. The desire to be more active and influential in politics is one important reason why young intellectuals join the Party. Not to join is to be left out of meetings which, for all their limitations, do provide real opportunities for extended debate on all sorts of political questions (including the writers' trials, Czechoslovakia, and international Communist Conferences). Such meetings allow for the exchange of different opinions and for divided votes. As we have already seen, intellectuals are accorded considerable representation in the Central Committee of the CPSU. While this is mainly the representation of the state bureaucracy and the party *apparat* there is also a token representation of scientists, writers and academics. At all levels of the party structure intellectuals are active and at all levels this facilitates access from wider groups of intellectuals to the leading organs of the Party, to the Central Committee, to the Central Committees of the Republican Parties and to Regional Committees.

(2) Important agencies of the intelligentsia such as the USSR Academy of Sciences and even individual research institutes are closely linked to the party apparatus. The link between the Academy of Sciences and the Communist Party is symbolized

by the inclusion of several academicians in the Central Committee. The Academy of Sciences has a direct channel to the government since it is formally an important part of the planning machinery and is directly linked not only to Gosplan but to the State Committee for Science and Technology. Educational establishments are linked to the USSR Council of Ministers through the Ministry of Higher and Secondary Specialist Education. Further, many research and teaching institutes are controlled by other ministries, and consequently the members of such institutes have favourable opportunities for influencing certain policy areas within the responsible ministry. Even in a sensitive area such as foreign affairs, the Institute of International Relations, which is controlled by the Ministry of Foreign Affairs, is engaged not merely in staff-training but in research. Since persons other than members of this particular institute hold part-time teaching and research posts there, many personal links must obviously exist between this and Academy of Science institutes.

Many direct links exist between Academy of Science institutes and the party *apparat*. Thus it seems likely that there is a direct link between the Institute of the International Workers' Movement and the Department of the Central Committee of the CPSU on liaison with non-bloc countries, and between the Institute of World Economics and International Relations and the Foreign Affairs Department of the Central Committee. This latter institute, one of the strongest in the sphere of capitalist economics and politics, also has direct links with the Ministries of Foreign Affairs and Foreign Trade. Such links allow the party and state apparatus to get information at short notice—a telephone call to an institute or even to a particular department in an institute will soon provide this. It also means that some at least of the research projects undertaken by an institute will be selected by the party bureaucracy for its own purposes. But such links also allow some influence to operate in the reverse direction, for in a Communist regime, as well as elsewhere, to act as a special adviser is to influence the administrator.

Other groups of intellectuals are linked to particular ministries. Thus most doctors come under the Health Ministry and most teachers under the Education Ministry. Other intellectuals are under the supervision of the Ministry of Culture or one of

the State Committees under the USSR Council of Ministers
—the State Committee on Professional and Technical Education,
the State Committee on Radio Broadcasting and T.V. and the
State Committee on Cinematography or the State Committee on
the Press.[15] Since such administrative agencies are the main
policy-making agencies within given fields it is only natural that
intellectuals working in these fields should place considerable
importance on co-operating with and influencing these agencies.
Such patterns of interaction and influence may be discerned in
the debates over recent years.

(3) Mention has already been made of the advisory and
policy-forming role of intellectuals through their service on such
agencies as Standing Commissions of Soviets, Scientific Councils
attached to ministries and departments and to the Presidium of
the Academy of Sciences. The precise role of intellectuals within
Standing Commissions of Soviets is difficult to estimate since
meetings of such agencies are not fully reported in the Soviet
press. Some tentative comments might be made about the
Standing Commissions of the USSR Supreme Soviet appointed
in August 1966.[16] The Legislative Proposals Commissions of the
Supreme Soviet, where non-*apparat* intellectuals might have
been anticipated, showed only a handful of them, and almost no
lawyers. However, amongst the intellectuals included was a
senior scientist and the rector of Tomsk University. On the other
hand, the Standing Commission on Foreign Affairs of the Soviet
of Nationalities had a number of prominent intellectuals among
its thirty-one members, including four writers (Korneichuk,
Sholokhov, Tikhonov and Ehrenburg) and the mathematical
scientist, Academician M. A. Lavrentiev. The Planning-Budget
Commissions, like most of the Commissions, contained a solid
core of party functionaries of the intermediate administrative
level, but they also contained a fair number of state administrators, managers and teachers. The only two Standing Commissions with a high representation of non-*apparat* intellectuals
proved to be the Standing Commissions on Education, Science
and Culture, and the Standing Commissions on Health and
Social Security. Thus the Standing Commission on Education,
Science and Culture of the Soviet of the Union was headed by S.
P. Trapeznikov, head of the Central Committee Department on
Science and Educational Establishments. While this Commis-

sion contained several *obkom* secretaries and government officials, twelve of the thirty ordinary members were non-*apparat* intellectuals, including an artist, several secondary teachers, a singer, a composer, an editor, a theatrical producer, and two mathematicians. The Standing Commission of the Soviet of the Union on Health and Social Security showed a somewhat similar pattern. The Chairman was Professor N. N. Blokhin, Chairman of the USSR Academy of Medical Sciences. Fourteen out of the remaining thirty commission members were non-*apparat* intellectuals. They included doctors drawn from various parts of the USSR, an engineer and plant director and a zootechnician and state farm director.[17] From the brief reports which have appeared in *Vedomosti Verkhovnovo Soveta SSSR* and in the Soviet press over recent years it can be seen that Standing Commissions of the Supreme Soviet are becoming more active and that they are less dominated by officials. However, it does seem that the Soviet Union has not yet sought to use the full opportunities of the system. There would seem to be no good reason other than power within the party structure for continued *apparatchiki* domination of most Standing Commissions. The role of the intellectual advisers is perhaps greater if the range is extended to include the subcommittees which advise the various Standing Commissions. However, even here there seems to be a policy of drawing advisers mainly from the ranks of conservative and establishment minded intellectuals.

From time to time the government has appointed special Commissions to prepare drafts of major legislation. Thus in April 1962 a Constitutional Commission of ninety-six members under the Chairmanship of the First Secretary, N. S. Khrushchev,[18] was appointed for the purpose of drafting a new Constitution for the USSR. The Commission was packed out with party and state officials but it included a number of non-*apparat* intellectuals, with writers (Korneichuk, Fedin and Sholokhov), mathematicians (Keldysh, Lavrentiev), jurists (A. I. Denisov and P. S. Romashkin), a geologist, an agricultural scientist and a philosopher (P. N. Fedoseev). Again the Commission worked through subcommissions which substantially increased the representation of the intelligentsia. Perhaps the intellectuals must bear some responsibility for the failure of this Commission to reach agreement for there is evidence that intellectual opinion was divided on many key issues of constitutional reform, including Soviet federalism and other nationality questions.[19] Be that as it may, the Commission was reconstituted in December 1964 (when L. I. Brezhnev became the Chairman), but it had not produced a draft of a new Constitution up to 1970. The Commission appointed by the Central Committee of the CPSU in January 1966 to prepare a new draft statute for collective farms had about the same proportion of non-*apparat* intellectuals among its 149 members,[20] including a lawyer (Professor V. M. Chkhikvadze), several agricultural scientists, agricultural economists and engineers. This Commission proceeded with greater urgency and the public debate on its new draft statute commenced in April 1969, while the statute, with minor amendments, was adopted by the 3rd All-Union Congress of Collective Farmers at the end of November 1969.[21]

Quite outside of the avenues for influencing major areas of government policy described above, intellectuals can exert considerable influence on scientific development and technology through the scientific councils attached to the ministries and state departments and to the Presidium of the USSR Academy of Sciences. Scientific institutes and university departments also often undertake specific research projects on behalf of government departments or party agencies. Such research findings must influence government and party policy, even if somewhat slowly.

(4) The public discussions which are organized from time to time in the Soviet Union around particular issues of public concern provide many opportunities for intellectuals to participate. Certainly the longer contributions to the public discussions on industrial reorganization (1957), educational reform (1958) and the new draft collective farm statute (1969) came from intellectuals. The precise role of such participation is somewhat difficult to determine. Some critics have suggested that public discussion merely serves to allow politicians to manipulate public opinion through the process of mobilizing their intellectual supporters to 'front' for them publicly against their political rivals. There was certainly a strong element of this in the 1957 industrial reorganization debate. But intellectuals do not always clearly represent the views of leadership factions, nor are their views always dependent views. For the most part intellectuals seem to use the occasion of an open discussion to ride their own hobby-

horses.[22] It also seems likely that on more limited discussions—as on such matters as the reform of the basic law codes—the views of experts are expressed more confidently and more successfully. Thus the opening salvo in the discussion on the new draft statute for collective farms was fired by a group (drawn mainly from the Agricultural Law Sector) of the Institute of State and Law. The contribution offered general acceptance of the draft statute but it urged a number of specific changes to the proposed statute.[23] Later letters in the discussion came mainly from intellectuals with a special interest in the question—from collective farm chairmen, from agricultural economists, agricultural engineers, agricultural scientists and jurists.

(5) Debates on economic, scientific and cultural matters are often generated within the intellectual establishment, within teaching and research institutes rather than within the Central Committee or within the Council of Ministers or individual ministries. Thus the pioneers of the economic reforms which were adopted in the Central Committee in September, and in the Supreme Soviet in October 1965, were groups of reforming economists and individual managers, who conducted a skilful campaign over several years until sufficient support was gained in the higher ranks of the party and state apparatus to enable the reform to be carried through. In the process of this long campaign the reformers employed every form of available publicity, including articles in the daily papers and scientific journals, press interviews, radio and T.V. commentaries, and lobbying of party leaders. They showed considerable skill in the tactics they used to bring about the reform, although they were less able to ensure successful implementation of the reforms and to resist bureaucratic opposition and delays.[24]

Intellectuals have a greater capacity to influence party and government policy when the policy decisions directly concern their own area of competency. Thus the party decision to establish the Siberian Division of the USSR Academy of Sciences (taken in May 1957, and implemented in the following year) was little more than the acceptance of an imaginative proposal put forward by leading scientists, including M. A. Lavrentiev, during the general public debate on industrial decentralization early in 1957.[25] The Scientific Councils (*nauchnye sovety*), which are playing such an important role in the development of science policy in the USSR today, were first suggested by V. Kirillin (then a Corresponding Member of the Academy of Sciences and Head of an important C.C. Department) in an article in *Pravda* on 15 March 1959. They were provided for in the new rules of the Academy of Sciences introduced on 28 March 1959, and have been rapidly expanded during the 1960s. Intellectual opinion—as distinct from governmental opinion—has had a considerable influence on the various reorganizations to the machinery of scientific research undertaken over the past decade, including the establishment of the State Committee for the Co-ordination of Scientific Research Work, which was established in April 1961.[26]

Intellectuals have usually taken the lead in the numerous campaigns over recent years to preserve natural resources from unscientific exploitation. Such struggles usually produce divisions within the community as between the economic exploitative agencies (particularly those associated with quarrying, mining, lumber- and wood-processing industries and fishing), and scientific agencies concerned with a scientific conservation policy. But since many experts are employed by the extractive industries (including industrial economists and engineers), expert opinion is often divided between those counselling rapid exploitation of resources and those advising caution.[27] On one occasion at least, such disputes between the experts led to the dismissal of the Minister of Forestry in June 1968. Following the dismissal of the Minister (I. Voronov), *Pravda* printed a long article entitled, 'The forester and the woodcutter: commentary on a conflict', written by a forestry specialist and a vice-chairman of the All-Russian Society for the Preservation of Nature. The writer of this article asserted that:[28]

> Timber procurement agents not only fell the forest on the principle of 'there is enough for our century', but they also attempt to provide scientific grounds for why they should act this way. In short, the art of forest destruction has its own theorists and followers. They make statements in the press and on the radio.

One such article referred to was by the head of the Department of the Economics of Forestry at the Leningrad Forest Technology Institute.

A key agency in struggles around the preservation of Lake Baikal in recent years has been the USSR Academy of Sciences Commission for the Study of Productive Forces and Natural Resources, under the Chairmanship of Academician N. Melnikov, established in May 1967,[29] as a direct counter to the attempt by the industrial lobby to exclude the Academy of Sciences from participation in these matters. Melnikov concluded his article in the *Literaturnaya gazeta* of 12 July 1967, with these words: 'Of course, science does have a consultative voice in the mastery of nature. But let us hope that managers will begin to listen to this sober voice more intensely than they have hitherto.' The warning was heeded, but not before a long political struggle. The outcome was that in February 1969 the USSR Council of Ministers issued a decision concerned with the preservation and rational use of the natural resources of the Lake Baikal basin. Under this measure the entire Lake Baikal basin has been placed under very stringent control and supervision and the cellulose plants in the area ordered to reduce lumber-extraction on steep slopes and to install special equipment for purifying the industrial waste. However, waste still flows into Lake Baikal.[30]

Similar struggles must frequently occur at the local as well as at the national level. Thus, recently scientists at the Crimean Astrophysical Observatory forced a local industrial plant to transfer its quarrying operations because it was causing so much dust that star gazing had become impossible. Another recent example from Sverdlovsk concerned architects urging the city Soviet to remove trees along Lenin Prospect in order to provide a more impressive view of the centre of the city. The matter was referred to intellectuals and others in the *aktiv* and this conference decided unanimously to reject the architects' plan and to preserve the trees. The city Soviet accepted the advice of the *aktiv* and the trees were saved, temporarily at least.[31]

Similar examples of intellectual policy-making initiative could be selected from the area of the social sciences. Thus the matter of constitutional reform gained only a brief mention by Khrushchev at the 21st Congress early in 1959. It was not taken up at the official level until much later, with the appointment of the Constitutional Commission in April 1962. But meanwhile academics had been holding discussions and conferences and producing recommendations. As early as May 1959 the State Law Sector of the Academy of Sciences held a conference at which papers presented by Professor V. Kotok and others recommended extensive changes to the description of the social structure and to the powers of various state agencies.[32]

An even better example is provided by the development of Soviet sociology over the past decade. Although the initial decisions which made this possible were taken by the Party (at the 20th, 21st and 22nd Congresses and in the Central Committee), the pace-setting and many of the consequential decisions were taken by the academics. Thus party definitions of the functions of sociology stressed only two functions—ideological struggle and problem-solving. But academics have consistently argued for a greater range of functions, some of which imply a greater measure of independence in relation to investigation of social problems and making policy recommendations than the party apparatus originally conceded.[33] The institutional structure of Soviet sociology bears all the earmarks of academic rather than governmental decision-making. The first small laboratories of Concrete Sociological Research were established in 1958-9. During the early 1960s they spread like a rash and by the end of 1968 they existed in more than a score of Soviet cities. In Moscow and Leningrad several independent centres existed, linked to Academy institutes, to University faculties, or to other higher educational institutes. Having established themselves, without any top-level party, government or Academy decision in this piecemeal and local way, the sociologists launched a campaign in 1965 for the integration and consolidation of existing institutes and for the development of undergraduate teaching in sociology. Not all of these objectives have been realized as yet, but in May 1968 the Presidium of the USSR Academy of Sciences agreed to establish an Institute of Concrete Social Research. This was formally set up in December 1968 and by May 1969 it already had about 170 staff.[34] The new institute will co-ordinate the work already being done in various Academy laboratories throughout the country.[35]

The dialectic of the development of Soviet sociology, especially over the years since 1965, has been provided mainly within the academic establishment. The success of the sociologists must be compared with the earlier failure to establish

Soviet political science. Notwithstanding the fact that the Association of Soviet Political Science was established in 1960, the campaign to establish political science as an academic discipline fizzled out less than a year after it was launched with the article by F. M. Burlatsky in *Pravda*, 10 January 1965. This was surprising since Burlatsky enjoyed considerable support from within the party leadership. As late as mid-June 1965 the campaign still seemed to have top party backing.[36] The discussion was fought out almost entirely by academics through conferences, articles and letters. Very soon the field divided into those who were generally in favour of the Burlatsky proposals and those who were opposed to them. The former group included some senior jurists such as Professor G. V. Tadevosyan, but it drew most support from younger scholars who had grown tired of the aridity of traditional Soviet legal studies. On the other hand, opponents of the proposal included such 'heavy weights' as Professors V. M. Chkhikvadze and S. L. Zivs of the Institute of State and Law, Moscow. Their line of argument, that there was no need for political science since all things studied under it could be better studied under Soviet Law and in the new subject, Scientific Communism, was tailored to attract support from the ideological specialists within the party apparatus.[37] It would seem therefore that an alliance between academic conservatives and party ideologists blocked this development. Perhaps Burlatsky's friendship with N. S. Khrushchev proved a liability. He became a political commentator shortly afterwards and dropped out of controversies until he resurfaced in 1968 as one of the leaders in the campaign for establishing sociology. But perhaps he is still a political scientist at heart, since in 1969 he headed the important Department on Public Opinion* within the newly established Institute of Concrete Social Research.[38]

(6) Intellectuals in recent years have achieved considerable success in developing theoretical analysis of political processes, especially international processes, beyond the limits of official ideological formulation. This is most obvious in the analysis of questions such as the national liberation movement,[39] the role of the military in developing societies,[40] the changing social structures and politics of capitalist and developing countries,[41]

---

* This department was abolished early in 1972 and Burlatsky and some other political sociologists were transferred to the Institute of State and Law.

regional studies (especially African and Latin American studies),[42] peaceful coexistence,[43] and the theory of the State. Having read a good deal of Soviet academic writing in all these fields I have found it to be increasingly well researched and well argued. One can only hope that these more careful academic assessments are fed back to, and are influencing the party theoreticians and government officials. Even if they aren't they at least indicate that the party leadership now shares with the academics the important function of reshaping the Marxist ideology.

(7) Intellectuals, in recent years at least, have achieved considerable success through their actions in defence of liberal opinions and in resistance to conservative pressures. A wide variety of forms of defence and protest has been used, including joint and individual letters to top party[44] and state[45] bodies. Important also have been the 'declarations of faith' issued by prominent members of particular groups of intellectuals[46] which have been widely circulated for criticism and support. Through these means and others, numerous overlapping circles of liberal 'opinion-makers' are emerging in the Soviet Union. Even in the Academy institutes it is noticeable that individuals whom the Party sought to victimize, because of their opposition to the writers' trials or over Czechoslovakia, have been protected and helped to survive. Indeed, something like a 'mutual protection network' seems to be operating in the Soviet Union today so that many of those who challenge or dissent from party policy in vital areas are given protection and alternative employment. Politics is an important present factor in the mobility of intellectuals, particularly in the social sciences. For many liberal-minded intellectuals there is a constant shifting of jobs and each shift is associated with hopes that the new position will be better and freer than the old.

(8) Implied throughout the above discussion is the point that personal contacts between intellectuals and the *apparat* exist at all levels. The *apparat* is not united and is divided by sectional, factional and policy differences. Under these circumstances intellectual groupings, whether progressive or conservative, will operate through contacts within the apparatus. Even quasi-legal oppositional groups such as the organized group of intellectuals operating the illegal *samizdat* (independent press)

in Moscow have their top-level contact men. Thus on one recent occasion when the KGB arrested the poet, Voznesensky, after a reading of protest poems at a Moscow concert hall, he was released within hours through the personal intervention of Politburo member, A. N. Shelepin.

Relations between the party apparatus and the intelligentsia

Relations between Soviet intellectuals and the party *apparat* are close, complex and contradictory. They are so full of contradictions that it would be hazardous to predict with confidence what they will be over the next two decades. However, a clear distinction cannot be drawn between intellectuals and the *apparatchiki*. The first reason for this is that the majority of Soviet intellectuals are either party members or close supporters of the Party. As such, they recognize the Party's leading role throughout society and they accept the need for the Party to maintain a strong apparatus and for this to be drawn increasingly from their own ranks. Second, many intellectuals hold positions which are *nomenklatura* positions i.e. party-controlled positions. Such *nomenklaturnye rabotniki* or 'Establishment men'[47] are in many ways an extension of the *apparatchiki* proper, and do in fact often move right into positions within the party apparatus. Third, there are no important distinctions between party officials and other intellectuals in terms of class, nationality, basic education or income. There are differences in career patterns but these are not so great as they were in pre-war days and they are probably of declining importance. There remain important differences in power and influence between party officials and other intellectuals.

Because of the importance of education and professional training in the recruitment and careers of Soviet intellectuals it is necessary to discuss at some length the position of the party officials. While it is still not a necessary prerequisite for all who join the party apparatus to have a tertiary qualification, many, perhaps most, do have this qualification. The future *apparatchik* is early distinguished by his greater activity within the *Komsomol* and by his early joining of the Party. Whereas most intellectuals seem to join the Party in their mid-thirties, after a decade or more of professional experience, the *apparatchik* usually joins the Party at twenty-three to twenty-five years of age, at the very outset of his professional career or even before he has graduated. Once in the party apparatus, his career depends primarily on his successful performance of party tasks and on nomination to higher or to different positions. Only a minority of positions held by intellectuals will be on the party *nomenklatura*, or job list. But those who begin their careers on the basis of a party recommendation are likely to continue to have their careers determined in this way.

To illustrate the above point I will refer briefly to the careers of three Soviet intellectuals known to me over several years. Each of the three graduated in history in the early fifties. They were all active party members at the time of graduation and they were all assigned to specialist work within the Central Committee apparatus. After a few years in research and information work in Moscow their careers began to diverge. One man was selected to go as an interpreter with the Soviet Olympic Team to the Olympic Games in Melbourne in 1956. He began to work up an Australian background. Unfortunately he became ill and got no further than Tashkent. He continued as an Australian specialist in Moscow and over the next few years made a trip to Australia as an interpreter, published two booklets on Australia and translated an Australian book on trade unions. In 1961 he was appointed as a lecturer in history at the Patrice Lumumba University in Moscow. He claims to have enjoyed the experience but he found the academic regimen rather tedious and not fully rewarding. In 1963 he was forced to take a long sick-leave and, on his doctor's advice, he did not return to academic work. He was well enough in 1964 to spend three months in Australia as an interpreter for a famous theatrical group. On his return from Australia late in 1964 he was posted to an important position in the APN newsagency. In the spring of 1965 he became the head of an APN agency in Western Europe.

The second of the trio moved from work in the Party Secretariat to the Ministry of Foreign Affairs. After some time working in Moscow he received an appointment as a First Secretary in a Soviet Embassy in the Antipodes. He continued to be interested in academic research and while abroad commenced collecting material for an advanced degree. However, after only three years he was posted back to Moscow. In the middle of 1965 he was appointed ambassador to a smaller English-speaking country, a post he held for four years. On his return to Moscow he again worked as a senior official dealing with South-West Pacific policy. He still dreams of gaining a higher degree and moving into academic work but his career has become thoroughly professionalized and tied to the Foreign Affairs Ministry.

The third man in the group has had a very different career to the other two. He has worked for the C.C. apparatus since graduation. He has risen steadily so that in the mid-sixties he was liaison secretary for an overseas Communist Party. This meant frequent consultations with visiting Communists and much time spent in arranging their itineraries, and in accompanying them on their trips to various places in the Soviet Union. He also received the requests of visiting delegations and did his best to meet them. This often involved him in lobbying for favours with the Academy of Sciences, universities and other academic institutions. By the end of the sixties he had moved up into a middle-ranking position in the central party apparatus. He was one of three private secretaries to a member of the Secretariat. As such he became less approachable to his many foreign acquaintances. While still friendly in face-to-face contacts, he often took shelter behind the party bureaucracy and became a master of formal, polite evasiveness. Much more than the other two, his career has become identified with the central party apparatus. He might still be transferred to work in the provinces or to some central state job but the chances are that he will remain working in the central apparatus.

An important training period in the life of many party and government officials is the years spent in a Higher Party School. The highest training of this sort is that provided in the Academy of the Social Sciences under the Central Committee of the CPSU. Only persons with tertiary qualifications are admitted to this Academy and, having graduated from the Academy, they move into senior scientific, academic and administrative positions. Higher Party Schools under the Central Committee of the CPSU and republican parties are used more to provide an alternative tertiary-type training for middle-aged, middle-level party and state officials. Graduates from these schools are less likely to enter the academic or scientific world, although they are quite likely to attain senior administrative, managerial or party posts. While some intellectuals other than party or state officials go through the party school system they are not very many. There were 33,000 graduates from Higher Party Schools over the years 1966–70 compared with more than two and a half million graduates from tertiary educational institutions.

Nothing that I have said above should be taken as evidence that everyone who joins the party apparatus does so at an early age. Many intellectuals move into the party *apparat* in the middle of their careers or even at the end of their careers. Some specialists in the field of communications and ideology will follow an intermittent career in the party apparatus, with important jobs outside the apparatus alternating with jobs in the apparatus. Senior scientists might acquire a top post inside the Central Committee apparatus by virtue of their long and outstanding career in science. Many scientists become closely associated with the party apparatus because they hold senior scientific positions. Some examples of these various patterns are given below.

Academician M. V. Keldysh, the President of the USSR Academy of Sciences, is a senior scientific administrator. Although he did not join the Party until he was thirty-eight, several years after he became a full member of the USSR Academy of Sciences, he has been a member of the Central Committee since 1961. His professional career began in 1932 when he became a lecturer in mechanical engineering at Moscow State University at the age of twenty-one. He gained his doctorate in physico-mathematical science in 1938 and became a full professor. He became a corresponding-member of the USSR Academy of Sciences in 1943, a full member in 1946 and a Presidium member in 1949, the year in which he joined the Party. In 1960 he became head of the department of applied mathematics of the Mathematics Institute of the USSR Academy of Sciences, and in 1961 the President of the Academy.

Academician M. A. Lavrentiev, a Vice-President of the USSR Academy of Sciences and the President of the Siberian Division since 1957, did not join the Party until 1952 when he was fifty-two, after thirty years as an academic scientist. On the other hand, another leading scientific administrator of the sixties, A. M. Samarin, joined the Party at the early age of twenty-three.

Notwithstanding this, he spent many years in teaching and research positions. He has been a professor at the Moscow Steel Institute since 1938, a corresponding member of the USSR Academy of Sciences since 1946 and Director of the Institute of Metallurgy within the Academy of Sciences since 1960.

G. P. Frantsov, rector of the Academy of Social Sciences under the Central Committee of the CPSU, holds many senior scientific and political posts. However, he did not join the Party until 1940 when he was thirty-seven. During the thirties he was an associate, and from 1937 to 1945 the Director of the Museum of the History of Religion of the USSR Academy of Sciences. Over the years 1945–9 he was Director of the Institute of International Relations, USSR Ministry of Foreign Affairs. Between 1949 and 1952 he was the Head of the Press Department of the Ministry of Foreign Affairs. Between 1953 and 1957 he was foreign editor of *Pravda*, and during 1957–9, deputy chief editor. He became a corresponding member of the USSR Academy of Sciences in 1958 and a full member in 1964. Since then he has been Chairman of the Soviet Sociological Association and of the Scientific Council (of the Academy of Sciences) for Co-ordinating Work on Atheism and Religious Criticism.

A. A. Gromyko, USSR Minister of Foreign Affairs, began his professional career as an academic. Born in 1909 he joined the Party in 1931. He graduated from the Minsk Institute of Agriculture in 1934 and completed a postgraduate course at the Leningrad Institute of Economics. He was a senior associate at the Institute of Economics, USSR Academy of Sciences, in Moscow 1936–9 and executive secretary to the editorial board of the journal *Voprosy ekonomiki*. In 1939 he became head of the department of American countries in the Commissariat of Foreign Affairs, then counsellor at the USSR Embassy in Washington. Since 1939 he has been a career diplomat.

V. A. Kirillin, a famous thermo-physicist and scientific administrator, joined the Party in 1937 at the age of twenty-four, barely a year after he had graduated from the Power Engineering Institute in Moscow. Between 1938 and 1941, and again in 1943–52, he was a lecturer at this institute. He became a doctor of technical science and a professor in 1952. In 1954 he became Deputy USSR Minister of Higher Education and in 1955 Deputy Chairman of the State Committee for New Technology.

Since 1955 he has held various positions in the Central Committee apparatus, including head of the Department of Science, Higher Educational Institutions and Schools over the years 1955–63. He was for a time the deputy head of the Ideological Commission of the C.C. For several years until 1961 he was Director of the Laboratory on High Temperatures of the USSR Academy of Sciences. He became a full member of the USSR Academy of Sciences in 1962 and a Vice-President in 1963. He also became Chairman of the Knowledge Society in 1963. Since 1965 he has been Chairman of the State Committee on Science and Technology and a Vice-Chairman of the Council of Ministers of the USSR.[48]

The above few biographies are not sufficient to enable the construction of a typology of Soviet officials. They do however suggest the convergence in the career patterns of senior scientists and government and party officials. Professor George Fischer[49] has recently developed a typology of Soviet officials on the basis of an analysis of 306 top party executives. He recognizes four basic types—the *dual executive*, the *technician*, the *hybrid executive*, and the *official*. The dual executive type is one with considerable technical and managerial experience alternating with party work. This basic type seems to be somewhat similar to the careers we have outlined over the last few pages. They seem to represent a career type that might be called either the *scientist-administrator* type or the *academic-apparatchik* type.

Positive aspects of the relationship

From the point of view of Soviet intellectuals the close relationship with the party *apparat* has both positive and negative features. I will begin my analysis of this relationship by first examining what might be called the positive aspects. In the first place, most Soviet intellectuals seem to accept the socialist system and are prepared to work within the Communist political system, to observe its rules and to respect its restraints. They are generally willing and often very anxious to assist in the improvement and further development of their social and political system.

Second, the Communist Party is fully committed to the rapid extension of Soviet science and culture and is, through its control of the state budget, providing the bulk of finance for its maintenance and development.[50] Third, the Soviet system provides for the direct representation of intellectuals in higher party and state bodies. This creates many access points through which intellectuals can hope to influence the determination of basic policy and especially the finer details of that policy. Fourth, in addition to the intelligentsia having its representatives on higher party bodies (such as the Central Committee of the CPSU, the Central Committees of republican parties, the apparatus of the Central Committees, etc.), intellectuals are extensively used for collecting information (*spravka*) and for giving advice on policy matters. These advisory channels, as we have already seen, are partly formal and partly informal.

A fifth positive feature of the relationship is the public recognition given to intellectuals through awards and honours. Far more than in other societies intellectuals get the medals and the honours. Leading academicians will sometimes hold as many as four or five Orders of Lenin, not to mention Stalin and Lenin Prizes and various Soviet and international awards. Furthermore, intellectuals have the main say in the allocation of their own special awards, the Lenin Prizes.

Sixth, the educational level of the apparatus, not merely at the central level but right down to the district level, has risen rapidly over recent years. Most secretaries of District Committees and Chairmen of District Soviet Executive Committees have tertiary education nowadays. This has probably improved the co-operation between intellectuals in the apparatus and intellectuals outside the apparatus.

Seventh and last, there is a great deal of interchange between the *apparat* and the intellectual establishment, and a considerable measure of interpenetration exists. Academics and scientists are frequently seconded to the apparatus as journalists, political commentators, heads of party educational institutes, editors, or even to serve a term on some agency of the Central Committee. Likewise scholars will be moved from a research institute to serve in a Soviet Embassy overseas, in the Foreign Affairs Ministry at home, or even in the United Nations Secretariat or in some specialized international agency. Most if not all such transfers are facilitated by the fact that senior academic and scientific posts are included in some party *nomenklatura*.

Negative aspects of the relationship

There are many friction points in the relationship between the apparatus and the intelligentsia. They include the following:

(1) Censorship, restrictions on foreign publications and restrictions on foreign travel. While intellectuals have greater freedom to use foreign information than have other sections of Soviet society their special need for free access to information makes existing restrictions all the more irritating. Restrictions on the use of books and other printed matter operate most severely against the social scientists. Although libraries such as the Fundamental Library of the Social Sciences contain a wide variety of foreign material much of it is on the 'specially reserved' shelves. Special written authorization is required each time *spets khran* material is used and it must be read in a special reading room. The same provisions operate in institute libraries and in university libraries. Personal possession of such books is prohibited, although it is not uncommon. This would perhaps not be so irksome if the books were few in number. But since whole categories of books are restricted, including most books written by Westerners on Soviet and Communist politics, many books printed in other socialist states, books on Nazism and comparative politics, the work conditions of Soviet social scientists must be somewhat frustrating. Although the censors systematically review the lists of 'reserved books' it usually takes years for a book to be reclassified. In the meantime new books are being added speedily. Since no published list of such books is available to Soviet scholars their research work carries an added frustration. Censorship also imposes difficulties on publication, and not merely for the creative intelligentsia. To avoid censorship, Soviet writers, social scientists as well as playwrights, make extensive use of veiled comment, 'esopian language'. They also use foreign approaches which they cannot apply to their writing on the Soviet system (functional analysis, behaviourism, etc.) when they are writing about the United States or China. Very many research projects (including approved projects) never result in publication. Perhaps half of completed manuscripts in the social sciences are never published.

Since 1965 the KGB has strengthened its supervision over

Soviet intellectuals. The 5th Department, which supervises intellectuals, has grown more rapidly than any other department of the KGB over recent years. Contacts with foreigners are carefully controlled, or at least controls are attempted. Many scientists suspect the presence of police agents in their research institutes. Sometimes individuals are called up for questioning and warning. If they neglect such warnings they might find themselves up before a court on a serious charge such as 'parasitism' or 'anti-Soviet propaganda'. Yet despite this increase in police activity Soviet intellectuals are prepared to run the risk and to talk openly about internal politics with foreign colleagues.

Restrictions on foreign travel are a lesser irritant although their impact may change as more Soviet intellectuals discover the desire and the need for travel.

(2) There is some irritation over the extent to which basic policy decisions relating to intellectual life are still taken at the highest party or state level. While formally the decision to establish a new institute or to reorganize an existing one will be made by the Presidium of the Academy of Sciences, such decisions are often the consequence of prior party decisions. It is therefore often difficult for intellectuals who wish to promote a new development to exercise enough leverage to carry it through, at least not without a prolonged struggle over years.

(3) Party control or influence on appointments in the academic and scientific world is widely criticized. While few intellectuals reject the system in its entirety many consider it too extensive. I have occasionally found criticisms of the system in the Soviet press.[51] In most Academy institutes between 30 and 50 per cent of the scientific staff are *nomenklatura* appointments. These include directors, deputy directors, academic secretaries, departmental heads and even associates of the institute. Quite minor administrative posts (such as minor academic secretaryships) are also *nomenklatura* appointments. In the social sciences at least, the sort of qualities that gain such appointments are ideological, political and bureaucratic rather than intellectual.

(4) An increasing irritant, especially over the past four or five years, has been the disorganization of research work caused by the party apparatus making excessive demands on the scientific institutes. Such demands include the organization of

innumerable political conferences to celebrate ideologically important birthdays and other occasions. The Institutes such as the Institute of State and Law and the Institute of the International Workers' Movement and the Academy of Social Sciences under the Central Committee of the CPSU, are particularly liable to such demands. Many scientists regard such activities as 'politicking'. They also resent the disruption caused by excessive requests for *spravka*. Sometimes as much as half a research worker's time (especially if he is employed in a sensitive social science institute) will go into this sort of routine fact finding. Intellectuals resent it not only because it distracts them from more serious matters, but because they regard it as a form of intellectual prostitution. On a slightly different level intellectuals sometimes resent the amount of time that goes into more routine political activities, in social organizations, in elections, and in the Party.[52]

(5) Despite some broad similarities between the career patterns of intellectuals and *apparatchiki*, especially in the early stages, they are significantly different in most cases. Soviet intellectuals consider the *apparatchik* an incurable bureaucrat. While there are some bureaucrats holding posts in scientific and educational institutes most of the members are scholars and scientists and tend to think and act as such. While some are 'careerists', many are not and will select a job which offers a reasonable income and interesting research prospects in a genuine collective rather than seek rapid promotion through political conformity. While academics do not seem to regret the steady movement of intellectuals across to the apparatus, they resent the attempt to fill top level scientific and academic posts with members of the *apparat*, especially if they regard them as conservatives. The Academy of Sciences, where the *nomenklatura* system does not operate at the level of the election of new members and corresponding members, has sometimes succeeded in excluding undeserving political applicants. Thus, while both Ponomarev and Ilichev were elected to the Academy in 1962 (as full member and corresponding member respectively), S. P. Trapeznikov failed to secure election in 1968.

Almost half of the scientific staff of the Academy are party members. In some institutes between 80 and 90 per cent of the scientific staff are party members. Scientists usually join the

Party (if they join at all) at about thirty-five years of age, some ten years after graduation, while they still hold junior and mainly non-*nomenklatura* positions. Some join much later, even in their fifties.[53] Leading *apparatchiki* tend to join the Party earlier, at twenty-three or even earlier. If they hold any academic or scientific position outside of the apparatus it is usually for brief periods. Because of these considerable differences in career patterns (often capped by a three, or four-year course in a Higher Party School for the *apparatchik*) their outlook tends to differ from that of other intellectuals, even though there are many cases of convergence and there is a career type of 'academic-*apparatchik*' just as there is one of 'managerial-*apparatchik*'.[54]

(6) Intellectuals do not seem to oppose the 'raiding' of their ranks by the apparatus. They do however complain that the persons recruited into the apparatus are generally the most socialized and the most conformist. They also note that such recruiting happens mainly at the lower and intermediate administrative levels. Few such intellectual recruits reach the top. Thus there is little likelihood of such intellectuals acting as a leavening, much less as a dissolving force on the apparatus. The practice is not wide enough to counter the renewed feeling, strongest among the younger intellectuals, of isolation and even alienation from the *apparat*.

These negative aspects of the relationship between the Soviet regime and the intelligentsia have been frequently referred to in various appeals sent by Soviet intellectuals over recent years to the party leadership. One recent statement (printed in *Newsweek*, 13 April 1970) drafted by three prominent scientists, A. D. Sakharov, V. F. Turchin and R. A. Medvedev, made the position very clear:

Freedom of information and creative labour are necessary for the intelligentsia due to the nature of its activities, due to the nature of its social function.

The desire of the intelligentsia to have creative freedom is legal and rational. The state, however, suppresses this desire by introducing various restrictions, administrative pressure, dismissals and even the holding of trials.

This brings about a gap, mutual distrust and complete lack

of understanding, which makes it difficult for the state and the most active strata of the intelligentsia to co-operate fruitfully.

In the conditions of the present-day industrial society, where the role of the intelligentsia is growing, this gap cannot but be termed suicidal.

8   The future of the intelligentsia

Predictions about the future of the Soviet intelligentsia are closely related to predictions about the future of the Soviet political system. It is therefore desirable that we should take a much closer look at the political attitudes and actions of Soviet intellectuals before proceeding to discuss the prospect before them.

Most of what has been written in the West over the past few years about the politics of Soviet intellectuals concerns the politics of a small and not very typical minority. No one would deny the claim made by Sidney Monas recently that:[1]

> Now there are once again in Russia something like an intelligentsia—not merely as Stalin defined them, 'a social segment' of professionals and 'white collars' recruited from among the workers and peasants, but a 'spiritual brotherhood' bearing a *special burden of conscience* and equipped with a special responsibility.

But the thrust of this approach, and even more of that taken by Crankshaw,[2] is to equate the intelligentsia with the small minority of it which carries dissent to the stage approved of by the writer. Since no worth-while sociological study has been made of the political attitudes of the Soviet intelligentsia it is impossible for any assessment to be other than subjective. But even so it is surely the duty of the writer to recognize the complexity of the problem. Any attempt at classifying Soviet intellectuals into two groups, the conformists and dissenters, is an absurd over-simplification. What follows is still a subjective evaluation of the problem but it has been made after considerable discussion with Soviet and foreign intellectuals.

Political approaches of the Soviet intelligentsia

I would suggest that there are at present four broad types of approaches to politics on the part of the Soviet intelligentsia. These types I define as the *careerist professionals*, the *humanist intelligentsia*, the *open oppositionists* and the *lost intelligentsia*. Some types have more than one subtype. This is particularly so in the case of the largest of the four groups, the *careerist professionals*, representing perhaps three-quarters of all intellectuals. The largest grouping within this type consists of the *party-minded loyalists*. Within this group are three classes of individuals, those who invariably (in private as well as in public) parrot the *Pravda* editorials, those who are sincere supporters of the Party and seek to apply the party line within their own professions, and those who are sincerely trying to apply Marxism-Leninism as individuals, to apply it as a methodology in their intellectual work as historians, philosophers, economists or social scientists. Members of this last group are often loyal to Leninist traditions rather than to present party leaders. Much of their effort is directed at reviving Leninism as a meaningful approach to politics. They are sensitive to any soft-pedalling of de-Stalinization and generally not very sympathetic to the manipulation of the ideology for the immediate advantages of the *apparat*. The second subtype recognized, the *pure careerists*, is probably not the most representative group within the intelligentsia. These are to be found in every professional group and are mainly upwardly mobile specialists of limited political competence. Many of them join the Party at the stage when it becomes professionally advantageous to do so. While outwardly rendering lip service to party ideals they really have little interest in the matter and sometimes—privately—will confess to boredom. The third subtype, the *loyal oppositionists*, is probably growing relative to the two other subtypes of careerist professionals. The loyal oppositionist is often very critical of the political establishment but he supports the socialist system and the leading role of the Party. He is usually a party member or a *Komsomol* member. He is much more critical of party policy in private than in public. But even in public, in party meetings, for example, he is quite likely to register dissent by abstaining on votes approving policies to which he is strongly opposed. The exact size of this subtype is hard to determine, but it probably amounted to only a small minority of *careerist professionals* by 1970.

The second broad type we recognize, the *humanist intelligentsia*, is drawn largely from the ranks of the creative intelligentsia, from the writers, artists, actors, musicians, cultural workers in other fields, and from those full-time tertiary students who are at present reacting against the narrow specialist training in the tertiary institutes. This type, which represents only a small minority of all intellectuals, is diverse in its professional and political interests. Generally its members are supporters of the Party and are often party members. Their quarrel with the Party is mainly over cultural policy. Many members of this section of the intelligentsia opposed the strengthening of ideological control over literature and art in 1960–3 and again since 1968. However the humanist intelligentsia is divided in its attitudes on this issue and so most groupings within the creative intelligentsia—writers, artists, actors, etc.—are divided into two politically active wings, a liberal and a conservative wing. Intermediate between these two wings is the body of the group which holds ambivalent attitudes. All these sections maintain direct links with individuals within the party leadership.

The third type, the *open oppositionist*, has received so much attention from Western writers that I hardly need to discuss it. Still a very small group, it fluctuates widely depending on the point of opposition. The highest point of protest reached in the sixties was in 1968 when 738 persons signed various collective and individual protests over the Galanskov-Ginsburg case. Of these, 45 per cent were academics and scientists, 22 per cent artists and writers, 13 per cent engineers and technicians, 9 per cent employees in the publishing industry, teachers, doctors and lawyers, 6 per cent were manual workers and 5 per cent were students.[3] On this analysis the groups contributing most actively to this new type of open protest are writers and artists, academics, students and scientists. Groups giving less support include manual workers and peasants, engineers, technicians, doctors and teachers.

The forms of protest vary from letters to the press, letters to senior party and state leaders, to the collection of signatures, distribution of leaflets and street demonstrations. Reactions of authorities have also varied but open support for any of these forms of protest is likely to lead to police questioning, house searches and intimidation. Repeated participation in such protests has led in most cases to dismissals from employment, exile or imprisonment. Consequently it is not surprising that only limited numbers of intellectuals—perhaps only one in three or four hundred—will accept the risks involved in such forms of protest.

The ideological motivation of open oppositionists is complex. It frequently stems from the consciousness that certain minorities are being discriminated against and persecuted by party leaders and government officials. Leaders are criticized for their failure to live up to Leninist principles on individual and nationality rights, for their failure to conform to the Soviet Constitution and to the Universal Declaration of Human Rights. Defence of specific minority rights often spreads to the defence of other minorities and individuals. Thus a Ukrainian nationalist writer will extend his protests to include Poles, Moldavians, Germans, Tartars, Jews, Latvians and others.[4] But the protests, generally speaking, are not directed against the regime or its principles but against actions which are held to be contrary to those principles. At the same time the severity of the persecution has forced many individuals to seek individual explanations of their suffering. Such personal evaluations vary considerably in detail and emphasis, reflecting the 'ideological personality'[5] of each victim. While some individuals undoubtedly draw on non-Communist belief systems for moral reinforcement, in the main their witness is to the humanism of the underlying ideals of Communism.[6] As Chornovil puts it:

> Man is not a soulless computer living in accordance with an established program. Man examines each program with his brain and with his heart. The meeting of thoughts, the contest of opinions, the crossing of ideas constitute a powerful lever which always has and always will continue to move humanity forward. The highest material saturation, without free thought and will, does not constitute communism. It constitutes a great prison, in which the food rations for the prisoners have been increased. Even under communism people will suffer—the sufferings of the ever-striving intellect. Even under communism there will be contradictions,

occasionally tragic ones—the contradictions of spirit and action; but they will not be solved by coercion and violence, but by a communist awareness of individuality and identity. The great minds of mankind have always dreamt of a society like this. It has been declared in our country today that communism is being transformed from dream to reality, that 'the present generation of the Soviet people will live under communism' (Program of the CPSU).

The fourth type, the *lost intelligentsia,* are those who are fully alienated from the Soviet system. Members of this group seek individual solutions by 'opting out' of the system. They live in a private, family or sectarian world of their own, although they will often give competent and loyal service as specialists or skilled workers during working hours. Such approaches are often found among older people, especially those living in rural and isolated areas, but there is abundant evidence that younger, alienated intellectuals, sometimes gravitate towards this position. When fully developed the *lost intellectual* becomes an 'integral émigré'.

While I have sought to indicate the relative frequency of the above four types of approaches to politics taken by the Soviet intelligentsia, it should be recognized that my types are artificial constructs or 'ideal types'.[7] They are derived from Soviet reality but they are not identical with it.

Control and coercion

The other side of the coin is the pattern of official control and coercion. This has often been mentioned elsewhere in the book but it has not yet been set out in detail.

Throughout the sixties the Communist Party sought to maintain its hegemony over Soviet intellectual life. This was a continuing campaign. There were periods of intensified political control interspersed with brief spells of relaxation, but there was never any abandonment of the struggle to maintain party hegemony. For the most part, the machinery through which this domination was exercised had been fashioned in earlier years. When changes occurred they were mainly adjustments to the existing mechanism of control. The removal of Khrushchev in

October 1964 and his replacement by a more stable oligarchy produced only marginal changes to the control mechanism. For a little over a year there was some relaxation of pressure on intellectuals, but since the end of 1965 controls have been re-established and extended. Among the various control mechanisms the following should be noted.

(1) *The mobilization of party members and supporters behind the decisions of the Party Congress.* This was done through various professional associations of the creative intelligentsia and through special conferences and meetings of representatives of particular groups of intellectuals with party and government leaders. Thus within a few weeks of the 22nd Congress (October 1961) the history department of the USSR Academy of Sciences heard a report on the tasks confronting Soviet historians in the light of the decisions of the 22nd Congress.[8] A similar report was delivered to the Board of the USSR Writers' Union in December 1961,[9] and an All-Union Conference on Questions of Ideological Work opened in Moscow on 25 December. The main speaker at the conference was L. F. Ilichev, the head of the newly-established Ideological Commission of the Central Committee of the CPSU.[10] During 1962 there were several ideological conferences, the All-Union Conference of Heads of Departments of Social Sciences of Higher Educational Institutions in February (with the main report by M. A. Suslov),[11] the general assembly of the USSR Academy of Sciences in October (with a report by L. F. Ilichev on the development of the social sciences), a meeting between party and government leaders and writers and artists on 17 December addressed by Ilichev,[12] and an All-Union Conference of Historians, which opened at Moscow State University, where the main report was given by party secretary and historian, B. N. Ponomarev.[13] At the end of December there was a meeting of the Ideological Commission which was attended by representatives of young writers, artists, composers, theatre and film workers, addressed by Ilichev.[14] The activity in December 1962 was a follow-up to Khrushchev's angry outburst at the Exhibition of Modern Art in Moscow on 1 December. In March 1963 there was a further meeting between party and government leaders and writers and artists at which both Khrushchev and Ilichev spoke. Several writers, including Yevtushenko, Ehrenburg, Nekrasov and Voznesensky were

singled out for rebuke. Ehrenburg in particular was held responsible for drafting a letter to the party leaders in which open competition between different approaches in art and literature was recommended.[15] Shortly after this March meeting there were plenary sessions of the Boards of the Writers' Union of the USSR and the RSFSR and a meeting of the *aktiv* of the creative intelligentsia of the Ukraine which was addressed by Podgorny on 'The place and role of ideologists today'.[16]

The drive to reassert ideological hegemony came to a climax in June 1963 when the full Central Committee heard L. F. Ilichev report on 'Current tasks of the Party's ideological work'.[17] N. S. Khrushchev and other party leaders joined in the attack. What was emphasized at this plenum and in earlier conferences and meetings was the obligation of all intellectuals to accept party leadership, to combat bourgeois ideology, and to promote Soviet ideological precepts such as 'socialist realism', party-mindedness and Communist ideology in art and literature.

The pressure slackened somewhat during 1964. There was a further expanded meeting of the Ideological Commission in June to consider the work of the creative intelligentsia. Four reports were presented by officials of the Writers' union, the Film Workers' Union, the Artists' Union, and the Composers' Union. Once again the main report was presented by Ilichev.[18]

These ideological assaults became less frequent after the fall of Khrushchev. In March 1965 the Ideological Commission was abolished and Ilichev lost his position in the Party Secretariat. The removal was widely applauded by Soviet intellectuals, although they were soon to realize that it did not herald a greater permissiveness on the part of the leadership. The new leadership soon showed a preference for more formal procedures. Pressure was brought to bear on intellectuals through meetings of the party primary organizations, through regular congresses of specific professions, through the press, and through massive campaigns around the jubilee of the revolution and the centenary of Lenin's birth.

(2) *Inner-Party discipline*. During the period 1962–5 the main party agency for keeping intellectuals on the line was the Ideological Commission of the Central Committee. The removal of this commission restored the importance of older Central Committee departments such as those on agitation and propaganda,

and of science, higher educational institutions and schools. Within the party structure the responsibility of primary organizations was extended, not only in relation to economic activity, but in relation to all forms of scientific and intellectual work. This made it possible in 1968–9 for the party leadership to use meetings of party primaries in scientific institutes, in educational establishments, in theatres and film studios, in newspaper offices and publishing houses, to force intellectuals into accepting actions such as those taken against dissident writers and against Czechoslovakia. Party primaries also extended their supervision of the scientific research work conducted in Academy institutes and in universities. At the 24th Congress in April 1971 party primaries were formally given power to control* the administration and research planning of all scientific research institutes.

Individual party members who acted according to their conscience and stood out against government decisions found it difficult to keep their positions. It is worth noting however that in several cases exclusion of dissidents from membership was carried out not by the primary organizations but by the district committee to which the primary belonged. This suggests a considerable amount of support for dissidents among peer groups.

(3) *Control through professional unions.* The Party has frequently sought to use professional unions such as the Writers' Union and the Artists' Union to bring pressure to bear on non-conformist members. If a writer cannot get his work published he must starve or find other employment. Since most of the avenues of publication are controlled by the Writers' Union or by government and party agencies, the Writers' Union is in a position of tremendous power. The treatment meted out to Solzhenitsyn since early 1963 is a clear example of how the pressure operates against even a major writer. Opposition within the Board of the Writers' Union probably lost him a Lenin Prize in 1964. There has been a virtual ban on publishing his work since 1963 and he has been subjected to repeated campaigns of vilification in the Soviet press. In September 1967 he had to defend himself against an inquiry into his activities and writings by the Board of the Writers' Union. In November 1969 he was formally ex-

*The Russian verb *kontrolirovat* means to supervise, to check up on, to inspect, but not to administer. Cf. French *contrôler.*

pelled from the Writers' Union for 'anti-social behaviour'. In 1970 he was prevented from accepting the Nobel Prize.

(4) *Administrative controls.* Administrative controls include economic penalties—demotion, transference to lower-paid jobs, and exclusion from professional employment. There are many cases over recent years of outstanding intellectuals, including writers, artists, teachers and scientists, who have been forced to accept poorly-paid manual work because professional employment was denied them.

(5) *Censorship and control over foreign travel.* Since early 1963 the Soviet censorship has been tightened. Notwithstanding considerable support for Solzhenitsyn within the Writers' Union and even in editorial boards, it has not been possible to publish either *The First Circle* or *Cancer Ward*. Many other writers and playwrights have had their works suppressed or heavily censored. Since 1963 editors have had to gain permission from the Central Committee before publishing major critical works. Other works are often refused publication by timid editors. If editors prove too persistent in their support for critical writing they are likely to be removed. Thus the liberal editor of *Novy mir* during the sixties, A. Tvardovsky, was finally forced to resign early in 1970 along with several other liberal members of the editorial board.

The perils of overseas visits were singled out for special emphasis by Khrushchev in his speech on literature and art on 8 March 1963. Before and since that date it has been exceedingly difficult for critical intellectuals in any field to gain permission to go overseas whether for study, for research, to attend conferences, or to perform. Temporary travel bans have been placed on outstanding writers, poets, artists and scientists.

(6) *Police control.* Since the beginning of the sixties the KGB, the courts, and the procuracy, have been used in an effort to force Soviet intellectuals into uniformity. Soviet citizens, especially intellectuals, have been arrested in a score of cases and charged with 'anti-Soviet propaganda', 'bourgeois nationalism' and similar crimes. They have been sentenced to imprisonment with hard labour for anything between two and seven years. In all, several hundreds of intellectuals suffered this fate over the decade. Others have been declared insane and put into lunatic asylums. In many cases the requirements of the Criminal Codes

have been blatantly circumvented. Persons arrested have been held for months without trial. They have been subjected to police brutality both before and after trial. Trials have often been held in closed courts and without adequate legal defence. Apart from those who received prison sentences many others have been exiled on the basis of the 'anti-parasite' laws, which operated throughout the sixties. The number of intellectuals subjected to police interrogation, brow-beating and seizure of manuscripts and private papers, must run into thousands.[19]

In order to sustain such an offensive the KGB has been steadily expanded, especially the 5th Section. There is active recruiting of agents from within the intelligentsia and most intellectual organizations contain police agents. However, it is questionable whether such reversion to Stalinist methods has proved effective. Many persecuted intellectuals have been driven into firmer opposition to government policy. This is amply borne out by the collection of statements published under the title, *The Chornovil Papers*, and by the regular appearance since April 1968 of a *samizdat* periodical, *Chronicle of Current Events*. It is also demonstrated by the continued and strengthened opposition of individuals such as Pyotr Grigorenko, Pavel Litvinov, Larissa Daniel and Alexander Solzhenitsyn. Even among the ranks of the 'loyal oppositionists' the same is true. Scientists such as A. D. Sakharov, Peter Kapitsa and others refuse to be silenced. On 16 November 1970 it was reported in Moscow that three prominent Soviet scientists, A. D. Sakharov, A. Tverdokhlebov and V. Chalidze had formed a Committee for Human Rights pledged to work within legal channels for the maintenance and extension of human rights in the Soviet Union. Writers such as Tvardovsky,* Leonov and K. Simonov have refused to sign statements issued by the Writers' Union in support of government actions such as the invasion of Czechoslovakia.[20] The KGB certainly recovered a great deal of power during the sixties but it has less power today than it had under Stalin. Its control over intellectuals is more selective and more restrained. The severity of the control is insufficient to check the steady growth of the movement for liberal reforms within the system. If, as seems feasible, the object of the Soviet leadership has been to produce

* Tvardovsky's death was reported in *Pravda*, 20 December 1971.

a 'functional opposition', a muzzled opposition which serves to release the pressures built up within an over-rigid political system, then it has been a limited success but by no means a complete success.

Future prospects

Late in 1969 the British journal, *Survey*,[21] published an article by a young Soviet intellectual entitled, 'Will the USSR survive until 1984?'. Amalrik, the writer of this article, argues that Soviet intellectuals are becoming increasingly alienated. Further, he argues that a minority of the intellectuals, those grouped around the *samizdat* (unofficial press) represent 'a new independent force which can now be regarded as a real political opposition to the regime, or at any rate, as the embryo of a political opposition.'[22] But this 'democratic movement', while it is well organized and in one sense a 'social movement', is not a political opposition or even a potential opposition. It is led by highly placed intellectuals, most of whom are party members. It depends for its survival on its limited programme (which is to criticize the censorship and to promote greater freedom of expression) and on its links with and even patronage from individuals within the party leadership. Were it to go beyond its present objectives it would lose its protectors and many of its present leaders. The 'democratic movement', like the 'cultural opposition' before it, is a functional opposition, which operates within the present political system to strengthen it. It is not likely to generate a revolutionary movement. While it may, as Amalrik claims, include elements of Christian and liberal ideologies, it is overwhelmingly Marxist. Its Marxism, however, is strongly influenced by humanism, idealized Leninism. It is not a different ideology to the official ideology but it aspires to be a purer version of it. This is clear from the many statements of its supporters. Consider, for example, 'My Ideology', written by Evgeny Yevtushenko in his most rebellious phase and published in *Izvestia* in January 1963, on the eve of his visit to France.[23]

My Ideology

My ideology is work
to the utmost, until complete exhaustion,

and for the people, not just for anyone—
Yes, for them, and only for them.
My ideology is care
for collective farm and factory affairs,
and for the affairs of my neighbour.

My ideology is grieving
for all on earth who fight against need,
who sob frenziedly at night
smearing their tears with their fists.
It is the throb of every heart,
it is the seething of all revolutions.

My ideology is the Revolutionary Committee
My ideology is a proclamation
to governments, the simple realization
that neither blade of grass nor building
nor even the earth itself, may survive.
It stands for co-existence,
but—damn it—it cannot co-exist
with any lousy rubbish.

My ideology is battle
with all who lie diligently from birth,
with all who for service to the Fatherland
have basely substituted toadying.
And forever in it—I have come to a decision—
I don't agree to disarmament.
Otherwise we might perish. Thus I sized it up.

In like manner the many protests since 1965 against the
arrests, trials and imprisonments of writers, and against the persecution of national minorities, have been made not only on the
basis of liberalism but on the principles of the Soviet Constitution. For it is an essential demand of the protest movement
that the Soviet system should really operate on the basis of
'socialist legality'.[24]

Amalrik does not forecast the victory of the democratic movement because he considers it to be too mediocre and too tied to
the bureaucracy. But under conditions of protracted war be-

tween Russia and China (which he expects to develop between 1975 and 1980) the regime will become weakened through defeats and be in danger of collapsing through pressure of the liberal movement on the one hand and destructive outbursts of the masses on the other. But this prediction is based on the analogies of 1905 and 1917 and it ignores the more relevant experience of the war of 1941–5. The evidence suggests that while a war between the USSR and China would not be popular it would be accepted if it proved unavoidable. It could easily strengthen the popular support for the regime. However, a war either with its capitalist enemies or with Communist China, whether brief or protracted, would certainly produce major changes in the regime. It might well produce a relative decline in the power of the Party and a rise in the authority of the state, especially of its military machine. But it would be a gross misreading of history to expect that it would produce massive rebellion on the part of the workers, peasants and intellectuals. The outcome of a really protracted war involving the Soviet Union in an attempt at occupying part of Manchuria and northern China—such as envisaged by Harrison Salisbury[25]—is more difficult to predict. Such a war could wreck the political systems of both countries.

My predictions about the future of the Soviet regime are based on the assumption that major war will be avoided. If this happens the social changes we have noticed during the fifties and sixties are likely to continue. On present trends the Soviet population will be about 64 per cent urban by 1980. The intelligentsia will number upwards of eighteen million. The number of scientific workers, if the present increase continues, will be above one and a half million. But these levels will only be realized if the regime substantially increases its investment in tertiary education and postgraduate teaching and research. Before that decision is taken there will probably be increased tension over admission to universities and other tertiary institutions.

The structure of the intelligentsia is likely to change. The student section of the intelligentsia will continue to grow, but since it is already expanding less rapidly than the output of graduates, its overall strength in the intelligentsia will fall. Both in the student population and in graduate streams there will be a slow process of redistribution. Disciplines such as agricultural science, veterinary science, biology, geology, chemistry and medicine will continue to decline, while mathematics and physics, mathematical-economics, cybernetics, technology and social sciences will become increasingly important. New disciplines will struggle for recognition, especially in the social sciences. It is probable that both sociology and political science will be firmly established within the coming decade.

Conflicts within the intelligentsia over the allocation of resources and over new developments will continue. The Academy of Sciences will certainly retain its privileged position, but it might be forced to restrict its rate of expansion as the government directs additional revenue to the universities and other tertiary teaching institutions. Within the intellectual establishment struggles will continue over new approaches and new techniques. As in the sixties, these disputes will be primarily intellectual but because of the interpenetration of the intellectual establishment with other establishments (governmental, party, military and industrial) major intellectual disputes will inevitably become politicized.

In most sections of the intelligentsia there will be conflict of generations between older, established authorities and youthful challengers. In most cases the division will not be exactly along generational lines and there will be grey heads in most rebel armies. This generational conflict is likely to be strongest in fields such as administration and management, where the challengers will be urging new techniques of business efficiency and practical competency against older leaders who have relied more on power than authority to maintain their position.[26]

It is more difficult to predict changes in the relations between the *apparat* and the intelligentsia. As the Party encourages and directs the scientific and technological revolution the interdependence of the intellectual establishment and the *apparat* is likely to increase. The alliance will not necessarily result in more liberal policies but policies are much more likely to be carefully researched and more rationally applied. The party *apparat* will perhaps be forced to withdraw even more from the ideological domination of science and intellectual activity, but if this happens it will be replaced by a more traditional bureaucratic system in which ministries and government departments will decide policy on the basis of their own experts and advisers. The general trend in Soviet politics since the fall of Khrushchev in October 1964 has been towards more regular, more rational but less spectacular policy-making, towards a modern bureaucracy. In this silent revolution the intellectuals have played and will continue to play a leading part.

Appendix I
The USSR Academy of Sciences

The USSR Academy of Sciences is a direct descendant of the Imperial Academy of Sciences established in 1724. The Academy of Sciences came under the control of the Commissariat of Education early in 1918 but it was many years before Communist Party influence became predominant in the Academy. As late as 1927 there wasn't a single Communist member of the Academy. During the 1920s the Party placed most emphasis on a rival academy, the Communist Academy under the Central Executive Committee. This was merged into the Academy of Sciences only in 1936.

In 1927 the Academy of Sciences was reorganized and enlarged. The 1927 Statutes brought the Academy under clear governmental and party control. There was a purge of the Academy in 1929 and a further reorganization in 1930. During the First Five Year Plan the Academy was brought more into the field of applied science.

The Academy of Sciences has grown steadily since 1930 so that in 1968 there were 226 institutes with 32,445 scientific workers within the USSR Academy of Sciences. At the same time there were 370 institutes with 33,163 scientific workers under the Academies of Sciences of the Union Republics.[1] As an American historian of the Academy has recently stated: 'Of all the scientific institutes in various countries of the world the one which is by far the most important, relative to the scientific life of its nation, is the Academy of Sciences of the USSR.'[2]

The USSR Academy of Sciences saw three reorganizations during the Khruschev era, in 1959, 1961 and 1963. The main problem at the back of all three reorganizations was that of co-ordination of research and government supervision of research. The 21st Congress of the CPSU, held early in 1959, approved an ambitious Seven Year Plan of Economic Development. Simultaneously a seven year plan for scientific research was worked out by the State Scientific and Technical Committee, the Ministry of Higher Education and the Academy of Sciences—'Basic Limits of Scientific Research in the

USSR for 1959–1965 in the fields of physics and mathematics, chemistry, technology, biology, geology and geography, economics, philosophy, law and history.'[3] Shortly afterwards, at the general assembly of the USSR Academy of Sciences on 28 March 1959 new statutes were adopted. Article 3 of these rules provided that:[4]

> The Academy of Sciences of the Union of Soviet Socialist Republics prepares and submits to the USSR Council of Ministers for approval long-range plans for the accomplishment in the USSR of complex scientific and technical tasks that are of the utmost theoretical and practical importance; it promotes the coordination of scientific work under way in the USSR; it offers conclusions and submits proposals regarding the organization of scientific work in the USSR.

At the time when the new statutes came into force in 1959 there were eight departments in the Academy, covering physics and mathematical sciences, chemistry, geology and geography, biological sciences, technology, history; economics, philosophy and law; and literature and languages. In addition, there was the rapidly growing Siberian Division based on Novosibirsk.

In 1961 reorganization was related to the establishment of a new state co-ordinating authority, the State Committee for the Co-ordination of Scientific Research Work under the USSR Council of Ministers. The decision establishing this new Committee emphasized the need to develop science and technology in the shortest possible time, the need to tackle fundamental research problems and for improved co-ordination of scientific research work.[5] The State Committee for the Co-ordination of Scientific Research Work was to supervise the work being done by various institutes, to co-ordinate the work of the USSR Academy of Sciences, the Academies of Sciences of the Union Republics, the ministries and departments in the USSR Council of Ministers. The new Committee was to be jointly responsible with the State Scientific Economic Council and Gosplan for drafting plans for basic scientific research. The President of the USSR Academy of Sciences was to be a member of the State Committee for the Co-ordination of Scientific Research Work. The 1961 reorganization transferred 92 scientific research establishments with 20,500 workers from the USSR Academy of Sciences to government committees and departments.

In May 1963 the Central Committee again resolved to reorganize the USSR Academy of Sciences and the Academies of Sciences in the Union Republics. The matter came up at the May and July 1963 general assemblies of the Academy and at the July assembly the new statutes and organization were approved. The main organizational change was the increase in the number of Departments to 15:

Department of Mathematical Sciences;
Department of General and Applied Physics;
Department of Nuclear Physics;
Department of Physical and Technical Problems of Energetics;
Department of Earth Sciences;
Department of Mechanics and Cybernetics;
Department of General and Technical Chemistry;
Department of Physical Chemistry and Technology;
Department of Biochemistry, Biophysics, and the Chemistry of Physiologically Active Compounds;
Department of Physiology;
Department of General Biology;
Department of History;
Department of Philosophy and Law;
Department of Economics;
Department of Literature and Languages.

Because of the greater complexity of this structure the Presidium was divided into three broad Sections. These Sections were:

Section of Physical-Technical and Mathematical Sciences;
Section of Chemical-Technological and Biological Sciences;
Section of Social Sciences.[6]

While there are thousands of scientific workers employed in the USSR Academy of Sciences the number of members of the Academy is quite small. Thus on 15 January 1966 there were 174 members and 360 corresponding members and 38 foreign members.[7] On 20 November 1967 there were 204 members and 382 corresponding members, including 31 full members and 79 corresponding members in the Social Sciences Section.[8]

The supreme policy-making body of the USSR Academy of Sciences is the General Assembly, consisting of both full and corresponding members of the Academy. It meets at least twice a year. Meetings usually last four to five days. The General Assembly hears reports from the main departments and decides the main lines of emphasis in research work. The General Assembly elects the Presidium, consisting of a President, Vice-Presidents and Academic Secretary. The Presidium elected in May 1967 consisted of:

President　　　　　M. V. Keldysh,
Vice-Presidents　　M. D. Millionshchikov, B. P. Konstantinov, N. N. Semenov, A. M. Rumyantsev, M. A. Lavrentiev, and A. P. Vinogradov.
Academic Secretary Yu. V. Peive.

In addition to the General Assembly of the Academy, each Department and the Siberian Division has its General Assembly and Presidium. Admission to membership of the Academy has sometimes been influenced by party pressure but this seems to be lessening in its effectiveness. Election is highly competitive. The number of new members is determined by the General Assembly. In order to secure election a candidate must first secure the support of two-thirds of his Departmental General Assembly. He must then secure an absolute majority of votes in the General Assembly of the Academy of Sciences. In 1962 there were 46 candidates for 13 vacancies to membership and 320 candidates for 26 vacancies for corresponding membership.[9] Only very top scientists are elected and few reach the Academy before middle age. The average age of persons elected to full membership over the fifty years 1917–66 was fifty-two to fifty-three years, while the average age of persons elected to corresponding membership was forty-six to forty-seven years.[10]

The dispersal of the Academy of Sciences has been thrice attempted during the Soviet era. By a decision of the General Assembly of the Academy in June 1931 several major centres for research were to be organized in outlying regions. Branches of the Academy were soon established and by March 1936 there were Branches of the Academy in Georgia, Azerbaidjan, Kazakhstan, Armenia, the Urals and the Far East. The War caused further dispersal and accelerated the process by which Branches were elevated to Union-Republican Academies. By 1961 there were Academies of Sciences in all Union-Republics, the last being the Moldavian Academy of Sciences established in 1961. The decentralization drive of the late 1950s affected scientific research as well as industry. Whereas in 1950 almost 90 per cent of USSR Academy of Sciences institutes were in Moscow or Leningrad, by 1966 only 65 per cent of institutes were in these two cities and over 70 institutes were based elsewhere. By far the biggest decentralization effort was the establishment of the Siberian Division. Established in 1958 it was a vast complex by 1967 with 44 institutes and 50 independent laboratories employing 5,300 scientific workers.[11]

The dispersal of scientific establishments has also gone on within individual republics. Thus in 1968 the Ukrainian Academy of Sciences established a Donets Branch which included an Institute of the Economics of Industry and an Institute of Applied Mathematics. The Siberian Division of the USSR Academy of Sciences manages the East Siberian Branch based on Irkutsk. This Branch already has several institutes, including Institutes of Geology, Biology, Chemistry and Energetics. Over recent years Branches of the USSR Academy of Sciences have been established in the Bashkir, Dagestan, Buryat and Komi Autonomous Republics. There are also older Branches in the Urals and the Kola Peninsula.[12]

The Academy of Sciences became more saturated with party members during the rapid expansion since 1950. By 1967, 43 per cent of all scientific workers employed by the Academy were party members. The prestige of the Academy is shown by the fact that no fewer than 46 academicians and corresponding members were elected as delegates to the 23rd Party Congress in April 1966.[13]

Expenditure on scientific research and capital construction of laboratories, libraries and other research facilities, rose from 3.3 billion rubles in 1959 to 7.7 billion rubles in 1966. In 1966 wages and salaries constituted 37 per cent of total expenditure on research. The amounts of the budgetary allocations for science are fixed each year by the State Committee of the USSR Council of Ministers for Science and Technology[14] in agreement with the USSR Finance Ministry. The USSR Academy of Sciences budget is a centralized one which forms a major part of the USSR Budget allocation on science. However, since the Union Republic academies come under the Union-Republican governments these academies largely control the allocations of that section of the USSR Academy of Sciences budget which is incorporated into Union Republican budgets. Almost all (91.5 per cent in 1965) of the revenue of the Academy of Sciences comes from government sources. However, the Siberian Division and some other Branches of the Academy secure some revenue from industrial establishments for successful solving of research problems and for the development of new equipment. Payment for these services most likely comes from enterprise rather than from state funds. Similarly, industrial enterprises sometimes pay for the cost of constructing new research laboratories which are designed to develop research in their industry. Such laboratories however are controlled by the Academy.

The Social Sciences Section of the USSR Academy of Sciences includes the Departments of History, Philosophy and Law, Economics, and Language and Literature. It has been expanding slowly and new institutes were being established at about the rate of one a year during the late 1960s. Thus the Institute of the International Workers' Movement was established in 1967, the Institute of the USA and the Institute of Concrete Social Research in 1968. The main institutes in the Social Sciences Section in June 1969 were as follows:

Institute of Eastern Affairs;
Institute of Sinology;
Institute of Slavic Studies;

Institute of Archaeology;
Miklukho-Miklai Institute of Ethnology;
Institute of History;
Institute of the History of Natural Science and Technology;
Institute of Economics;
Institute of Russian Language;
Institute of Linguistics;
Gorky Institute of World Literature;
Institute of Russian Literature;
Institute of World Economics and International Relations;
Institute of the Economics of the World Socialist System;
Institute of State and Law;
Institute of Philosophy;
Institute of the International Workers' Movement (1967);
Institute of Concrete Social Research (1968);
Institute of Africa;
Institute of Latin America (1961);
Institute of the USA (1968);
Central Institute of Economics and Mathematics;
Ufa Institute of History, Language and Literature.

Most of these institutes are based on Moscow but many of them have branches at Leningrad and other places. The area and regional institutes are generally inter-disciplinary, including departments on language, literature, history, philosophy, law, etc.

Appendix II
Decision of the Central Committee of the CPSU and the Council of Ministers of the USSR

Concerning Measures for the Improved Co-ordination of Scientific Research Work in the Country and the Activities of the Academy of Sciences of the USSR.

(Izvestia, 12 April 1961)

The Central Committee of the CPSU and the Council of Ministers of the USSR have examined the question of the means of improving the conditions of scientific research work in the country and the activities of the Academy of Sciences of the USSR.

The Central Committee of the CPSU and the Council of Ministers of the USSR consider that the development of national science and technology has achieved outstanding successes. The historical achievements of Soviet science and technology are the clear expression of the creative genius of the Soviet people and the high industrial-technical level of the country.

In the Soviet Union a broad network of scientific research establishments and higher educational institutions has been established in which work over 350,000 scientific workers. In our country science has become truly popular; its achievements are widely used for the successful development of the national economy, for the development of the material welfare and cultural level of the toilers.

There have been great successes in the development of science, in the development of national cadres of scientific workers and the creation of a wide network of scientific research establishments in the Union Republics.

Soviet scientists selflessly work for the good of our country. The Soviet people are justly proud of their spectacular scientific achievements.

The great successes of national science have been attained thanks to the unlimited possibilities which the socialist system has established for the creative activity of scientists, thanks to the continued care of the Communist Party and the Soviet Government and of all Soviet people for the development of science.

At the present time, when our country is entering the period of the all-round construction of communist society, the role and importance of science and technology will grow still more. Soviet science and technology must in the shortest period attain the foremost position in the world in all decisive spheres of science and technology.

Of particular importance in contemporary circumstances is the acquiring of the greatest strengthening of theoretical research into the most important scientific problems having the greatest economic significance, bringing science closer to production and securing the swiftest application of the results of scientific research work to the national economy of the USSR.

For the solving of these important tasks it is necessary to carry out a fundamental reconstruction of the system of leadership of the work of the scientific research establishments of the country in order to liquidate unnecessary parallelism in the fulfilment of scientific research.

In the contemporary epoch of the development of science and technology, questions of the perfecting of the system of long-range and short-range planning of scientific research and the co-ordination of scientific research work acquires major significance.

The existing forms of leadership of the work of scientific research establishments, the co-ordination of the planning of scientific research in the country, requires the greatest possible improvement.

In resolving the problems confronting Soviet science the Academy of Sciences of the USSR is called upon to play the greatest role, because, in contemporary circumstances, still higher demands will be placed on the leadership of the work of scientific research establishments.

The presence in the Academy of Sciences of the USSR of a great number of separate scientific establishments distracts it from the solving of perspective problems in science, disperses its strength and resources on working over a great many technical questions of diverse character which could be decided more successfully in specialized scientific research establishments.

These shortcomings in the work of the USSR Academy of Sciences and in other scientific research establishments to a significant degree are the consequences of the fact that there isn't in the country a general governmental organ which is able to exercise the co-ordination of scientific research. The absence of such an organ in a number of cases leads to unjustified duplication of scientific research and irrational use of scientific cadres and material resources.

With the aim of guaranteeing the necessary co-ordination in the work of the scientific research establishments of the country, improving the planning of scientific research and the inculcation of the achievements of science and technology in the national economy and also the liquidation of unnecessary parallelism in the fulfilment of scientific work, the Central Committee of the CPSU and the Council of Ministers of the USSR have recognized the necessity for organizing the State Committee of the Council of Ministers of the USSR for the Co-ordination of Scientific Research Work.

On the State Committee of the Council of Ministers of the USSR for the Co-ordination of Scientific Research Work rests the leadership of the work of the scientific research establishments for the fulfilment of important complex scientific-technical problems in conformity with the directives of the Party and the government and the co-ordination of the activities of the Academy of Sciences of the USSR, the Academies of Sciences of the Union Republics, and the ministries and departments of the USSR on the fulfilment of important complex scientific research work and also in guaranteeing the unbroken development of scientific research and the application of their results in the national economy.

The State Committee of the Council of Ministers of the USSR must work out jointly with the State Economic Council of the USSR and with USSR Gosplan and also on the basis of the proposals of the Councils of Ministers of the Union Republics and the ministries and departments of the USSR, draft plans for scientific research work in the country and the application of the achievements of science and technology to industry, guaranteeing the development of all branches of the national economy and bring these plans for the ratification of the Council of Ministers of the USSR.

The State Committee of the Council of Ministers of the USSR for the Co-ordination of Scientific Research Work shall exercise:

General governmental control over the fulfilment by all ministries, departments and organizations of the most important scientific research and the putting into operational order of measures for the most rapid application of the achievements of science and technology into the national economy;

Prepare proposals on important scientific-technical questions having major national economic importance, and also on questions arising out of new discoveries and inventions;

Prepare proposals on questions guaranteeing the scientific research establishments of the country with unmatched equipment, apparatus and instruments.

To study and generalize the achievements of science and technology with the aim of applying these achievements to the national economy of the USSR, and also to co-ordinate the international contacts of ministries, departments, and scientific research organizations on questions of science and technology, and the leadership of the task of scientific-technical information in the country.

The State Committee of the Council of Ministers of the USSR for the Co-ordination of Scientific Research Work will work out in agreement with USSR Gosplan, the State Economic Council of the USSR, and the Ministry of Finance of the USSR, and recommend to the Council of Ministers of the USSR on the basis of the draft plans of the Councils of Ministers of the Union Republics of the ministries and departments, draft annual and long-range plans for finance and material-technical guarantees of scientific research work, and also of draft plans of capital investment for the development of science.

The co-ordination of scientific research work not having inter-departmental character will be exercised by the ministries, the departments and the *sovnarkhozes*.

The State Committee of the USSR Council of Ministers for the Co-ordination of Scientific Research Work consists of the following:

The Chairman of the Committee is a Vice-Chairman of the Council of Ministers of the USSR.

Deputy Chairmen and also *ex-officio* members of the Committee are—the Chairman of the State Committee of the Council of Ministers of the USSR on Automation and Machine Construction, the Chairman of the State Committee of the Council of Ministers on Chemistry, the President of the USSR Academy of Sciences, the Vice-Chairman of the State Economic Council of the USSR, the Vice-Chairman of USSR Gosplan, the USSR Minister of Higher and Secondary Specialist Education, and the Chairman of the Committee on Affairs of Invention and Discovery under the Council of Ministers of the USSR.

For the examination of important problems connected with the development of science and technology and the determination of the basic direction of scientific research in the country there will be established a Scientific Council of the State Committee of the Council of Ministers of the USSR for the Co-ordination of Scientific Research Work consisting of senior scholars from separate branches of science and technology and leaders of the main scientific research establishments.

The State Committee of the Council of Ministers of the USSR for the Co-ordination of Scientific Research Work is commissioned to create jointly with the USSR Academy of Sciences, with interested Union Republican Ministries and departments, Scientific Councils on separate problems in which should be included the greatest scholars and specialists.

In connection with the carrying out of the measures for the reconstruction of the system of leadership of the scientific research establishments in the country and the creation of the State Committee of the Council of Ministers of the USSR for the Co-ordination of Scientific Research Work, with the aim of improving the work of the USSR Academy of Sciences, the C.C. of the CPSU and the Council of Ministers of the USSR have recognized the necessity of concentrating the activities of the Academy of Sciences of the USSR on the working out of the most important perspectives and quickly developing the main direction of science assisting the development of the national economy and the culture of the country.

The USSR Academy of Sciences must:

Provide the scientific and systematic leadership in the carrying out of research in the natural (physics, mathematics, chemistry, biology, astronomy and geology) sciences and social sciences, with the aim of using the results of scientific research work accomplished for the development of the national economy and culture.

Render maximum help to the Academies of Sciences of the Union Republics in the pursuit of scientific research and carry out the co-ordination of the activities of subordinate scientific research institutes, scientific establishments of the Academies of Science of the Union Republics, and higher educational establishments on theoretical problems of natural and social sciences.

Maintain scientific liaison with scientific establishments in foreign countries.

Carry out the training of scientific cadres.

With the aim of concentrating the USSR Academy of Sciences on the fulfilment of the most important scientific research work in the field of natural and social sciences and also for the improvement of the activities of the institutes' separate profiles, on the recommendation of the Presidium of the USSR Academy of Sciences or of the USSR Academy of Sciences, to transfer to the competency of State Committees of the Council of Ministers of the USSR, ministries, departments and the Council of Ministers of the RSFSR, a range of institutes and other scientific establishments and also Branches of the Academy of Sciences of the USSR. The scientific-methodological leadership of the Branches remains with the USSR Academy of Sciences.

The main task of the Branches transferred to the competency of the Council of Ministers of the RSFSR will be to provide the required help to the *sovnarkhozes* in the study of the natural resources for the development of the industrial strength of corresponding regions.

The State Committee of the Council of Ministers of the USSR for the Co-ordination of Scientific Research Work is commissioned to work out jointly with the Councils of Ministers of the Union Republics measures for the further improvement of scientific establishments.

The C.C. of the CPSU and the Council of Ministers of the USSR have entrusted the State Committee of the Council of Ministers of the USSR for the Co-ordination of Scientific Research Work to confirm the list of heads of scientific research institutes in all branches of the national economy and the standard regulations concerning these institutes, and also the preparation, with the participation of the Council of Ministers of the Union Republics, ministries and departments, and to present to the Council of Ministers of the USSR proposals about the improved leadership of the heads of the scientific research institutes and their subordinate agencies.

The organization of new scientific research establishments irrespective of their departmental subordination shall be exercised in agreement with the State Committee of the Council of Ministers of the USSR for the Co-ordination of Scientific Research Work.

In connection with the organization of the State Committee of the Council of Ministers of the USSR for the Co-ordination of Scientific Research Work, the State Scientific-Technical Committee of the Council of Ministers of the USSR is abolished. Organizations under the competency of the State Scientific-Technical Committee of the Council of Ministers of the USSR will be transferred to the control of the State Committee of the Council of Ministers of the USSR for the Co-ordination of Scientific Research Work.

The Councils of Ministers of the Union Republics and the State Committee of the Council of Ministers of the USSR for the Co-ordination of Scientific Research Work are commissioned to carry out the reorganization of the leadership of the scientific research establishments in the Union Republics resulting from the problems and measures with which the present decision is concerned.

The C.C. of the CPSU and the Council of Ministers of the USSR consider that the most important tasks of all scientific research establishments is the further strengthening of research into all fields of science and technology and above all, in the widening of scientific research work into basic scientific problems having the greatest mutual economic significance so that Soviet science and technology in the shortest possible time will achieve new, still greater, major successes.

Appendix III
Resolution of the 4th Writers' Congress to the Central Committee of the CPSU

(Pravda, 18 May 1967)

The Fourth Congress of Soviet Writers representing all the diverse national literatures of the country sends warm greetings to the Central Committee of the Communist Party of the Soviet Union!

Our Congress is taking place in the year of the fiftieth anniversary of the Great October Socialist Revolution, on the captain's bridge of which the world sees and always will see, Vladimir Ilych Lenin, creator of the mighty party of Communists.

We, practitioners of Soviet literature, in all our thoughts, in all our creative activity, are bound to the Party which expresses the deepest interests of the people. 'Communists forward!' That rousing slogan of the epoch has sounded on the fields of the Civil War, in the construction of the Five Year Plan, and through the storming of Berlin, and it sounds in the great achievements of recent years.

Summing up the results of literature over the past half century, full of heroism, victory and difficult experiences, we first of all consider it necessary to say that we have examined and are examining our literature as a part of our general party, our Communist duty.

Keeping sacred the best traditions of national and world literature, we Soviet writers value literature as a social act, as a powerful factor of progress. It comes from the people and belongs to the people; it faithfully serves the people in the struggle for the great principles of freedom, equality, fraternity, and justice, for the lofty ideals of Communism.

We openly and proudly call our literature party-minded because it hasn't got and cannot have any interests other than those of the people as expressed by our Party. We call our literature party-minded because we see in the policy of the Party the fullest embodiment of the cherished desires of progressive mankind. And we say today in the name of our multi-national literature, 'Having chosen Communism as our ideal—we will be true to it to the end!'

For fifty years our people have battled and built, and literature was with them in deeds of work and war. Today the Soviet Union has become one of the most powerful states in the world. We are the country which delivered the decisive blow to fascism and which has stood unceasingly for the cause of peace. We are the country of ideas, of example, the experience of which has inspired and inspires the nations in their struggles against various forms of social and national oppression. And if today the world has become different, the merit for this lies in the literature of socialist realism. The awareness of that for us Soviet writers is a source of pride and creative inspiration.

We acknowledge that in our literary affairs there are not a few shortcomings, that there are difficulties and unsolved problems. It is essential for us to perfect the activities of our Union, to develop the creative initiative and civic activity of each writer, always remembering the high responsibility of the Soviet artist before time and people.

We cannot for a moment forget that our activities are taking place under circumstances of the sharpest ideological struggle which knows no truce and which completely excludes ideological coexistence or neutralism.

All this was said with great force and clarity in the greetings of the C.C. of the CPSU to our Congress. We evaluate this important document as yet another witness of the unceasing care of the Party for the development of Soviet literature.

The Fourth Congress of Writers assures the Central Committee of the Communist Party of the Soviet Union that Soviet writers will apply all their strength in order to justify the confidence of the Party and the people, acknowledging the highest award of the country— the Order of Lenin—by a general lifting of creative activity, bringing by their labour a worthy contribution to the building of communism, embodying in artistic productions the life of the people, creating a wide picture of the struggles and achievements.

Soviet writers, together with the writers of the entire socialist community and the progressive artists of all continents, will passionately defend peace in the future, will raise their voices against imperialist adventures and the resurgent face of neofascism. We will always remember that the unity of the progressive forces is the guarantee of success in the struggle against the dark forces of reaction and war.

Long live the Communist Party—the great helmsman of revolution!

Long live the union of life and creative work, of art and revolution!

IV Congress of Writers of the Soviet Union

Appendix IV
A Reform Charter of the
Intelligentsia

(An excerpt from the Appeal of Soviet Scientists to the government-party leaders, 1970. Signed by A. D. Sakharov, V. F. Turchin, and R. A. Medvedev. Text taken from *Survey*, Summer 1970, pp. 165–8).

The course leading towards democratization would remove the rift dividing the Party-State apparatus from the intelligentsia. Mutual misunderstanding would give way to close collaboration. The course leading towards democratization would call up a huge enthusiasm comparable to the twenties. The best intellectual forces would be mobilized for the solution of national economic and social problems.

Carrying out democratization is no easy process. Its normal course would be threatened from the one side by individualistic, anti-socialist forces and from the other by adherents of 'strong government', demagogues of the fascist model who would be able to exploit for their own ends the economic difficulties of the country, the mutual misunderstanding and mistrust of the intelligentsia and the Party-State apparatus, and those philistine and nationalistic trends which exist in certain sections of society. But we should realize that our country has no other way out, that this difficult task has to be faced. If democratization were to be carried out on the initiative and under the control of the higher organs the process could proceed according to plan, and it would give units of the Party-State apparatus time to adjust to the new style of operations which differ from the past in that they allow greater publicity, openness and broader discussion of all problems.

There is no doubt that the majority of members of the Party apparatus, having been educated in a modern, highly developed country, would be capable of adjusting to this style of operations and would quickly come round to appreciate its benefits. Sifting out the few that are incapable of adjustment would be all to the general good.

We propose the following tentative programme of measures which could be implemented over four or five years:

1. A statement to be issued by the higher Party-Government organs regarding the need for further democratization, the speed and method of putting it into effect. Publication in the press of a number of articles discussing problems of democratization.

2. Restricted distribution (via Party organs, enterprises and institutions) of information regarding the state of the country and of theoretical works on social problems which, for the time being, it is inexpedient to make the object of wide-scale discussion. Such materials should be gradually made available to more and more people until finally restrictions are removed altogether.

3. Wide-scale organization of complex production combines (firms) endowed with a large measure of independence in questions of production planning, technological processes, sales and supplies, financial and personnel matters. Extension of the same rights to the smaller production units. Scientific assessment after painstaking research of the forms and level of State control.

4. An end to the jamming of foreign broadcasts. Free sale of foreign books and periodicals. Membership of the country in the international copyright system. Gradual (three to four years) extension and facilitation of international two-way tourism. Facilitation of international correspondence and also other measures to extend international contacts, in the first place the extension of these tendencies in regard to Comecon countries.

5. Setting up of a public opinion research institute. Initially restricted and later complete publication of materials showing the attitude of the population to the most important questions of domestic and foreign policy as well as other sociological materials.

6. An amnesty for political prisoners. A decree to establish the obligatory publication of full stenographic reports of trials of a political nature. Public control of places of detention and psychiatric institutions.

7. Certain measures to improve the work of courts and the Public Prosecutor's Office, which would be made independent of the executive authorities and local influences, prejudices and connections.

8. Abolition of registration of nationality in passports and questionnaires. A single passport system for all inhabitants of town and country. Gradual abandonment of the system of registration of passports, carried out in parallel with the levelling out of territorial inequalities in economic and cultural development.

9. Reforms in the field of education. Increased funds for primary and secondary schools, improvement in the material status of teachers, their autonomy and rights to experiment.

10. Passing of a press and information law. Provision of means for

public organizations and groups of citizens to set up new press organs.

11. Improvement of the training of leaders in the art of management. Establishment of practical training periods for probationers. Improvement in the information available to leaders at all levels, their rights to autonomy, to experiment, to defend and test their opinions in practice.

12. Gradual introduction of the practice of nominating more than one candidate to a single seat at elections to Party and Soviet organs at all levels, including indirect elections.

13. Extension of the rights of Soviet organs. Extension of the rights and the responsibilities of the Supreme Soviet of the USSR.

14. Restoration of all rights to nations forcibly resettled under Stalin. Restoration of national autonomy to resettled peoples and the possibility for them to return (where this has not yet been done).

15. Measures designed to increase publicity in the work of leading organs within limits determined by the interests of state. Creation of consultative scientific committees including highly qualified specialists in different branches attached to leading organs at all levels.

This, of course, should be regarded as a tentative plan. Moreover, it should clearly be complemented by a plan for economic and social measures drawn up by specialists. We would stress that of itself democratization by no means offers solutions to economic problems. It only creates the prerequisites for their solution. But without these prerequisites economic and technological problems cannot be solved. From our friends abroad we sometimes hear the USSR compared to a huge truck, whose driver presses one foot hard down on the accelerator and the other on the brake. The time has come to make more intelligent use of the brake!

In our opinion the proposed plan demonstrates that it is entirely possible to chart a programme for democratization which would be acceptable to the Party and State and, at first approximation, meet the most pressing needs of the country's development. Naturally a broad discussion and profound scientific, sociological, economic and socio-political research as well as life experience would suggest essential amendments and additions. But it is important, as the mathematicians say, to prove the 'theorem of the existence of a solution'.

It is also necessary to consider the international consequences of our country's acceptance of a course leading towards democratization. Nothing could so enhance our international authority and strengthen the progressive communist forces throughout the world as further democratization, accompanied by intensified technological and economic progress in the first socialist country in the world. Without doubt the possibilities of peaceful coexistence and international co-operation would be strengthened, the attraction of the Communist ideology would grow and our international position would become more secure. It is especially vital to shore up the moral and material position of the USSR vis-à-vis China; opportunities would grow for us to use technological and economic aid, for example, in order to indirectly influence the situation in the country in the interests of both peoples.

Notes

INTRODUCTION
1 This is very similar to the distinction drawn by Edward Crank-shaw in his article, 'Is this where I came in?', *Observer*, 22 December 1968.

CHAPTER I
1 Karl Mannheim (1960), pp. 136–46.
2 Nikolai Bukharin (1970), pp. 282–5.
3 First Russian edition, *Osnovy Marksizma-Leninizma*, Moscow, 1959. English Translation, *Fundamentals of Marxism-Leninism*, FLPH. Moscow, 1961. Quotation from pp. 190–1.
4 *Politichesky slovar* (1958), p. 211.
5 J. V. Stalin, 'On the Draft Constitution of the U.S.S.R.', 25 November 1936, 'Report on the Work of the Central Committee to the 18th Congress of the C.P.S.U.(B.)', 10 March 1939. *Problems of Leninism* (1945), pp. 541–7; 638–40.
6 M. P. Kim (1968), p. 4. L. K. Erman (1966), ch. 1.
7 A. Gramsci (1957), pp. 118–25.
8 See the contributions of Soviet scholars to the Conference held at the Institute of the International Labour Movement, Moscow, April 1967. Papers by M. K. Mamardashvili and M. A. Lifshits, dealt with the intelligentsia and made reference to Gramsci, but without any attempt at applying his approach to the Soviet Union. *Problemy rabochevo dvizhenia*, Akad. Nauk SSSR, Moscow 1968, pp. 21–39.
9 L. K. Erman (1966), pp. 7–8.
10 M. N. Rutkevitch (1966). V. S. Semenov (1966).
11 There are several useful accounts of the growth of the Soviet intelligentsia. See: M. P. Kim (1968), K. T. Galkin (1958), M. Vlasov (1968), G. D. Komkov *et al.* (1968), Loren R. Graham (1967 and 1968), UNESCO, *Science Policy and Organization of*

Research in the U.S.S.R. (1967), Nicholas de Witt (1961) and J. H. Billington (1968).

12 For a general description of this concept from a Communist viewpoint, see Radovan Richta (1967). See also, S. A. Kugel (1969 b).

13 Less than 10 per cent of all scientific workers are employed in the Academy of Sciences Institutes. Research and Development estimates usually go beyond the 770,000 scientific workers. Richta (1967) gives the figure of 2,497,000 for 1965, but this is probably an exaggeration.

14 Many statements by Soviet workers and peasants contain an anti-intellectualism that is reminiscent of the attitude of Waclaw Machajski in his work, *The Intellectual Worker* (Geneva, 1905). In the unofficial transcript of the trial of Josef Brodsky in February 1964 the following is recorded:
Conversation in the Courtroom
—Writers! They should be thrown out!
—Intellectuals! They've forced themselves on our necks!
—So what's wrong with the intelligentsia? Don't they work? They work, too.
—What do you mean? Didn't you see how they work? They use other people's work!
(The *New Leader*, 31 August 1964.)

15 Raymond A. Bauer *et al.*, *How the Soviet System Works* (1956), ch. 23. See also Alex Inkeles (1969), ch. 2. For an interesting discussion of the 'we'—'they' dichotomy, see Robert C. Tucker (1964), ch. 4, 'The image of a dual Russia'.

16 See, for example, the various approaches taken to this problem by Professor John N. Hazard, *The Soviet System of Government*, in the 1957, 1964 and 1968 editions.

CHAPTER 2
1 Ts. A. Stepanyan and V. S. Semenov (1968), ch. 1.
2 V. S. Semenov (1966). Semenov includes the semi-intelligentsia with the intelligentsia.
3 'Understanding the social structure of socialist society', ch. 4 of Ts. A. Stepanyan and V. S. Semenov (1968).
4 Alex Inkeles (1950). Reprinted in Alex Inkeles (1969), pp. 150–74.
5 Alex Inkeles (1969), pp. 154, 156.
6 F. Burlatsky, *The State and Communism*, Progress Publishers, Moscow, n.d., p. 84.

7 Cf. the chapter 'Social group differences in Soviet society' by K. P. Buslov, L. I. Feinburg, B. D. Parygin and V. A. Gavridov in Ts. A. Stepanyan and V. S. Semenov (1968).

8 *Nar.kh.SSSR v 1967*, p. 78.

9 *Nar.kh.SSSR v 1967 g.*, p. 812.

10 The main decisions were:

1 Decision of the Central Committee of the CPSU and the USSR Council of Ministers, 'On measures for improving the quality of dissertations and the procedure for awarding academic degrees and titles', *Pravda*, 7 February 1960.

2 Decision of the Central Committee of the CPSU and the USSR Council of Ministers, 'On measures for improving the co-ordination of scientific research work in the country and the work of the USSR Academy of Sciences', 3 April 1961.

3 Decision of the Central Committee of the CPSU and the USSR Council of Ministers, 'On measures for further improving the selection and training of scientific personnel', *Pravda*, 18 May 1962.

4 Decision of the Central Committee of the CPSU and the USSR Council of Ministers, 'Concerning measures for improving the activities of the USSR Academy of Sciences and the Academies of Sciences of the Union Republics', 11 April 1963.

11 Calculated from the Tables in *Nar.kh.SSSR v 1967 g.*, pp. 12, 849.

12 S. A. Kugel, 'Changes in the social structure of socialist society under the impact of the scientific-technological revolution', 1969 b, pp. 13–22. Statistics taken from the Table on p. 19.

13 *Chislennost, sostav i razmeshchenie naseleniia SSSR*, Moscow 1961, p. 35.

14 M. A. Vyltsan (1967).

15 P. I. Simush (1969).

16 M. Rodionov (ed.), (1970), p. 53.

17 *Ibid.*, p. 54.

18 *Ibid.*, p. 50.

19 *Ibid.*, p. 51.

20 A. Aleksandrov, M. Garin, N. Shtanko, '430 interviews at the village crossroads', *Izvestia*, 12 November 1964.

21 M. Garin, A. Druzenko, 'At the same village crossroads', *Izvestia*, 12 July 1970.

22 *Soviet Union: 50 years*, p. 242.

23 *Nar.kh.SSSR v 1967 g.*, p. 809.

24 *Ibid.*, p. 802.

25 Alex Nove and J. A. Newth (1967), pp. 81–2.

26 Based on the percentage of national groups not speaking their native language as given in the January 1959 census.

27 On the other hand, national feeling and prejudice seems to be stronger amongst the educated sections of national minorities. Cf. Yu.V. Arutyunyan (1969 b).
28 In 1959 44.3 per cent of Armenians lived outside of Armenia, while only 3.4 per cent of Georgians lived outside of Georgia.
29 Ivan Dzyuba (1968). See also, V. Chornovil (1968), and Michael Browne (1971).
30 Peter J. Potichnyj and Grey Hodnett, *The Ukraine and the Czechoslovak Crisis*, Occasional Paper No. 6, Department of Political Science, Research School of Social Sciences, Australian National University, Canberra, 1970.
31 Alex Nove and J. A. Newth (1970), p. 146.
32 Gene Sosin (1969), pp. 63–75.
33 Alex Nove and J. A. Newth (1970), pp. 146–7.
34 Bernard D. Weinryb (1970), p. 311.
35 Alex Nove and J. A. Newth (1970), p. 154.
36 M. Rodionov (ed.) (1970), p. 90.
37 *Ibid.*, p. 105.
38 *Ibid.*, p. 97.
39 *Ibid.*, p. 81.
40 1960–1 figures from Nove and Newth (1970), p. 154. Later figures from *Nar.kh.SSSR v 1967 g.*, *v 1968 g* and *v 1969 g*.
41 *Nar.kh.SSSR v 1967 g.*, p. 811.
42 This practice offends some particular nationalists in the USSR. Cf. Ivan Dzyuba (1968), pp. 110–11 and elsewhere.

CHAPTER 3
1 Z. Katz, 'Hereditary elements and social structure in the USSR', Project on Social Structure and Social Mobility in the USSR, University of Glasgow, Institute of Soviet and East European Studies, 1969, p. 44. Katz's estimate is 6:1 but this seems to me to be somewhat exaggerated.
2 *Nar.kh.SSSR v 1967 g.*, pp. 779, 791.
3 Report of the Central Statistical Administration published in *Pravda*, 25 January 1970.
4 Cf. Z. Katz, *op. cit.*, p. 60.
5 *Ibid.*, pp. 24–5. An investigation of school leavers made in the city of Sverdlovsk showed that 95–98 per cent planned to go on to higher study. A study of 2,000 school graduates in Sverdlovsk and Province showed that 91 per cent planned to continue study. A Novosibirsk survey showed that 93 per cent of school leavers planned to continue study. A Vilnius (Lithuania) survey in 1968

showed that all but 12 out of 526 school leavers polled planned a professional career (*Sovetskaya Litva*, 30 May 1968). A survey of *Komsomol* school leavers in Estonia in 1969 showed that 45 per cent wanted to go on to university (*Molodezh Estonii* 3 July 1969). Taken from *Soviet Studies*: *Information Supplement*, January 1970, p. 41.

6 For example, V. V. Bodzimskaya, 'On the question of social conditions on the choice of a profession', *Chelovek i obshchestvo* (University of Leningrad), no. 2, 1967, pp. 74–91. See also the long article in English by Murray Yanowitch and Norton T. Dodge (1969).

7 Decision of the Central Committee of the CPSU and the USSR Council of Ministers, *Pravda*, 13 August 1964. The decision reduced the number of years spent in advanced secondary education from three to two, thus virtually abandoning Khrushchev's scheme for one year work experience. According to one Soviet source 39 per cent of all tertiary students in 1964–5 were workers by social origin. M. P. Kim (1968), p. 406.

8 *Pravda*, 6 September 1969.

9 Z. Katz, *op. cit.*, pp. 20–1, 43.

10 Based on the Table in *Nar.kh.SSSR v 1967 g.*, p. 792.

11 Interview with the rector, Professor S. V. Rumyantsev, *Pravda*, 7 February 1970, p. 4.

12 Professor Kovalov as reported in *New World Review* (N.Y.), fourth quarter 1969, p. 25.

13 *Sov. Stud. Information Supp.*, April 1965, p. 5.

14 Calculated from the Table in *Nar.kh.SSSR v 1967 g.*, p. 788.

15 In 1969 stipends ranged from 35 rubles a month in first year to 43.75 rubles a month in fifth year, with special scholarships going up to 50–60 rubles a month.

16 *Nar.kh.SSSR v 1967 g.*, p. 797.

17 *USSR: Questions and Answers*, Novosti Press Agency, Moscow, 1967, p. 356.

18 See the article by the rector of the Institute, Professor K. A. Mokichev in *Sovety*, no. 1, 1968, pp. 70–3.

19 M. P. Kim (1968), pp. 338–44.

20 The breakdown is as follows:

Academy of Social Sciences under the C.C.	2,920
Higher Party Schools	6,791
Corresp. Higher Party Schools	33,744
Higher Party Schools–Republican & Oblast-Krai Committees (2–4 years, 1957–66)	24,774

(2–3 years, 1946–56)   60,570
Soviet-Party Schools   31,649
V. I. Strukov (1969), p. 103.

21 Thus an opinion poll taken in the Spring of 1967 among 1,500 students in Estonia showed that 30.77 per cent were interested in political discussion. A similar finding was made in an investigation at Vilnius. *Sov.Stud.*: *Information Supp.*, October 1968, p. 27.

22 G. N. Kolokolova (ed.) (1970), pp. 113–38.

23 *Ibid.*, pp. 81–97.

24 For a vivid account of how this works in Moscow State University, see William Taubman (1968).

25 In 1966 only 5,000 out of almost 50,000 students and staff at Moscow State University belonged to the Party. 30 out of 39 members of the University Party Committee were professors or lecturers. See B. Mochalov, *Kommunist*, no. 10, July 1966, pp. 34–42.

26 Another reason for these misfits is that courses and training methods have not always kept up with the demands of industrial technology and scientific and administrative change. Cf. the article by two economists, N. Bugaev and B. Yakovlev, 'Profile of an economist in the making', *Ekonomicheskaya gazeta*, no. 17, April, 1969.

27 *Komsomolskaya Pravda* has published a good deal of information on these problems over recent years. E.g., *Kom.Pravda*, 16 January 1968, 30 January 1968. *Sov.Stud: Information Supp.*, April 1968, p. 30. Also, January 1970, p. 16.

28 Decision of the USSR Ministry of Higher and Secondary Specialist Education, 13 December 1961. G. N. Kolokolova (1970), p. 62.

29 A recent survey of a Tallinn Professional-Technical School showed that 70 per cent of the students had no idea of the choice of subjects in advance of starting their course. Of 45,000 persons who changed jobs in Estonia in 1968, 35 per cent were below twenty-four years of age. Professional counselling offices are to be set up in Tallinn and other cities. *Molodezh Estonii*, 19 August 1969, *Sov.Stud.*; *Information Supp.*, January 1970, p. 40.

CHAPTER 4

1 G. Sharp and D. White, 'Features of the intellectually-trained', *Arena* (Greensborough, Victoria), no. 15, 1968, pp. 30–3; and G. Sharp, 'A revolutionary culture', *Arena*, no. 16, 1968, pp. 2–11.

2 P. P. Amelin (1970), p. 43.

3 'In our country, since all of us work for the state, we all have the psychology of officials—writers who are members of the Writers' Union, academics employed in government establishments, workers or collective farmers—just as much as KGB or MVD officials.' André Amalrik (1969), p. 55.

4 S. A. Kugel, 'Professional mobility and the tendencies to change under conditions of the scientific and technological revolution', (1969 a).

5 G. D. Komkov *et al.* (1968), pp. 210–14.

6 An investigation into student opinions at Vilnius University in 1968 found that 98.3 per cent of respondents gained their information mainly from Soviet sources but that 35.4 per cent listened regularly to broadcasts from capitalist countries. *Sov.Stud.*: *Information Supp.*, October 1968, pp. 14–15.

7 The 5th Department is mainly concerned with surveillance of Soviet intellectuals, including their foreign contacts. Its increase in size and position within the KGB is the subject of frequent comment in the Soviet Union.

8 'How party organizations supervise scientific organizations', *Part.zh.*, no. 16, August 1963, pp. 32–9.

9 A recent Soviet investigation of professionals found that they spent much of their free time in associating with professional colleagues. They spent more time in such associations than they spent with relatives or neighbours. The reverse was true for industrial workers, construction workers and service personnel. *Sotsiologicheskiye isledovania goroda*, Moscow, 1969, p. 100.

10 General Statute on USSR Ministries. Text in *Ekon.gaz.*, no. 34, August 1967. English trans. in C.D.S.P., XIX, no. 37, pp. 4–8. Art. 19: 'For the purpose of examining the proposals for the main directions in the development of science and technology, defining a scientifically sound, uniform technical policy in the branch, working out recommendations for the application in production of the latest achievements of domestic and foreign science, technology and advanced experience, a scientific-technical (or scientific) council of prominent scientists, highly skilled specialists, production innovators and representatives of scientific and technical societies and other organizations is organized in the USSR Ministry.'

11 Thus the All-Russian Association of Engineers was liquidated in 1929. See Jeremy A. Azrael (1967), pp. 54–6.

12 This was re-named the Soviet Association of Political Science(s) in January 1965. See my article 'Towards a Soviet political science' (1966 b).

13 M. A. Sholokhov complained about the ageing of the members of the Writers' Union in his speech to the 4th Writers' Congress. Whereas 71 per cent of delegates to the 1st Writers' Congress were under forty, only 12.2 per cent of delegates to the 4th Writers' Congress in May 1967 were under forty. *Pravda*, 28 May 1967.

14 See Appendix III.

15 Thus Sergei Narovchatov speaking at the 4th Writers' Congress demanded major changes in the Soviet copyright law. *Lit.gaz.*, no. 22, 31 May 1967.

16 *USSR: Questions and Answers* (1967), p. 179.

17 *Sovetskaya kultura*, 11 April 1963. For an account of the work of Neizvestny see John Berger (1969).

Membership figures for 1967 are given in *Spravochnik chlenov i kandidatov v chleny Soyuza Khudozhnikov SSSR*, Moscow, 1968.

18 *Pravda*, 21, 24, 25, 26 and 27 November 1965.

19 Text in *Pravda*, 16 November 1959.

20 Text in *Pravda*, 15 November 1959.

21 Besides the Journalists' Union, the Union of Writers, the Union of Soviet Societies of Friendship and Cultural Relations with Foreign Countries, and the USSR Knowledge Society participated in this venture.

22 *USSR: Questions and Answers* (1967), p. 181.

23 M. P. Kim (1968), p. 351.

24 See the report by the chairman of the Russian Section of this Society, Professor V. I. Kochemasov, in *Istoria SSSR*, no. 5, September–October 1967, pp. 197–203. The report deals with the work of this Society over its first year.

25 V. M. Chkhikvadze (1967), pp. 330–3.

26 For the text of this Statute see *Izvestia*, 13 October 1967. Art. 35: 'Representatives of state bodies, public organizations, scientific institutions, specialists and scientists, may be invited to meetings of the Commissions of the Soviet of the Union and the Soviet of Nationalities and participate in meetings of the Commissions with the right to consultative votes.

If necessary, a Standing Commission can decide to hold a closed meeting.'

CHAPTER 5

1 Cf. Max Weber, 'Class, status, party', in H. H. Gerth and C. Wright Mills (1947), pp. 180–95. I do not altogether follow Weber in the above analysis.

2 A. Inkeles (1950), pp. 466ff.
3 V. S. Semenov (1966). See also M. N. Rutkevich (1966).
4 L. Kolakowski (1970), p. 202.
5 *Sovety*, no. 8, 1970, pp. 59–60; pp. 60–3 of the same number reports an investigation made into the above complaint by a special correspondent of *Sovety* which fully supported cde. Kharlamova.
6 V. N. Shubkin (1966), p. 90.
7 Murray Yanowitch, Norton T. Dodge (1969). The quotation is from p. 629.
8 *Nar.kh.SSSR v 1967 g.*, pp. 657–8.
9 For a useful discussion on this problem see David Lane (1970 b), pp. 398–403.
10 Abbreviation for *Zhilishchno-ekspluatatsionnaya kontora* (Housing allocation office).
11 Cf. Henry W. Morton (1968).
12 Raymond A. Bauer (1965). The nine portraits cover students, a woman collective farmer, a woman doctor, a party secretary, a housewife, a writer, a factory director, a tractor driver, and a secret police agent.
13 T. H. Rigby (1969), pp. 383–8.
14 Several sociological surveys made in the USSR during the 1960s showed that men had much more leisure time than women, in most cases between 60 and 80 per cent more time. Men also spent on the average more time each week on self-education. See G. V. Osipov and S. A. Frolov, 'Nonworking time and its use', in *Sotsiologia v SSSR*, G. V. Osipov (1966), pp. 227–44.
15 The contrast between the two life styles is vividly portrayed by Daniel Granin in his account of the career of Krylov in the novel, *Into the Storm* (1965).
16 For one of the best collections of individual life styles of writers and artists in the Moscow district see, Mihajlo Mihajlov, *Moscow Summer: 1964*. Solzhenitsyn's novels, *The First Circle* and *Cancer Ward*, while they deal with the fifties rather than the sixties, nevertheless contain many realistic portraits of Soviet intellectuals.
17 *Komsomolskaya Pravda*, 10 September 1967. See also, Valeri Kondrakov, 'Portrait of the young researcher', *Sputnik*, May 1968, pp. 128–33.
18 Daniel Granin's novel, *Iskateli* (*The Seekers*), Leningrad, 1954, has as its central character a young engineer, Andrei Lobanov. Lobanov feels that academicians are 'the generals of science' and all others, like himself, 'common soldiers'.

CHAPTER 6

1 Frank Knopfelmacher (1968), pp. 1off.

2 T. H. Rigby (1969), p. 407 estimates that 27 per cent of all graduates are party members.

3 Decision of the C.C. of the CPSU, 'On History Teaching in Schools', *Pravda*, 16 September 1959.

4 Decision of the C.C. of the CPSU and the USSR Council of Ministers, 'On Measures for Improving the Quality of Dissertations and the Procedure for Awarding Academic Degrees and Titles', *Pravda*, 7 December 1960.

5 Decision of the C.C./C.M., 'On Measures for Further Improving the Selection and Training of Scientific Personnel', *Pravda*, 8 May 1962.

6 Decision of the C.C./C.M. 'On Measures for Further Development of Biological Science and Strengthening its Ties with Life', *Pravda*, 15 January 1963.

7 Decision of the C.C./C.M., 'On Measures to Improve the Activity of the USSR Academy of Sciences and the Union Republican Academies of Science', *Pravda*, 17 May 1963.

8 Decision of the C.C. of the CPSU, 'Concerning Measures for Further developing Jurisprudence and Improving Legal Education in the Country', *Pravda*, 4 August 1964.

9 Decision of the C.C. of the CPSU, 'On Measures for Further Developing the Social Sciences and for Strengthening their role in Communist Construction', *Pravda*, 22 August 1967.

10 Decision of the C.C./C.M., 'On Measures for Further Improvement of Health Services and the Development of Medical Science in the Country', referred to in *Pravda*, 3 February 1969.

11 This matter is the subject of frequent editorials and special articles in the Soviet press. Cf. R. Kosolapov, P. Simush, 'The intelligentsia in socialist society', *Pravda*, 25 May 1965; the article by A. Rumyantsev, *Pravda* 21 February 1965; *Pravda* editorial, 'For a new development of the social sciences', 18 June 1968; *Pravda* editorial, 'Our Soviet intelligentsia', 11 October 1969; *Pravda* editorial, 'The lofty vocation of the artist', 13 December 1969.

12 In 1967, 19.1 per cent of party members had a completed or unfinished tertiary education, but only 3.9 per cent of the total population had reached this educational level. Rigby (1969), p. 401, gives 16.7 per cent of party members in 1967 as having a completed higher education. His estimate for student membership of the CPSU in 1967 is 200,000 (*ibid.*, p. 346). This would suggest that 2,314,000 intellectuals, as we have defined them, or

21.7 per cent of the total, were party members. Cf. Rigby's estimate of 27 per cent of graduates.

13 The percentage of delegates with a higher education was 52.4 at the 22nd Congress (October 1961) and 55.5 at the 23rd Congress (April 1966); and almost 58 per cent at the 24th Congress in April 1971.

14 1965 figures from K. F. Sheremet (1968), p. 151. 1967 figures from B. Bayanov, *et al.* (1968), p. 117. 1969 figures calculated from the Table in *Sovety*, no. 9, 1969, pp. 46-50.

15 For Estonian surveys see; *S.G. i P.*, no. 10, 1965, pp. 65-70; no. 9, 1966, pp. 3-14; and no. 3, 1967, pp. 65-72. See also Kh.Rapp, I. Tamm (1969).

16 On Kazakhstan, see the report of the research investigation of 1965 in *S.G. i P.*, no. 7, 1965, pp. 3-12.

17 For the Institute of State and Law survey of Armenia, see, I. Azovkin (1968). See also *S.G. i P.*, no. 7, 1968, pp. 3-11.

18 T. H. Rigby (1969), p. 439.

19 V. P. Elyutin (USSR Minister of Higher and Secondary Specialist Education) in his speech to the C.C. of the CPSU, 19 June 1963. *Izvestia*, 20 June 1963.

20 G. D. Komkov *et al.* (1968), p. 189.

21 N. de Witt estimated the percentage of employed professionals who were party members at 30.5 in 1956 and 30.8 in 1959. See T. H. Rigby (1969), p. 408. Soviet estimates of party membership amongst teachers gave 25 per cent in 1964, 1966 and 1968.

22 M. P. Kim (1968), p. 428.

23 John M. Cammett (1967), pp. 201-4.

24 P. P. Amelin (1970), pp. 52-3.

25 Cf. A. Rumyantsev, 'The Party and the intelligentsia', *Pravda*, 21 February 1965:

Moreover, in the process of building socialism, the general level of the population's culture grows steadily, which effaces the difference between physical and mental labour. The labour of front-rank workers in industry and agriculture increasingly approximates intellectual labour, the increase in leisure time expands for all people the opportunity to master the achievements of world culture. (Trans. from C.D.S.P., 1965.)

26 L. G. Churchward (1966 b).

27 *Nar.kh.SSSR v 1968 g.*, pp. 549, 601, 603.

28 L. G. Churchward (1966 a).

29 *Nar.kh.SSSR v 1968 g.*, p. 695.

30 See Loren R. Graham (1968).

31 See Appendix I.

32 The best known of these statements was the *samizdat* publication by Andrei D. Sakharov. This was first published in the West in 1968 under the title, *Progress, Coexistence and Intellectual Freedom.*

33 Jessica Smith, 'Siberian science city' (1969).

34 Lavrentiev on 'Freeing Creativity', *New World Review,* fourth quarter, 1969, p. 69.

35 Cf. references for n.11 above.

36 All three biographies based on information given in *Who's Who in the USSR 1965/66.*

37 Cf. the interesting article, 'Most important part of general party duty', dealing with the Moscow *gorkom* and the creative intelligentsia in Moscow. *Pravda,* 12 May 1967, pp. 2–3.

38 *Vest.Akad.Hauk SSSR,* no. 1, 1967, p. 144. A summary of this article is contained in *Soviet Studies,* Information Supp., April 1967, p. 7.

39 B. I. Marushkin (1969).

40 The article dealt with events in Poland. *Pravda,* 1 April 1968.

41 Yu. Frantsev, 'Concerning certain features of the contemporary ideological struggle', *Pravda,* 22 September 1968.

42 T. Timofeev, 'The leading revolutionary force', *Pravda,* 24 December 1968.

43 *Pravda,* 25 September 1968.

44 *On Events in Czechoslovakia*: facts, documents, press reports and eye-witness accounts. Press Group of Soviet Journalists, Moscow 1968.

45 On the general role of symbols in communication see Hugh Dalziel Duncan (1969).

46 A. Shishkov (1970).

47 *Ibid.,* p. 72.

48 Decision of the C.C., 'Concerning the Measures for Improving the Activity and Performance of the Soviet Press' (1962); and, 'Concerning the Improvement of the Work of Examining Letters and the Organization of Interviewing Toilers' (29 August 1967).

49 For an interesting discussion of this point see V. M. Chkhikvadze (1967), pp. 247ff.

50 Text from *Izvestia,* 12 April 1961.

51 Hugo Wolfsohn, 'The ideology makers', in *Australian Politics,* Henry Mayer (ed.), 1967, pp. 70–81.

52 Decision of the Supreme Soviet of the Armenian SSR, 29 March 1968, 'Concerning Further Improvement in the Working of Local Soviets of deputies of Toilers in the Light of Decisions of the XXIII Congress of the CPSU', *S.G. i P.,* no. 7, 1968, pp. 3–11.

53 Academician A. Rumyantsev, 'Economic science and the building of communism', *Pravda*, 9 October 1967, pp. 2–3.
54 *Vedomosti Verkh.Sov.SSSR*, no. 28, 10 July 1968.
55 *Vedomosti Verkh.Sov. SSSR*, no. 6, 5 February 1969.
56 *Vedomosti Verkh.Sov.SSSR*, no. 17, 26 April 1967.
57 Thus Keldysh has five Orders of Lenin while P. Kapitsa and N. N. Semenov have four each.

CHAPTER 7
1 To answer the question about the actual relationship of the intelligentsia to the top decision-making machinery, we simply have not got enough information. We must know precisely how much, how often, and under what circumstances the men of the Party Presidium, the Secretariat, or the Central Committee, consult the experts, in various fields. We do not know the channels through which consultation takes place, the directness of access professionals have to top politicians, or precisely what kind of experts do, and do not, have access. We have insufficient knowledge of any tests of strength that might have taken place or the form which such tests might have assumed. We take it for granted that in any real test of strength the Party will inevitably win (Alfred G. Meyer, 1965, p. 457).
2 John H. Kautsky (1966).
3 John N. Hazard (1957), p. 30.
4 *The Soviet System of Government*, 3rd ed., 1964, p. 32.
5 Herman F. Akhimov (1958).
6 One of the most influential writers supporting this thesis is Carl L. Linden (1967). For a similar analysis of the influence of Soviet economists, see Gertrude R. Schroeder (1968).
7 Thus H. Gordon Skilling, Brzezinski and Huntington, Roger Pethybridge, D. Richard Little, and Milton C. Lodge all, in varying degrees, assume that Soviet groups such as the military, the economists, writers, lawyers, educationalists, industrialists, and managers, have a reasonable degree of group cohesion. See Bibliography for books and articles by the above writers.
8 See Morris Bornstein (1969). See also Philip D. Stewart (1969).
9 T. H. Rigby and L. G. Churchward (1962), pp. 32–42.
10 Milton C. Lodge, *Soviet Elite Attitudes Since Stalin* (1970), pp. 115f.
11 Philip D. Stewart (1969).
12 Franklyn Griffiths, ch. 2 of Skilling and Griffiths (1971). The views in this chapter were first presented in a paper to the Canadian Political Science Association Congress in 1968.

13 Philip D. Stewart, *op. cit.*, p. 47.
14 T. H. Rigby (1970).
15 Alex Inkeles, 'Developments in Soviet mass communications' in *Social Change in Soviet Russia* (1969), ch. 14. This article provides a useful summary of the Soviet agencies of mass communication.
16 For a brief description of this committee system see, L. G. Churchward (1968), pp. 126–9.
17 The full list of members of all Standing Commissions is given in *Vedomosti Verkhovnovo Soveta SSSR*, no. 32, 1966. Short biographies of all deputies are given in *Sostav deputatov Verhkovnovo Soveta SSSR*, 1966.
18 *Izvestia*, 26 April 1962.
19 See Grey Hodnett, 'The debate over Soviet federalism' (1967).
20 *Pravda*, 26 January 1966.
21 *Pravda*, 25–9 November 1969.
22 A large number of articles have been published analysing the more important of these public discussions. These include R. Schlesinger (1956), J. Miller (1957), L. G. Churchward (1958), Jaroslav Bilinsky (1962), Vladimir G. Tremi (1968), D. Richard Little (1968), Philip D. Stewart (1969).
23 The article was signed by the Director of the Institute of State and Law, Professor V. M. Chkhikvadze (a member of the Drafting Commission) and three others, all from the Agrarian Law Sector of the Institute. *Pravda*, 28 April 1969.
24 Vladimir G. Tremi (1968).
25 See the letter by Academicians Lavrentiev and Khristianovich in *Pravda*, 2 April 1957. See also, *Pravda*, 8 March 1968. See also, Komkov G. D. *et al.* (1968), p. 197.
26 *Izvestia*, 12 April 1961. For full text of this decision, see Appendix II.
27 For a brief general survey of the current interest in pollution problems in the Soviet Union see, Victor Zorza, 'Now pollution becomes an issue in Russia', *Age* (Melbourne) 9 March 1970.
28 *Pravda*, 6 June 1968. Trans. in *C.D.S.P.*, XX, no. 23, pp. 13–16, 1968.
29 See the article by Melnikov in *Lit.gaz.*, no. 28, 12 July 1967. Trans. in *C.D.S.R.*, XIX, no. 32, pp. 22–39, 1967.
30 Eric Thornton, 'A boost for Baikal', *Tribune* (Sydney) 6 August 1969.
31 See the Foreword to *Sovety*, no. 5, 1969, pp. 3–6.
32 *S.G.i.P.*, no. 9, 1959, pp. 111–16.
33 Thus the Leningrad sociologist, V. A. Yadov, in an article in *Lit.gaz.*, no. 9, 28 February 1968, formulated the following six functions for Soviet sociology:

(i) Informational function—the location of social problems, scientific description and classification of social problems;
(ii) Critical function—collation of new facts and evaluation of them;
(iii) Theoretical function—the need to build non-contradictory, integrated, conceptual models;
(iv) Prognosis function—forecasting possible paths of development or changes in social processes and evaluating the reliability of the forecasts;
(v) Applied function—the sociologist proposes the optimum paths for active intervention in social processes in a socially desirable direction; and,
(vi) Educational function—increasing the understanding of the process of social change, of Marxism, etc.

34 For important articles in the early stages of this campaign see: G. Grushin, 'Sociology and the sociologists', *Lit. gaz.*, 25 September 1965; V. Shubkin, 'Problems and prospects of sociology', *Pravda*, 13 March 1966; D. A. Kerimov, A. Kharchev, 'Sociology and its needs', *Izvestia*, 13 November 1966; P. Fedoseev, 'Marxist sociology and concrete sociological research', *Part.zh.*, no. 20, October 1967; A. Rumyantsev, G. Osipov, F. Burlatsky, *Izvestia*, 8 June 1968.

35 There have been many articles dealing with the development of Soviet sociology published in English. Several of these are included in the book by Alex Simirenko (1967).

36 See the summary of the first six months' discussion in *Pravda*, 13 June 1965, 'Concerning the working out of the problems of political science'.

37 Cf. G. V. Tadevosyan's summary, 'The discussion concerning political science', *Vop.fil.*, no. 10, 1965, pp. 164–6.

38 For the background to this movement, see my article in *AJPH* (1966 b). Since 1968 Soviet writers have produced a Russian word for political scientist—*politolog*.

39 E.g. V. L. Tyagunenko (1969).

40 E.g. G. I. Mirsky (1970) and earlier articles.

41 E.g. *Rabochii klass stran Azii i Afriki*, Moscow, 1964; *Klassy i klassovaya borba v razvivayushchikhsya stranakh*, 3 vols, Moscow, 1968; S. M. Menshikov (1964); Yu. M. Sheinin (1963).

42 See the two articles by Georg A. von Stackelberg (1960). See also the article by J. Gregory Oswald (1968).

43 Cf. the following articles; Yu. A. Krasin (1960), (1962); V. B. Knyazhinsky (1960); G. E. Glezerman (1961); V. A. Shishkin (1962); V. G. Trukhanovsky (1963).

44 The most celebrated letter to the C.C. of the CPSU was the protest sent on the eve of the 23rd Congress against the threatened abandonment of de-Stalinization. This was signed by twenty-five leading Soviet scientists, artists and academics.

45 The letter signed by sixty-three Moscow writers protesting against the arrest and trial of writers, Daniel and Sinyavsky, was sent to the 23rd Congress, to the Presidium of the USSR Supreme Soviet, and to the Presidium of the RSFSR Supreme Soviet. For the text of this letter, see Labedz and Hayward (1967), pp. 290–1.

46 The Sakharov testament has recently been published with an introduction by Harrison E. Salisbury under the title, *Progress, Coexistence and Intellectual Freedom*, London, 1968.

47 Borrowed from Alec Nove, *Soviet Studies*, January 1971, p. 453.

48 Based mainly on the biographies supplied in Lebed (ed.), *Who's Who in the USSR 1965–66*.

49 George Fischer (1968).

50 Some Academy institutes gain revenue by research done under contract for specific industrial firms.

51 See the interview with Liberman reported in *Komsomolskaya Pravda*, 12 April 1966, and the article by G. Popov in *Izvestia*, 27 May 1966. In one example quoted by Popov, the Research Institute for Lake, River, and Fishing Resources, only one out of fourteen laboratory heads and two out of sixty-eight senior staff positions had been filled by competitive selection.

52 Thus S. Lichiskin in *Novy mir*, no. 8, 1967, included this as a point of criticism in his comparison of the relative effectiveness of R and D in the USA and the USSR.

53 An analysis of 50 senior scientists (selected at random) showed that 34 were party members. For these, the average joining age was 35 years. In the case of the members of the party leadership (full members of the Politburo and/or Secretariat, 1966) it was 22 years. A part analysis (23 out of 84) of members of the Council of Ministers of the USSR, August 1966, showed 25 years as the average joining age.

54 Cf. George Fischer's dual type. Fischer (1968).

CHAPTER 8

1 Sidney Monas, 'Engineers or martyrs: dissent and the intelligentsia' (1968). The quotation is from p. 3.

2 Edward Crankshaw, 'Is this where I came in?', The *Observer*, 22 December 1968.

3 André Amalrik (1969).

4 Vyacheslav Chornovil (1968), pp. 198–206. Petition drafted by S. Karavansky and sent to the Chairman of the Soviet of Nationalities, USSR Supreme Soviet.
5 V. Chornovil (1968), p. 91.
6 *Ibid.*, p. 68.
7 Max Weber (1962), pp. 29–58.
8 *Vop.ist.*, no. 1, 1962, pp. 3–13.
9 *Lit. gaz.*, 23 December 1961. The main report was given by G. Markov, Secretary of the Board on the theme, 'The 22nd Congress and the tasks of Soviet writers'.
10 *Izvestia*, 26, 27, 28 December 1961.
11 *Pravda*, 4 February 1962.
12 *Pravda*, 18 December 1962.
13 *Pravda*, 19 December 1962.
14 *Sovetskaya kultura*, 10 January 1963.
15 *Pravda*, 8, 9, 10 March 1963. References to the writers' letter were also made by Ilichev in his speech on 17 December 1962.
16 *Pravda Ukrainy*, 10 April 1963.
17 *Izvestia*, 19 June 1963.
18 *Lit.gaz.*, 9 June 1964.
19 The main court cases involving writers are summarized in Anatole Shub (1970).
   Other accounts may be found in Labedz and Hayward (1967), Ivan Dzyuba (1968), Peter Reddaway (1969), André Amalrik (1970), Labedz (1970), Michael Browne (1971).
20 *Lit.gaz.*, no. 43, 1968.
21 *Survey*, no. 73, autumn 1969, pp. 47–79.
22 *Ibid.*, p. 50.
23 *Izvestia*, 8 January 1963. Translated by L. G. C. Originally published in *Overland* (Melbourne), no. 37, 1967, p. 15. Reproduced with permission.
24 See the letters printed in Labedz and Hayward (1967), pp. 290–304, and in C. R. Hill (1969), pp. 100–20.
25 Harrison E. Salisbury (1969).
26 Cf. Jack Miller (1965).

APPENDIX I
1 *Nar.kh.SSSR v 1968 g.*, p. 699.
2 Loren R. Graham (1968), p. vii. See also Vucinich's chapter in Kassof (1968).
3 Academician A. N. Nesmeyanov's speech to the 21st Congress. *Pravda*, 5 February 1959.

4 *Vest.Akad.Nauk SSSR*, no. 5, May 1959, pp. 7–17. A full translation is given in *C.D.S.P.*, 1959.
5 For a full translation of this decision, see Appendix II.
6 *Pravda*, 5 July 1963.
7 UNESCO: *Science Policy and Organization of Research in the USSR* (1967), p. 46.
8 G. D. Komkov *et al.* (1968), p. 185.
9 *Ibid.*, p. 180.
10 *Ibid.*, p. 182.
11 *Ibid.*, pp. 199–201.
12 *Pravda* editorial, 'Advance posts of science', 3 September 1969.
13 G. D. Komkov *et al.* (1968), p. 189.
14 The State Committee for Science and Technology was established 2 October 1965. See Art. 8 of the Statute on the Reorganization of the Industrial Administrative Structure, *Izvestia*, 3 October 1965. It replaced the earlier Committee for the Coordination of Scientific Research Work.

Bibliography

AFANASIEV, G. V. (1968) *Nauchnoe upravlenie obshchestvom*, Moscow.

AKHIMOV, Herman F. (1958) 'The Soviet intelligentsia', included in *Soviet Society Today*, Institute for the Study of the USSR, pp. 64–87.

AMALRIK, A. (1969) 'Will the USSR survive until 1984?', *Survey*, no. 73, pp. 47–79.

AMALRIK, A. (1970) *Involuntary Journey to Siberia*, London: Collins & Harvill.

AMELIN, P. P. (1970) *Intelligentsia i Sotsializm*, Leningrad.

ANANEV, B. G. and KERIMOV, D. A. (eds) (1967) *Chelovek i Obshchestvo*, no. II, Leningrad.

ANDREEVA, G. M. (1965) *Sovremennaya burzhuaznaya empiricheskaya sotsiologia*, Moscow.

APTER, D. E. (ed.) (1965) *Ideology and Discontent*, London: Collier-Macmillan.

APTHEKER, H. (1965) *Marxism and Alienation*, New York: Humanities Press.

ARMSTRONG, John A. (1959) *The Soviet Bureaucratic Elite*, London: Stevens.

ARMSTRONG, John A. (1965) 'Sources of administrative behaviour: some Soviet and Western comparisons', *American Political Science Review*, lix, pp. 643–55.

ARMSTRONG, John A. (1967) *Ideology, Politics and Government in the Soviet Union*, New York: Praeger.

ARON, Raymond (1957) *The Opium of the Intellectuals*, New York: Norton.

ARON, Raymond (1961) *Eighteen Lectures on Industrial Society*, London: Weidenfeld & Nicolson.

ARUTYUNYAN, Yu. V. (1966) 'The social structure of the rural population', *Vop. fil.*, no. 5, pp. 51–61.

ARUTYUNYAN, Yu. V. (1969a) 'Social aspects of the cultural development of the rural population', *Vop. fil.* no. 3, pp. 119–31.

ARUTYUNYAN, Yu. V. (1969b) 'Concrete sociological research into national relations', *Vop. fil.*, no. 12, 129–39.

ASPATURIAN, Vernon V. (1968) 'The non-Russian nationalities', included in Kassof, *Prospects for Soviet Society*, pp. 143–98.

AVRICH, Paul (1965) 'What is Makhaevism?', *Soviet Studies*, xvii, pp. 66–75.

AZOVKIN, I. (1968) 'Becoming acquainted with Kafan raion', *Sovety*, no. 6, pp. 76–81.

AZRAEL, J. R. (1967) *Managerial Power and Soviet Politics*, Harvard U.P.

BACON, Elizabeth E. (1967) *Central Asia under Russian Rule*, Cornell U.P.

BARGHOORN, F. C. (1966a) *Politics in the USSR*, Boston: Little.

BARGHOORN, F. C. (1966b) 'Observations on contemporary Soviet political attitudes', *Soviet Studies*, xviii, pp. 66–70.

BARRY, Donald D. (1964) 'The specialists in Soviet policy-making: the adoption of a law', *Soviet Studies*, xvi, pp. 152–65.

BAUER, R. A. (1965) *Nine Soviet Portraits*, M.I.T. Press.

BAUER, R. A., INKELES, A. and KLUCKHOHN C. (1956) *How the Soviet System Works*, M.I.T. Press.

BAYANOV, B., UMANSKY, Y. and SHAFIR, M. (1968) *Soviet Socialist Democracy*, Moscow.

BEDENIN, N. N. (1969) 'The defence of nature in the USSR', *S.G.i.P.*, no. 10, pp. 151–3.

BENDIX, R. (1965) *Nation Building and Citizenship*, Wiley.

BERGER, John (1969) *Art and Revolution: Ernst Neizvestny and the Role of the Artist in the USSR*, London: Weidenfeld & Nicolson.

BERMAN, Harold (1963a) *Justice in the USSR*, New York: Random House.

BERMAN, H. J. (1963b) 'The struggle of Soviet jurists against a return to Stalinist terror', *Slavic Rev.*, xxii.

BESTUSHEV-LADA, Igor (1969) 'Forecasting—an approach to the problems of the future', *Int.Soc.Sc.J.*, xxi, pp. 526–34.

BILINSKY, Yaroslav (1962) 'The Soviet educational laws of 1958–59 and Soviet national policy', *Sov.Stud.*, xiv, pp. 138–57.

BILLINGTON, James H. (1968) 'The intellectuals', in Kassof (ed.), *Prospects for Soviet Society*, pp. 449–70.

BLACK, Cyril E. (1960) *The Transformation of Russian Society*, Cambridge, Mass.: Harvard U.P.

BLACK, Cyril E. (1970) 'Marxism and modernization', *Slavic Rev.*, xxix, pp. 182–6.

BLAKE, Patricia and HAYWARD, Max (1964) *Dissonant Voices in Soviet Literature*, London: Allen & Unwin.

BOCIURKIW, B. R. (1964) 'The post-Stalin thaw in Soviet political science', *The Canadian J. of Econs and Pol. Sc.*, no. 1, pp. 22–48.

BONDAREVSKY, G. L. *et al.* (1964) *Politika S Sh A v stranakh dalnevo vostoka*, Moscow.

BORNSTEIN, M. (1969) 'The Soviet debate on agriculture, price and procurement reforms', *Soviet Studies*, xxi, pp. 1–20.

BOTTOMORE, T. B. (1964) *Elites and Society*, London: Watts.

BOTTOMORE, T. B. (1965) *Classes in Modern Society*, London: Allen & Unwin.

BROWN, Emily Clark (1966) *Soviet Trade Unions and Labor Relations*, Harvard U.P.

BROWN, W. J. (1970) *Socialism and Today's Mass Media*, Sydney: W. J. Brown.

BROWNE, Michael (ed.) (1971) *Ferment in the Ukraine*, London: Macmillan.

BRZEZINSKI, Z. (1966) 'The Soviet political system: transformation or degeneration', *Problems of Communism*, pp. 1–15.

BRZEZINSKI, Z. and HUNTINGTON, S. P. (1964) *Political Power: USA/USSR*, London: Chatto & Windus.

BUKHARIN, Nikolai (1970) *Historical Materialism: A System of Sociology*, University of Michigan Press.

BURIN, Frederic S. (1963) 'The Communist doctrine of the inevitability of war', *American P.S.R.*, lvii, pp. 334–54.

BURLATSKY, F. (n.d.) *The State and Communism*, Moscow.

BURLATSKY, F. (1968) *Maoizm—ugroza sotsializmu v Kitae*, Moscow.

BURLATSKY, F. M. (1970) *Lenin, Gosudarstvo, Politika*, Moscow.

CAMMETT, John M. (1967) *Antonio Gramsci and the Origins of Italian Communism*, Oxford U.P.

CARR, E. H. (1969) *1917: Before and After*, London: Macmillan.

CARR, E. H. and DAVIES, R. W. (1969) *A History of Soviet Russia: Foundations of a Planned Economy 1926–1929*, 2 vols, London: Macmillan (vol. 2, ch. 21, 'The specialists').

Chislennost, sostav i rasmeshchenie naselenie SSSR, Central Statistical Administration, Moscow, 1961.

CHKHIKVADZE, V. M. (1964) 'Problems of Soviet legal science in the contemporary period of Communist construction', *S.G.i.P.*, no. 9, pp. 3–14.

CHKHIKVADZE, V. M. (1967) *Politicheskaya organizatsia sovetskovo obshchestva*, Moscow.

CHKHIKVADZE, V. M. (ed.) (1969) *The Soviet State and Law*, Moscow.

CHORNOVIL, V. (1968) *The Chornovil Papers*, Toronto: McGraw.

CHURCHWARD, L. G. (1958) 'The agricultural reorganization and the rural district Soviets', *Soviet Studies*, x, pp. 94–7.

CHURCHWARD, L. G. (1962) *see* RIGBY and CHURCHWARD.

CHURCHWARD, L. G. (1966a) 'Soviet local government today', *Soviet Studies*, xvii, pp. 431–52.

CHURCHWARD, L. G. (1966b) 'Towards a Soviet political science', *Australian J. of Pol. and Hist.*, xii, pp. 66–75.

CHURCHWARD, L. G. (1968) *Contemporary Soviet Government*, London: Routledge & Kegan Paul.

CLARKE, R. A. (1967) 'The composition of the USSR Supreme Soviet', *Soviet Studies*, xix, pp. 53–65.

CLEARY, J. W. (1967) 'Politics and Administration in Soviet Kazakhstan 1955–1964', Ph.D. Thesis, A.N.U., Canberra.

COHN-BENDIT, Gabriel (1969) *Obsolete Communism: The Left-Wing Alternative*, London: Penguin.

CONQUEST, Robert (ed.) (1968a) *Soviet Nationalities Policy in Practice*, London: Bodley Head.

CONQUEST, Robert (ed.) (1968b) *The Politics of Ideas in the USSR*, London: Bodley Head.

CONQUEST, Robert (ed.) (1968c) *The Soviet Police System*, London: Bodley Head.

CONQUEST, Robert (1970) *The Nation Killers*, London: Macmillan.

CORNELL, Richard (ed.) (1970) *The Soviet Political System*, New Jersey: Prentice-Hall.

CRANKSHAW, Edward (1966) *Khrushchev*, London: Collins.

DALLIN, A. and LARSEN, T. B. (ed.) (1968) *Soviet Politics Since Khrushchev*, Prentice-Hall.

DAVIDSON, Alastair (1968) *Antonio Gramsci: The Man, His Ideas*, Sydney: Australian Left Review Publications.

DEBORIN, G. D. (1961) 'Economics and politics of contemporary imperialism', *Vop. fil.*, no. 5, pp. 20–33.

DEINEKO, M. (n.d.) *Public Education in the USSR*, Moscow.

DEUTSCHER, Isaac (1966) *Ironies of History*, Oxford U.P.

DEUTSCHER, Isaac (1967) *The Unfinished Revolution*, Oxford U.P.

DEUTSCHER, Tamara (1970) 'Soviet oppositionists', *New Left Review*, no. 60, pp. 52–8.

DE WITT, Nicolas (ed.) (1961) *Education and Professional Employment in the USSR*, National Science Foundation, Washington D.C.

DRESSLER, A. (1960) 'The Third Writers' Congress', *Soviet Studies*, xi, pp. 327–41.

DUNCAN, Hugh D. (1969) *Symbols in Society*, Oxford U.P.

DYMSHITS, A. (ed.) (1968) *Art and Society*, Moscow.

DZYUBA, Ivan (1968) *Internationalism or Russification?* London: Weidenfeld & Nicolson.

EHRENBURG, Ilya (1961–6) *Men, Years-Life*, 6 vols, London: Macgibbon & Kee.

Bibliography

ENGEL, S. (1970) *Equality and Authority: A Study of Class, Status and Power in Australia*, Melbourne: Cheshire.

ERMAN, L. K. (1966) *Intelligentsia v pervoi russkoi revolyutsii*, Moscow.

FAINSOD, Merle (1963) *How Russia is Ruled*, revised ed., Oxford U.P.

FEDOSEEV, P. (1967) 'Marxist sociology and concrete sociological research', *Part.zhizn*, no. 20, pp. 34–41.

FEIFER, George (1964) *Justice in Moscow*, London: Bodley Head.

FERRIS, Paul (1965) *The Doctors*, London: Penguin.

FEUER, L. S. (1965) 'Meeting the philosophers', *Survey*, no. 55, April, pp. 10–23.

FISCHER, George (1960) 'The intelligentsia and Russia', in C. E. Black, *The Transformation of Russian Society*.

FISCHER, George (1965) 'The number of Soviet party executives: a research note', *Soviet Studies*, xvi, pp. 330–3.

FISCHER, George (1968) *The Soviet System and Modern Society*, New York: Atherton.

FLERON, Frederic J. Jr. (1969a) 'Cooptation as a mechanism of adaption to change', *Polity*, ii, winter, pp. 176–9.

FLERON, Frederic J. Jr. (1969b) *Communist Studies and the Social Sciences*, Chicago: Rand, McNally.

FLERON, Frederic J. Jr. (1970) 'Representation of career types in the Soviet political leadership', in R. B. Farrell, *Political leadership in Eastern Europe and the Soviet Union*, Chicago: Aldine Publishing Co.

FRANTSOV, G. P. (1965) *Istoricheskie puti sotsialnoi mysli*, Moscow.

FRAYN, Michael (1967) *The Russian Interpreter*, London: Penguin.

FREDERIKSEN, O. J. (ed.) (1958) *Soviet Society Today: A Symposium*, Munich.

FROLIC, B. Michael (1970) 'The Soviet study of Soviet cities', *The Journal of Politics*, 32, no. 3, pp. 675–95.

GALAY, Nikolai (1965) 'The new generation in the Soviet Armed Forces', *Studies on the Soviet Union*, v, no. 2, pp. 29–46.

GALDYAEV, P. K. (1965) *Kritika sovremennoi burzhuarznoi sotsiologii*, Moscow.

GALKIN, K. T. (1958) *Vysshee obrazovania i podgotovka nauchnykh kadrov v SSSR*, Moscow.

GEERTZ, C. (1965) 'Ideology as a cultural system', in D. Apter, *Ideology and Discontent*, Collier-Macmillan.

GERTH, H. H. and MILLS, C. WRIGHT (eds) (1947) *From Max Weber: Essays in Sociology*, London: Routledge & Kegan Paul.

GILL, Richard R. (1967) 'Problems of decision-making in Soviet science policy', *Minerva*, v, winter, pp. 198–208.

GINSBURG, Evgenia (1967) *Into the Whirlwind*, London: Penguin.

GLEZERMAN, G. E. (1961) 'The Marxist-Leninist characterization of the contemporary epoch', *Vop.fil.*, no. 2, pp. 25–38.

GLEZERMAN, G. E. (1968) 'The social structure of Socialist society', *Kommunist*, no. 15, pp. 28–39.

GRAHAM, Loren R. (1967) 'Reorganization of the USSR Academy of Sciences' in P. H. Juviler and H. W. Morton (eds), *Soviet Policy-Making: Studies of Communism in Transition*, Praeger.

GRAHAM, Loren R. (1968) *The Soviet Academy of Sciences and the Communist Party 1927–1932*, Oxford U.P.

GRAMSCI, A. (1957) *The Modern Prince and Other Writings*, London: Lawrence & Wishart.

GRANICK, David (1960) *The Red Executive*, London: Macmillan.

GRANIN, D. (1955) *Iskateli*, Leningrad.

GRANIN, D. (1964) *Posle svadby*, Moscow.

GRANIN, D. (1965) *Into the Storm*, Moscow.

GRANT, Nigel (1964) *Soviet Education*, London: Penguin.

HAZARD, John N. (1957) *The Soviet System of Government*, 4th ed. 1968, University of Chicago Press.

HEINMAN, S. (1969) 'The scientific and technological revolution and structural changes in the economy', *Kommunist*, no. 14, pp. 63–75.

HILL, C. R. (ed.) (1969) *Rights and Wrongs*, London: Penguin.

HODGES, D. C. (1963) 'Class, stratum and intelligentsia', *Science and Society*, xxvii, pp. 49–61.

HODNETT, Grey (1967) 'The debate over Soviet federalism', *Soviet Studies*, xviii, pp. 458–81.

HODNETT, Grey and POTICHNYJ, Peter J. (1970) *The Ukraine and the Czechoslovak Crisis*, Canberra: A.N.U.

HOUGH, Jerry F. (1967) 'The Soviet élite', *Problems of Communism*, xvi, nos. 1 & 2.

HOUGH, Jerry F. (1969) *The Soviet Prefects*, Oxford U.P.

H. H. (1966) 'Education and social mobility in the USSR', *Soviet Studies*, xviii, pp. 57–65.

INKELES, Alex (1950) 'Social stratification and mobility in the Soviet Union 1940–1950', *Am.Soc.Rev.*, xv, pp. 465–79.

INKELES, Alex (1969) *Social Change in Soviet Russia*, Oxford U.P.

INOZEMTSEV, N. N. (ed.) (1967) *Uchenie V.I. Lenina ob imperializme i sovremennost*, Moscow.

IONESCU, Ghita (1967) *The Politics of European Communist States*, London: Weidenfeld & Nicolson.

IRELAND, P. R. (1965) 'Soviet writing: towards a new situation', included in Miller and Rigby, *The Disintegrating Monolith*, Canberra: A.N.U.

Bibliography

ISKENDEROV, A. A. *et al.* (1964) *Rabochii klass stran Azii i Afriki*, Moscow.

JOHNSON, Priscilla (1963) 'The regime and the intellectuals: a window on party politics, winter 1962–summer 1963', *Problems of Communism*, xii, no. 4, July–August.

JORAVSKY, David (1966) 'Soviet ideology', *Soviet Studies*, xviii, pp. 1–19.

KALENSKY, V. G. (1969) *Politicheskaya nauka v S.Sh.A.*, Moscow.

KAMENKA, Eugene (1965) 'Pluralism and Soviet culture', in Miller and Rigby, *The Disintegrating Monolith*, Canberra: A.N.U.

KASER, Michael (1970) *Soviet Economics*, London: Weidenfeld & Nicolson.

KASSOF, Allen (1965a) 'American sociology through Soviet eyes', *Am. Soc.Rev.*, February, pp. 114–21.

KASSOF, Allen (1965b) *The Soviet Youth Program: Regimentation and Rebellion*, Oxford U.P.

KASSOF, Allen (ed.) (1968) *Prospects for Soviet Society*, Praeger.

KATZ, Z. (1969) 'Heredity elements in education and social structure in the USSR', University of Glasgow, Institute of Soviet and East European Studies.

KATZ, Z. (1970) 'After the Six-Day War', included in Kochan, *The Jews in Soviet Russia Since 1917*, pp. 321–36.

KAUTSKY, John H. (1966) *Political Change in Underdeveloped Countries: Nationalism and Communism*, Wiley.

KAZIMIRCHUK, V. P. (1967) 'Sociological research in law', *S.G.i.P.*, no. 10, pp. 37–45.

KEECH, William R. (1968) *see* SCHWARTZ and KEECH.

KEEP, John (1969) 'The Soviet Union and the Third World', *Survey*, no. 72, pp. 19–28.

KELLER, Suzanne (1963) *Beyond the Ruling Class*, New York: Random House.

KHRUSHCHEV, N. S. (1963) 'The great strength of Soviet literature and art', London: Soviet Booklet no. 108.

KIERNAN, V. G. (1969) 'Notes on the intelligentsia', in Miliband and Saville, *The Socialist Register 1969*, London: Merlin, pp. 55–84.

KIM, M. P. (ed.) (1968) *Sovetskaya intelligentsia*, Moscow.

KIRIMAL, Edige (1970) 'The Crimean Tatars', *Studies on the Soviet Union*, new series, x, no. 1, pp. 70–97.

KNOPFELMACHER, Frank (1968) *Intellectuals and Politics*, Melbourne.

KNYAZHINSKY, V. B. (1960) 'The problem of peaceful co-existence and bourgeois falsification of world history', *Vop.ist.*, no. 10, pp. 18–35.

KOCHAN, Lionel (ed.) (1970) *The Jews in Soviet Russia Since 1917*, Oxford U.P.

Bibliography

KOLAKOWSKI, Leszek (1968), 'Intellectuals and the Communist movement', in *Towards a Marxist Humanism*, New York: Grove, pp. 158–72.

KOLAKOWSKI, Leszek (1970) 'The fate of Marxism in Eastern Europe', *Slavic Review*, 29, pp. 175–81, 201–2.

KOLARZ, W. (1964) *Communism and Colonialism*, London: Macmillan.

KOLKOWICZ, R. (1967) *The Soviet Military and the Communist Party*, Oxford U.P.

KOLOKOLOVA, G. N. (ed.) *O pravakh i obyasonnostyakh molodykh spetsialistov*, Moscow.

KOMKOV, G. D. *et al.* (1968) *Akademia Nauk SSSR: Shtab Sovetskoi Nauki*, Moscow.

KONSTANTINOV, F. (1959) 'The Soviet intelligentsia', *Kommunist*, no. 15, pp. 48–65.

KORNHAUSER, W. (1960) *The Politics of Mass Society*, London: Routledge & Kegan Paul.

KOROL, A. G. (1965) *Soviet Research and Development: Its Organization, Personnel and Funds*, M.I.T. Press.

KRASIN, Yu. A. (1960) 'V. I. Lenin and the problem of peaceful coexistence', *Vop. fil.*, no. 9, pp. 9–23.

KRASIN, Yu. A. (1962) 'Peaceful co-existence and the contradictions of capitalism', *Vop. fil.*, no. 8, 23–35.

KUGEL, S. A. (1969a) 'Professional mobility in science and its tendencies to change under conditions of the scientific and technological revolution', *Vop. fil.*, no. 11, pp. 109–16.

KUGEL, S. A. (1969b) 'Changes in the social structure of socialist society under the impact of the scientific and technological revolution', *Vop. fil.*, no. 3, pp. 13–22.

KURSANOV, G. A. *et al.* (1965) *Sovremenny kapitalizm i burzhuarznaya sotsiologia*, Moscow.

KURYLEV, A. K. *et al.* (1969) *Iz opyta konkretnykh sotsiologicheskikh isledovanii*, Moscow.

LABEDZ, Leopold (1961) 'The structure of the Soviet intelligentsia', in R. Pipes, *The Russian Intelligentsia*, Columbia U.P., pp. 63–79.

LABEDZ, Leopold (1963) 'Sociology as a vocation', *Survey*, July, pp. 57–65.

LABEDZ, Leopold (1966) 'Sociology and social change', *Survey*, no. 60, pp. 18–39.

LABEDZ, Leopold (ed.) (1970) *Solzhenitsyn: A Documentary Record*, London: Allen Lane.

LABEDZ, Leopold and HAYWARD, Max (1967) *On Trial: The Case of Sinyavsky (Tertz) and Daniel (Arzhak)*, London: Collins & Harvill.

Bibliography

LAN, V. I. (1964) *S.Sh.A. v voennye i poslevoennye gody* (1940–1960), Moscow.

LANE, David (1970a) 'Ideology and sociology in the USSR', *Brit. J. of Sociology*, xxi, pp. 43–51.

LANE, David (1970b) *Politics and Society in the USSR*, London: Weidenfeld & Nicolson.

LEBED, Andrei (1965) 'The Soviet administrative élite: selection and deployment procedures', *Studies on the Soviet Union*, v, no. 2, pp. 47–55.

LEBED, Andrei, *et al.* (1966) *Who's Who in the USSR 1965–66*, 2nd ed., New York and London: Scarecrow Press.

LEPESHKIN, A. I. *Sovety- vlast naroda 1936–67*, Moscow.

LINDEN, Carl A. (1967) *Khrushchev and the Soviet Leadership 1957–1964*, Johns Hopkins Press.

LITTLE, D. R. (1968) 'The Academy of Pedagogical Sciences—its political role', *Soviet Studies*, xix, pp. 387–97.

LITVINOV, Pavel (1969) *The Demonstration in Pushkin Square*, London: Harvill.

LODGE, Milton C. (1969) ' "Groupism" in the post-Stalin period', in Fleron, *Communist Studies and the Social Sciences*, pp. 254–78.

LODGE, Milton C. (1970) *Soviet Elite Attitudes Since Stalin*, Prentice-Hall.

LYUBIMOV, N. N. (1962) *Kolonializm i mezhimperialisticheskie protivorechia v Afrike*, Moscow.

MCAULEY, Mary (1969) *Labour Disputes in Soviet Russia 1957–1965*, Oxford: Clarendon Press.

MALAKHOVSKY, K. V. (1969) *Avstralia i Azia*, Moscow.

MANNHEIM, Karl (1960) *Ideology and Utopia: An Introduction to the Sociology of Knowledge*, London: Routledge & Kegan Paul.

MARCUSE, Herbert (1964) *One Dimensional Man*, London: Sphere Books.

MARKO, Kurt (1968) 'Soviet ideology and Sovietology', *Soviet Studies*, xix, pp. 65–81.

MARUSHKIN, B. I. (1969) *Istoria i Politika (Amerikanskaya burzhuaznaya istoriografia sovetskovo obshchestva)*, Moscow.

MEDLIN, William K. (1968) 'Education', in Kassof, *Prospects for Soviet Society*, pp. 241–62.

MELMAN, S. M. (1964) *Razvitie promyshlennosti nezavisimoi Indii*, Moscow.

MENSHIKOV, S. M. (ed.) (1964) *Ekonomicheskaya politika pravitelstva Kennidi 1961–63*, Moscow.

MEYER, Alfred G. (1965) *The Soviet Political System*, New York: Random House.

MEYER, Alfred G. (1966) 'The functions of ideology in the Soviet political system', *Soviet Studies*, xvii, pp. 273–85.

MIHAJLOV, M. (1965) *Moscow Summer 1964*, Melbourne: Partisan Special.

MIKHAILOV, S. S. (1964) *Osvoboditelnoe dvizhenia v Latinskoi Amerike*, Moscow.

MILLER, J. (1957) 'The decentralization of industry', *Soviet Studies*, ix, pp. 65–82.

MILLER, J. (1965) 'Tomorrow's industrialists', *Studies on the Soviet Union*, v, pp. 23–8.

MILLS, C. Wright (1947) *see* GERTH and MILLS.

MIRSKY, G. I. (1970) *Politicheskaya rol armii v stranakh Azii i Afriki*, Moscow.

MOCHALOV, B. (1966) 'Party work in tertiary institutes', *Kommunist*, no. 10, pp. 34–42.

MOKICHEV, K. A. (1968) 'We present: the Faculty of Soviet Construction', *Sovety*, no. 1, pp. 70–3.

MONAS, S. (1968) 'Engineers or martyrs: dissent and the intelligentsia', *Problems of Communism*, xvii, n. 5, pp. 2–17.

MORTON, Henry W. (1968) 'The Leningrad district of Moscow—an inside look', *Soviet Studies*, xx, pp. 206–18.

MOORE, Barrington Jr., (1969) *Social Origins of Dictatorship and Democracy*, London: Penguin.

MUKSINOV, I. SH. (1969) *Sovet ministrov soyuznoi respubliki*, Moscow.

NECHKINA, M. V. (ed.) (1968) *V. I. Lenin i istoricheskaya nauka*, Moscow.

NOVE, Alec (1966) 'Ideology and agriculture', *Soviet Studies*, xvii, pp. 397–407.

NOVE, Alec (1969) 'History, hierarchy and nationalities: some observations on the Soviet social structure', *Soviet Studies*, xxi, pp. 71–92.

NOVE, Alec and NEWTH, J. A. (1967) *The Soviet Middle East*, London: Allen & Unwin.

NOVE, Alec and NEWTH J. A. (1970) 'The Jewish population: demographic trends and occupational patterns', in Kochan, *The Jews in Soviet Russia Since 1917*, pp. 125–58.

OMAROV, A. M. (ed.) (1969) *Besedy ob ekonomicheskoi reforme*, Moscow.

On Events in Czechoslovakia: Facts, Documents, Press Reports and Eyewitness acounts (1968), Moscow.

OSIPOV, G. V. (1964) *Sovremennaya burzhuaznaya sotsiologia*, Moscow.

OSIPOV, G. V. (ed.) (1966) *Sotsiologia v SSSR*, 2 vols, Moscow.

OSIPOV, G. V. (1968) *see* RUMYANTSEV and OSIPOV.

OSIPOV, G. V. (1969) *Sociology*, Moscow.

OSSOWSKI, S. (1963) *Class Structure and the Social Consciousness*, London: Routledge & Kegan Paul.

OSWALD, D. J. G. (1968) 'The development of Soviet studies on Latin America', *Studies on the Soviet Union*, vii, no. 3, pp. 70–83.

PARSONS, Talcott (1965) 'An American impression of sociology in the Soviet Union', *Am.Soc.Rev.*, February, pp. 121–5.

PARSONS, Talcott (1970) 'The impact of technology on culture and emerging new modes of behaviour', *International Soc.Sc.Journal*, xxii, no. 4, pp. 607–27.

PAUSTOVSKY, Konstantin (1964–9) *Story of a Life*, 5 vols, London: Harvill.

PETHYBRIDGE, Roger W. (1961) *A Key to Soviet Politics*, London: Allen & Unwin.

PIPES, Richard (ed.) (1961) *The Russian Intelligentsia*, New York: Columbia U.P.

PLOSS, Sidney (1965) *Conflict and Decision-Making in Soviet Russia: A Case Study of Agricultural Policy 1953–1963*, Oxford U.P.

PRICE, Don K. (1962) *Government and Science*, New York.

PROKHOROV, G. M. (1965) *Dve mirovye sistemy i osvobodivshiesya strany*, Moscow.

RAPP, KH. and TAMM, I. (1969) 'Experiences of research into the apparatus of district soviets', *Sovety*, no. 9, pp. 69–75.

RASPORKIN, F. (1971) *Partiiny rabotnik: oblik i stil*, Moscow.

REDDAWAY, Peter (1969) 'The Soviet treatment of dissenters and the growth of a civil rights movement', in C. R. Hill, *Rights and Wrongs*, pp. 79–120.

RICHTA, Radovan (ed.) (1967) *Civilisation at the Crossroads*, Sydney: Australian Left Review Publications.

RICHTA, Radovan and SULC, Ota (1969) 'Forecasting and the scientific and technological revolution', *Int.Soc.Science. J.*, xxi, no. 4, pp. 563–73.

RIGBY, T. H. and CHURCHWARD, L. G. (1962) *Policy Making in the USSR 1953–1961: Two Views*, Melbourne: Lansdowne Press.

RIGBY, T. H. (1965) 'The deconcentration of power in the USSR—1953–1964', in Miller and Rigby, *The Disintegrating Monolith*, pp. 17–45.

RIGBY, T. H. (1969) *Communist Party Membership in the USSR, 1917–1967*, Oxford U.P.

RIGBY, T. H. (1970) 'The Soviet leadership: towards a self-stabilizing oligarchy', *Soviet Studies*, xxii, October.

RODIONOV, M. (ed.) (1970) *Struktura sovetskoi intelligentsii*, Minsk.

RUMYANTSEV, A. M. (ed.) (1963) *Structure of the Working Class*, New Delhi: People's Publishing House.

RUMYANTSEV, A. M. and OSIPOV, G. V. (1968) 'Marxist sociology and concrete sociological research', *Vop.fil.*, no. 6, pp. 3–13.

RUMYANTSEV, A. M., et al. (1968) *Problemy rabochevo dvizhenia*, Moscow.

RUNCIMAN, W. G. (1963) *Social Science and Political Theory*, Cambridge University Press.

RUSH, Myron (1968) *Political Succession in the USSR*, Columbia U.P.

RUTKEVICH, M. N. (1966) 'The changing social structure of Soviet society and the intelligentsia', in Osipov, *Sotsiologia v SSSR*, vol. 1, pp. 391–413.

SAKHAROV, Andrei D. (1969) *Progress, Coexistence and Intellectual Freedom*, London: Penguin.

SALISBURY, Harrison E. (1967) *Anatomy of the Soviet Union*, London: William Clowes.

SALISBURY, Harrison E. (1969) *The Coming War Between Russia and China*, London: Pan Books.

SCHAPIRO, L. (1965) *The Government and Politics of the Soviet Union*, London: Hutchinson.

SCHLESINGER, R. (1956) 'Soviet historians before and after the XX Congress', *Soviet Studies*, viii, pp. 157–84.

SCHLESINGER, R. (1962) 'Marxist theory and the new program of the Soviet Communist Party', *Science and Society*, xxvi, pp. 129–52.

SCHROEDER, Gertrude E. (1968) 'Soviet economic reforms: a study in contradictions', *Soviet Studies*, xx, pp. 1–21.

SCHWARTZ, Benjamin (1961) 'The intelligentsia in Communist China: a tentative comparison', in R. Pipes, *The Russian Intelligentsia*, pp. 164–81.

SCHWARTZ, Joel J. and KEECH, William R. (1968) 'Group influence and the policy process in the Soviet Union', *Am.Pol.Sc.Rev.*, lxii, pp. 840–51.

SCOTT, Derek J. (1969) *Russian Political Institutions*, 4th ed., London: Allen & Unwin.

SEALE, Patrick and MCCONVILLE, Maureen (1968) *French Revolution: 1968*, London: Penguin.

SEMENOV, V. S. (1966) 'Concerning changes in the intelligentsia and office workers in the process of the building of Communism', included in Osipov, *Sotsiologia v SSSR*, vol. i, pp. 314–28.

SHARP, G. B. and WHITE, D. (1968) 'Features of the intellectually-trained', *Arena* (Greensborough, Victoria), no. 15, pp. 30–3.

SHARP, G. B. (1968) 'A revolutionary culture', *Arena*, no. 16, pp. 2–11.

SHEININ, Yu. M. (1963) *Nauka i Militarizm v S.Sh.A.*, Moscow.

SHELTON, William (1970) 'The Soviet scientist today', *The Russian Review*, vol. 25, pp. 25–37.

SHEREMET, K. F. (1968) *Kompetensia mestnykh Sovetov*, Moscow.

SHISHKIN, V. A. (1962) 'Bourgeois historiography and the question of peaceful coexistence', *Vop. ist.*, no. 9, pp. 3–21.

SHISHKOV, A. (1970) 'The party and the means of mass information', *Kommunist*, no. 4, pp. 63–75.

SHKARATAN, O. I. (1967) 'The social structure of the Soviet working class', *Vop.fil.*, no. 1, pp. 28–39.

SHUB, Anatole (1970) *An Empire Loses Hope*, New York: Norton.

SHUBKIN, V. N. (1966) 'Social mobility and choice of occupation', in G. V. Osipov (ed.), *Industry and Labour in the U.S.S.R.*, London: Tavistock, pp. 86–98.

SIMIRENKO, Alex (ed.) (1967) *Soviet Sociology*, London: Routledge & Kegan Paul.

SIMUSH, P. I. (1969) 'The impact of the scientific and technological revolution on the socialist village', *Int.Soc.Sc.Journal*, xxi, no. 2, pp. 256–64.

SKILLING, H. Gordon (1963) 'In search of political science in the USSR', *The Canadian J. of Econ. and Pol.Sc.*, pp. 519–29.

SKILLING, H. Gordon (1966) *The Governments of Communist East Europe*, New York: Crowell.

SKILLING, H. Gordon and GRIFFITHS, Franklyn (1971) *Interest Groups and Soviet Politics*, Princeton, New Jersey.

SMITH, Jessica (1969) 'Siberian Science City', *New World Review*, third quarter, pp. 86–101.

SNOW, C. P. (1961) *Science and Government*, London: Oxford U.P.

SNOW, C. P. (1962) *A Postscript to Science and Government*, London: Oxford U.P.

SOLZHENITSYN, A. (1968) *Cancer Ward*, 2 vols, London: Bodley Head, also Penguin.

SOLZHENITSYN, A. (1970) *The First Circle*, London: Collins, Fontana Books.

SOSIN, Gene (1969) 'Judaism in the Soviet Union', *Studies on the Soviet Union*, new series, ix, no. 2, pp. 63–75.

STEPANYAN, TS. A. and SEMENOV, V. S. (eds) (1968) *Problemy izmeneniya sotsialnoi struktury sovetskovo obshchestva*, Moscow.

STEWART, P. D. (1969) 'Soviet interest groups and the political process: the repeal of production education', *World Politics*, xxii, pp. 29–50.

STROIKA, A. (1969) 'The theory of "Stages of Economic Development" of W. Rostow—a falsification of social-economic development', *Vestnik Moskovskovo Universiteta*, Ekonomika I, pp. 81–90.

STRUKOV, V. I. (1969) *Naglyadnoe posobie po partiinomy stroitelstvy*, Moscow.

SULLIVAN, W. (1968) 'The Akademgorodok: a new look at Soviet science', in Harrison E. Salisbury, *The Anatomy of the Soviet Union*, pp. 299–322.

SWANSON, J. M. (1964) 'Reorganization: 1963', *Survey*, July, pp. 36–40.

TAMM. I. (1969) *see* RAPP and TAMM.

TATU, Michael (1968) *Power in the Kremlin*, London: Collins.

TAUBMAN, William (1968) *The View from the Lenin Hills: Soviet Youth in Ferment*, London: Hamish Hamilton.

TERTZ, A. (Sinyavsky A.) (1960) *On Socialist Realism*, New York: Random House.

TOMA, Peter A. (ed.) (1970) *The Changing Face of Communism in Eastern Europe*, University of Arizona Press.

TRAPEZNIKOV, S. P. (1967) 'The development of the social sciences and the raising of their role in Communist construction', *Vop.fil.*, no. 11, pp. 3–27.

TREMI, V. G. (1968) 'The politics of Libermanism', *Soviet Studies* xix, pp. 567–72.

TRUKHANOVSKY, V. G. (1963) 'The principle of peaceful coexistence and its bourgeois critics', *Vop.ist.*, pp. 62–96.

TSIRLIN, A. D. (ed.) (1970) *Inzhenernye voiska v boyakh za sovetskuyu rodinu*, Moscow.

TUCKER, Robert (1964) *The Soviet Political Mind*, Praeger.

TUMANOV, V. A. (ed.) (1967) *Sovremenny burzhuazny uchenie o kapitalisticheskom gosudarstve*, Moscow.

Two Universities: An Account of the Life and Work of Lumumba Friendship University and Moscow State University, London: Soviet News Booklet no. 110.

TYAGUNENKO, V. L. (1969) *Problemy sovremennykh natsionalno-osvoboditelnykh revolyutsii*, Moscow.

ULYANOVSKY, R. A. (1963) *Neokolonializm S.Sh.A. i slaborazvitye strany Azii*, Moscow.

ULYANOVSKY, R. A. (1965) *The Dollar and Asia*, Moscow (English trans. of the previous title).

UNESCO (1967) Science Policy and the Organization of Research in the USSR, Science Policy Studies and Documents, no. 7, Paris.

URBAN, P. (1964) 'Soviet historical science and the position of Soviet historians', *Bulletin* of the Institute for the Study of the USSR, xi, September, pp. 24–37.

UTECHIN, S. V. (1966) 'A new institute for social research in Leningrad', *Soviet Studies*, xvii, pp. 388–9.

VARDY, A. (1970) 'Party control over Soviet science', *Studies on the Soviet Union*, new series, x, no. 1, pp. 52–60.

VASILIEV, V. I. (1967) *Sovetskoe stroitelstvo*, Moscow.

VLASOV, M. (1968) *Rozhdenie sovetskoi intelligentsii*, Moscow.

VOLKOV, M. (1968) *Politicheskaya organizatsia obshchestva*, Moscow.

VON STACKELBERG, G. A. (1960) 'Soviet African studies as a weapon of

Soviet policy', *Bulletin* of the Institute for the Study of the USSR, vii, September, pp. 3–14.

VON STACKELBERG, G. A. (1966) 'The Soviet concept of the revolutionary democratic state and its political significance', *Bulletin* of the Institute for the Study of the USSR, xiii, April, pp. 3–13.

VORONITSYN, S. (1964) 'Soviet sociology since Stalin', *Bulletin* of the Institute for the Study of the USSR, xi, March, pp. 18–43.

VUCINICH, Alexander (1968) 'Science', in Kassof, *Prospects for Soviet Society*, pp. 318–54.

VYLTSAN, M. A. (1967) 'Composition and structure of the rural population of the USSR over 50 Years', *Istoria SSSR*, no. 6, pp. 43–63.

WADEKIN, K. (1971) 'Soviet rural society: a descriptive stratification analysis', *Soviet Studies*, xxii, pp. 512–38.

WATSON, James D. (1968) *The Double Helix*, London: Weidenfeld & Nicolson.

WEBER, Max (1962) *Basic Concepts of Sociology*, translated with an introduction by H. P. Secher, Peter Owen.

WEINRYB, B. D. (1970) 'Antisemitism in Soviet Russia', in Kochan, *The Jews in Soviet Russia since 1917*, pp. 288–320.

WERTH, Alexander (1969) *Russia: Hopes and Fears*, London: Penguin.

WETTER, G. A. (1966) *Soviet Ideology Today*, London: Heinemann.

WHITE, D. (1968) *see* SHARP and WHITE.

WOLFSOHN, Hugo (1967) 'The ideology makers', in Henry Mayer, *Australian Politics*, London: Dawson pp. 70–81.

YAKOVLEVA, N. (1970) 'The Labor semester: student building teams', *New World Review*, vol. 38, no. 4, pp. 107–11.

YAMPOLSKAYA, TS. A. (1965) 'Towards a methodology of the science of administration', *S.G. i P.*, no. 8, pp. 12–21.

YANOWITCH, M. and DODGE, N. T. (1969) 'The social evaluation of occupations in the Soviet Union', *Slavic Review*, vol. 28, pp. 619–43.

YEVTUSHENKO, Y. (1963) *A Precocious Autobiography*, London: Collins & Harvill.

ZALESKI, E., KOZLOWSKI, J. P., WIENERT, H., DAVIES, R. W., BERRY, M. J. and AMANN, R. (1969) *Science Policy in the U.S.S.R.*, Organization for Economic Co-operation and Development, Paris.

ZHAMIN, V. (1963) 'The transformation of science into immediate industrial power', *Kommunist*, no. 10, pp. 26–36.

ZHDANOV, A. A. (1950) *On Literature, Art and Philosophy*, London: Lawrence & Wishart.

ZHUKOV-VEREZHNIKOV, N. (1970) 'Popular universities: a Soviet experiment in adult education', *New World Review*, vol. 38, no. 3, pp. 85–9.

Index

Index

Index

Russian language, 29–30, 36
Russians, 11, 29–35, 36, 44–6, 82

Sakharov, A. D., 96, 103, 133, 144,
164–7
Samarin, A. M., 126
Samizdat, 123, 144–5
Science, 12, 76, 95–8
see also Scientists, Research,
Academy of Sciences,
Technology
Scientific Councils, 63, 116–17
Scientific Olympiad, 97
Scientists, 12, 17–24, 32–4, 76–7,
87, 95, 103, 107, 126–9, 132, 137
see also Agricultural scientists,
Research workers, Social
scientists, Technologists
Semenov, V. S., 16, 70
Shelepin, A. N., 123
Sholokhov, M., 114–15
Social Sciences, 22, 46, 57, 105–6,
119–20, 131, 140, 148
Social scientists, 12, 90, 103, 105–6,
130
Sociology, 46, 63–4, 120–1, 148
Soviet Sociological Association,
63–4
Solzhenitsyn, A., 142–3
Soviets
Standing Commissions of Soviets,
114–16
Standing Commissions of
Supreme Soviet of USSR, 69
Students
aspirations of, 26, 37, 75–9
categories of, 41–3
dissent of, 50, 137
post-graduate, 46–8
tertiary, 6–7, 37, 44–50, 92
Suslov, M. A., 66–7, 140

Tadevosyan, G. V., 121
Tadjiks, 11, 29–35, 45
Tartars, 11, 29–35, 45
Teachers, 19–20, 23–5, 46, 79, 90,
92, 107, 114
Technology, 12, 19, 22, 34, 46, 76,
96–7
see also Science
Theatre, 101–2
Sovremenik, 87
Tikhonov, N., 101, 114
Timofeev, T., 100
Trapeznikov, S. P., 114, 132
Turchin, V. F., 133, 164–7
Turkmen, 11, 44
Tvardovsky, A. T., 101, 143
Tverdokhlebov, A., 144

Ukrainians, 11, 29–35, 45, 82, 141,
153
Unions, *see* Professional
organizations
Uzbeks, 11, 29–35, 45

Voronov, I., 118
Voznesensky, A. A., 123, 140

Writers, 10, 17, 56, 90, 94, 107,
111–15, 130–7, 139–43
4th Writers' Congress, 162–3
Union of Soviet Writers, 65, 102,
107, 111, 140–3
see also Intelligentsia, creative
Writers' trials (1966–8), 50, 82, 146

Yevtushenko, E., 140, 145–6

Zhukov, Yu., 100
Zivs, S. L., 121
Znanie (Knowledge Society), 68, 94